AC340 Risk Management Cas
Xiaoquan Liu
University of Essex

Australia • Brazil • Japan • Korea • Mexico • Singapore • Spain • United Kingdom • United States

AC340 Risk Management Casebook
Xiaoquan Liu
University of Essex

Publishing Director: John Yates
Production Controller: Maeve Healy
Custom Solutions Manager: Jeni Evans

© 2008, Cengage Learning EMEA

All rights reserved by Cengage Learning 2008. The text of this publication, or any part thereof, may not be reproduced or transmitted in any form or by any means, electronic or mechanical, including photocopying, recording, storage in an information retrieval system, or otherwise, without prior permission of the publisher.

While the publisher has taken all reasonable care in the preparation of this book, the publisher makes no representation, express or implied, with regard to the accuracy of the information contained in this book and cannot accept any legal responsibility or liability for any errors or omissions from the book or the consequences thereof.

For product information and technology assistance, contact **emea.info@cengage.com**.

For permission to use material from this text or product, and for permission queries, email **clsuk.permissions@cengage.com**

Products and services that are referred to in this book may be either trademarks and/or registered trademarks of their respective owners. The publishers and author/s make no claim to these trademarks.

British Library Cataloguing-in-Publication Data
A catalogue record for this book is available from the British Library.

ISBN: 978-1-84480-987-5

Cengage Learning EMEA
High Holborn House, 50-51 Bedford Row
London WC1R 4LR

Cengage Learning products are represented in Canada by Nelson Education Ltd.

For your lifelong learning solutions, visit **www.cengage.co.uk**
Purchase e-books or e-chapters at: **http://estore.bized.co.uk**

Printed by TJI Digital
1 2 3 4 5 6 7 8 9 10 – 10 09 08

Acknowledgements

The content of this text has been adapted from the following product(s):

Applications for Financial Futures: Mason, Scott P.; Durdan, Sally E.
ISBN-10: (0-324-46570-X)
ISBN-13: (978-0-324-46570-9)

Basel II: Assessing the Default and Loss Characteristics of Project Finance Loans : Esty, Benjamin C.; Sesia Jr., Aldo
ISBN-10: (0-324-46457-6)
ISBN-13: (978-0-324-46457-3)

Basel II: Assessing the Default and Loss Characteristics of Project Finance Loans (B): Esty, Benjamin C.; Sesia Jr., Aldo
ISBN-10: (0-324-46495-9)
ISBN-13: (978-0-324-46495-5)

Cephalon, Inc.: Tufano, Peter; Verter, Geoffrey; Mullarkey, Markus F.
ISBN-10: (0-324-46865-2)
ISBN-13: (978-0-324-46865-6)

Note on Risk Arbitrage: Chacko, George; Cohen, Randolph B.; Chennault, Marc
ISBN-10: (0-324-46446-0)
ISBN-13: (978-0-324-46446-7)

Syscom Computers: Froot, Kenneth A.; Tufano, Peter; Marshall, Christopher L.
ISBN-10: (0-324-46734-6)
ISBN-13: (978-0-324-46734-5)

Overview of Credit Derivatives: Das, Sanjiv; Lynagh, Stephen
ISBN-10: (0-324-46810-5)
ISBN-13: (978-0-324-46810-6)

Pine Street Capital: Chacko, George; Strick, Eli Peter
ISBN-10: (0-324-46385-5)
ISBN-13: (978-0-324-46385-9)

Farallon Capital Management: Risk Arbitrage (A): Perold, Andre F.; Howard, Robert
ISBN-10: (0-324-46892-X)
ISBN-13: (978-0-324-46892-2)

Foreign Exchange Hedging Strategies at General Motors: Desai, Mihir A.; Veblen, Mark F.
ISBN-10: (0-324-46479-7)
ISBN-13: (978-0-324-46479-5)

Table Of Contents

1. Applications for Financial Futures: Mason, Scott P.; Durdan, Sally E.. 1
2. Basel II: Assessing the Default and Loss Characteristics of Project Finance Loans : Esty, Benjamin C.; Sesia Jr., Aldo... 25
3. Basel II: Assessing the Default and Loss Characteristics of Project Finance Loans (B): Esty, Benjamin C.; Sesia Jr., Aldo... 49
4. Cephalon, Inc.: Tufano, Peter; Verter, Geoffrey; Mullarkey, Markus F.. 55
5. Pine Street Capital: Chacko, George; Strick, Eli Peter... 73
6. Foreign Exchange Hedging Strategies at General Motors: Desai, Mihir A.; Veblen, Mark F...................... 91
7. Note on Risk Arbitrage: Chacko, George; Cohen, Randolph B.; Chennault, Marc............................... 119
8. Overview of Credit Derivatives: Das, Sanjiv; Lynagh, Stephen.. 131
9. Farallon Capital Management: Risk Arbitrage (A): Perold, Andre F.; Howard, Robert......................... 141
10. Syscom Computers: Froot, Kenneth A.; Tufano, Peter; Marshall, Christopher L................................ 169

 **Harvard Business School**

9-286-109
Rev. July 28, 1986

Applications for Financial Futures

1. Peoples Federal Savings Bank

On August 20, 1982, Richard Myers, president of Peoples Federal Savings Bank, was appalled to learn that Peoples had paid out $1,830,000 in variation margin calls on its Treasury bill futures position while he was enjoying a two-week seaside holiday. When added to the $690,000 in variation margin Peoples had paid prior to Myers's departure on August 6, the magnitude of these futures losses was staggering. As Myers studied the hedging report (**Exhibit 1**) his assistant had provided to him earlier in the morning, he wondered how a strategy designed to reduce risk could have produced such disastrous results. Richard knew that the bank's board of directors would expect an explanation for these huge cash outflows at the board's next meeting on August 27.

As of June 1982, Peoples Federal Savings Bank, based in Franklin, New Jersey, had accumulated assets totaling $556 million and consisting principally of fixed-rate first mortgage loans (**Exhibit 2**). The bank funded these assets with short-term consumer deposits, consisting largely of three-month fixed rate savings certificates. The maturity mismatch between Peoples' assets and liabilities had produced large losses as short-term interest rates rose over the period 1979-1982, severely eroding the thrift's capital base (**Exhibit 3**).

In the second quarter of 1982, Richard Myers realized that the bank would soon violate regulatory capital requirements if its losses were not controlled. Fearing rising Treasury bill rates, Richard had approached a major brokerage firm for advice on hedging its interest rate exposure. The firm's financial futures analyst, Joseph Rose, had advised Peoples to hedge the risk of interest rate fluctuations in the futures market. Impressed with this proposal, Mr. Myers had decided to hedge the cost of the September 1 rollover of its $400 million in savings certificates by taking a position in 90-day Treasury bill futures. Mr. Rose had assured Mr. Myers that any increase in savings certificate rates between May and September would be offset by gains on this futures position. Anxious to lock in an acceptable cost of funds through the end of the calendar year, Richard Myers sold short September 1982 T-bill futures contracts on May 20, 1982.

Because Peoples' savings certificates were priced at a fixed spread over T-bill rates, T-bill futures represented an effective vehicle for hedging the thrift's short-term interest rate exposure. In order to fully hedge its position, Peoples had sold short 400 September 1982 T-bill futures contracts. Upon initiating this position, the bank had been required to post initial margin of $2,500 per contract, or $1,000,000. At that time, Mr. Rose had explained to Myers that at the close of each day Peoples' margin account would be credited or debited with an amount equal to the daily change in the value

---

This case was prepared by Associates Fellow Sally E. Durdan, under the supervision of Associate Professor Scott P. Mason, as the basis for class discussion rather than to illustrate either effective or ineffective handling of an administrative situation.

Copyright © 1986 by the President and Fellows of Harvard College. To order copies or request permission to reproduce materials, call 1-800-545-7685, write Harvard Business School Publishing, Boston, MA 02163, or go to http://www.hbsp.harvard.edu. No part of this publication may be reproduced, stored in a retrieval system, used in a spreadsheet, or transmitted in any form or by any means—electronic, mechanical, photocopying, recording, or otherwise—without the permission of Harvard Business School.

of its short position. In the event Peoples' margin balance fell below the maintenance level of $2,000 per contract, Peoples would be required to post variation margin sufficient to restore its margin balance to the initial margin level. Peoples would accrue interest on its margin account balance, but not on variation margin payments. Although all variation margin cash flows would be realized prior to the thrift's September 1 savings certificate issuance date, FHLBB accounting standards would allow Peoples to defer net profits or losses on its futures position, matching them with interest payments on the September 1 savings certificate obligation being hedged.

Through late June, Peoples' expectations for rising rates proved correct and the thrift's margin balance rose to nearly $8 million. However, as rates began to fall in July the value of Peoples' futures position dropped precipitously. By the time Myers left for his vacation on August 6 the thrift had been forced to meet variation margin calls totaling $690,000. Although Myers had expressed concern over these losses to Mr. Rose before his departure, Rose had indicated that the dip in rates was expected to be temporary and advised that Peoples retain its futures position.

Today, on August 20, Myers could hardly believe the results of his "hedging" strategy: the bank had paid out over $2.5 million in cash against its futures position, and would be required to post another $540,000 to close out the bank's position at the end of the day. Upon questioning, Mr. Rose contended that the hedge was working precisely as planned. However, Myers considered the magnitude of the bank's futures losses totally unacceptable. He commented ruefully:

> It's not the fact that we lost money that upsets me. It's the fact that we lost so much. There really should be some downside protection.

As he slammed down his telephone, Myers wondered how he could possibly explain the results of his "risk reduction" strategy to the board on August 27.

1. Should Peoples Federal Savings have hedged its September 1 savings certificate rollover?

2. What would you have advised Mr. Myers to do on August 6?

3. How should Mr. Myers explain his futures losses to the board on August 27?

Applications for Financial Futures

Exhibit 1 Peoples Federal Savings Bank

Hedging Report: August 20, 1982

Position: Sold Short 400 September 1982 T-Bill Futures Contracts on May 20, 1982

Total Position	400 Contracts
Denomination of Contract	$1,000,000
Initial Margin per Contract	$2,500
Maintenance Margin per Contract	$2,000

Month	Day	Futures Price (IMM Index)	Daily Profit/Loss per Contract	Margin Balance per Contract	Daily Variation Margin Call per Contract	Cumulative Variation Margin Calls per Contract
May	20	88.58		$2,500		
	21	88.40	($450)	$2,950	$0	$0
	24	88.42	($50)	$2,900	$0	$0
	25	88.32	$250	$3,150	$0	$0
	26	88.18	$350	$3,500	$0	$0
	27	88.23	($125)	$3,375	$0	$0
	28	88.34	($275)	$3,100	$0	$0
June	1	87.74	$1,500	$4,600	$0	$0
	2	87.67	$175	$4,775	$0	$0
	3	87.65	$50	$4,825	$0	$0
	4	87.37	$700	$5,525	$0	$0
	7	87.64	($675)	$4,850	$0	$0
	8	87.49	$375	$5,225	$0	$0
	9	87.72	($575)	$4,650	$0	$0
	10	87.52	$500	$5,150	$0	$0
	11	87.67	($375)	$4,775	$0	$0
	14	87.11	$1,400	$6,175	$0	$0
	15	87.11	$0	$6,175	$0	$0
	16	87.10	$25	$6,200	$0	$0
	17	86.83	$675	$6,875	$0	$0
	18	86.67	$400	$7,275	$0	$0
	21	86.80	($325)	$6,950	$0	$0
	22	86.62	$450	$7,400	$0	$0
	23	86.72	($250)	$7,150	$0	$0
	24	86.52	$500	$7,650	$0	$0
	25	86.41	$275	$7,925	$0	$0
	28	86.61	($500)	$7,425	$0	$0
	29	86.83	($550)	$6,875	$0	$0
	30	86.94	($275)	$6,600	$0	$0
July	1	87.16	($550)	$6,050	$0	$0
	2	87.03	$325	$6,375	$0	$0
	6	87.09	($150)	$6,225	$0	$0
	7	87.35	($650)	$5,575	$0	$0
	8	87.86	($1,275)	$4,300	$0	$0
	9	88.01	($375)	$3,925	$0	$0
	12	88.01	$0	$3,925	$0	$0
	13	87.76	$625	$4,550	$0	$0
	14	87.73	$75	$4,625	$0	$0
	15	87.93	($500)	$4,125	$0	$0
	16	88.41	($1,200)	$2,925	$0	$0
	19	88.43	($50)	$2,875	$0	$0
	20	88.64	($525)	$2,350	$0	$0
	21	88.36	$700	$3,050	$0	$0
	22	88.74	($950)	$2,100	$0	$0
	23	88.78	($100)	$2,500	$500	$500
	26	88.45	$825	$3,325	$0	$500
	27	88.40	$125	$3,450	$0	$500
	28	88.16	$600	$4,050	$0	$500
	29	88.38	($550)	$3,500	$0	$500
	30	88.67	($725)	$2,775	$0	$500
August	2	89.27	($1,500)	$2,500	$1,225	$1,725
	3	88.93	$850	$3,350	$0	$1,725
	4	89.14	($525)	$2,825	$0	$1,725
	5	89.09	$125	$2,950	$0	$1,725
	6	88.81	$700	$3,650	$0	$1,725
	9	89.17	($900)	$2,750	$0	$1,725
	10	88.96	$525	$3,275	$0	$1,725
	11	89.01	($125)	$3,150	$0	$1,725
	12	89.52	($1,275)	$2,500	$625	$2,350
	13	89.78	($650)	$2,500	$650	$3,000
	16	90.18	($1,000)	$2,500	$1,000	$4,000
	17	90.60	($1,050)	$2,500	$1,050	$5,050
	18	90.65	($125)	$2,375	$0	$5,050
	19	91.10	($1,125)	$2,500	$1,250	$6,300

Exhibit 2 Peoples Federal Savings Bank Comparative Statement of Conditions[a]

	As of June 30	As of December 31		
	1982 (6 mo.)	1981	1980	1979
Assets				
First mortgage loans	406,124	430,201	384,667	304,812
Loans on savings accounts	821	1,282	823	927
Consumer and other loans	84,423	34,621	6,786	2,986
Cash on hand and in banks	2,301	1,880	2,426	2,260
Liquid Investment securities	28,562	16,282	16,823	17,782
Other investment securities	1,526	2,621	7,028	8,200
Investment in subsidiary corporations	6,721	5,261	6,201	2,460
Federal Home Loan Bank stock	4,162	2,721	2,864	2,350
Building and equipment (net)	4,012	3,081	1,823	1,626
Deferred charges and other assets	19,961	10,428	4,826	7,311
TOTAL	555,613	509,378	434,267	350,714
Liabilities and Reserves				
Deposits	410,477	381,940	328,146	282,960
Advances from Federal Home Loan Bank	45,891	43,826	44,567	26,462
Other advances	2,587	2,647	2,632	3,031
Other borrowed money	53,821	43,862	27,161	10,643
Loans in process	–	311	4,032	4,492
Deferred income	24,311	14,286	4,823	3,106
Other liabilities	7,124	9,026	6,301	4,215
Reserves and undividend profits	11,402	13,480	16,605	15,805
TOTAL	555,613	509,378	434,267	350,714

[a] In thousands of dollars

Applications for Financial Futures 286-109

Exhibit 3 Peoples Federal Savings Bank Comparative Statement of Operations[a]

	6 month		For the year ending December 31		
	1982	1981	1981	1980	1979
	(Jan.-June)				
Income					
Interest on mortgage loans	22,035	22,764	41,732	30,940	23,750
Income from other loans & investments	6,426	1,482	3,026	3,453	3,162
Loan fees	896	1,493	2,920	2,300	1,150
All other income	2,261	2,001	4,264	1,827	302
TOTAL INCOME	31,618	27,740	51,942	38,520	28,364
Expenses					
Operating expenses	4,327	3,102	6,240	49261	3,153
Non-operating expenses[b]	7,834	6,061	10,261	6,292	2,450
Dividends[c]	22,602	19,982	40,162	26,781	19,660
Income taxes	(1,067)	(491)	(1,596)	386	932
TOTAL EXPENSES	33,696	28,654	55,067	37,720	26,195
NET INCOME	(2,078)	(914)	(3,125)	800	2,169

[a] Figures in thousands of dollars
[b] Involves interest payments on borrowings other than deposits
[c] Denotes interest paid or credited to members

Exhibit 4 Peoples Federal Savings Bank

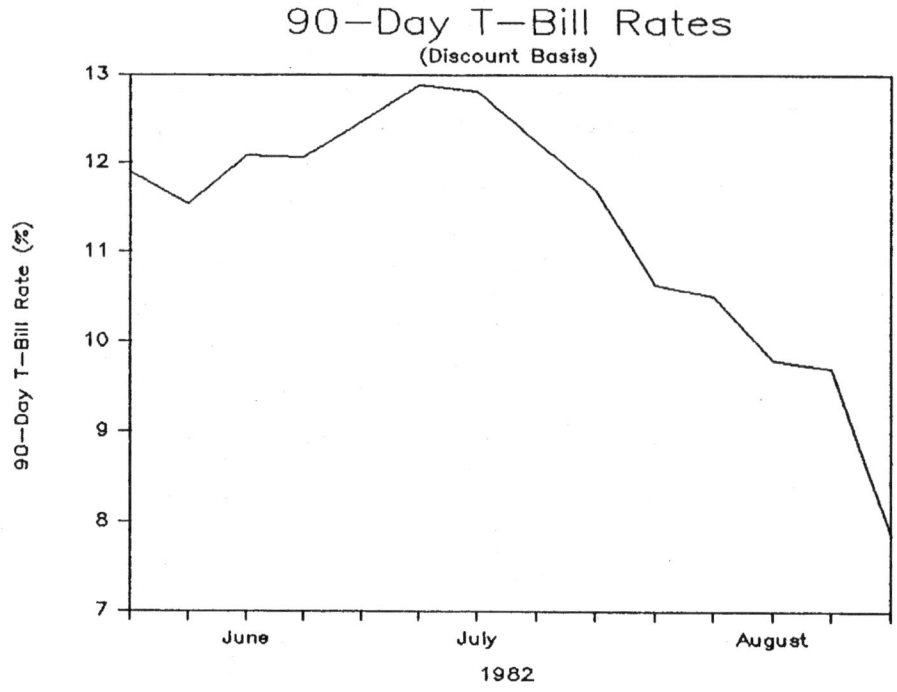

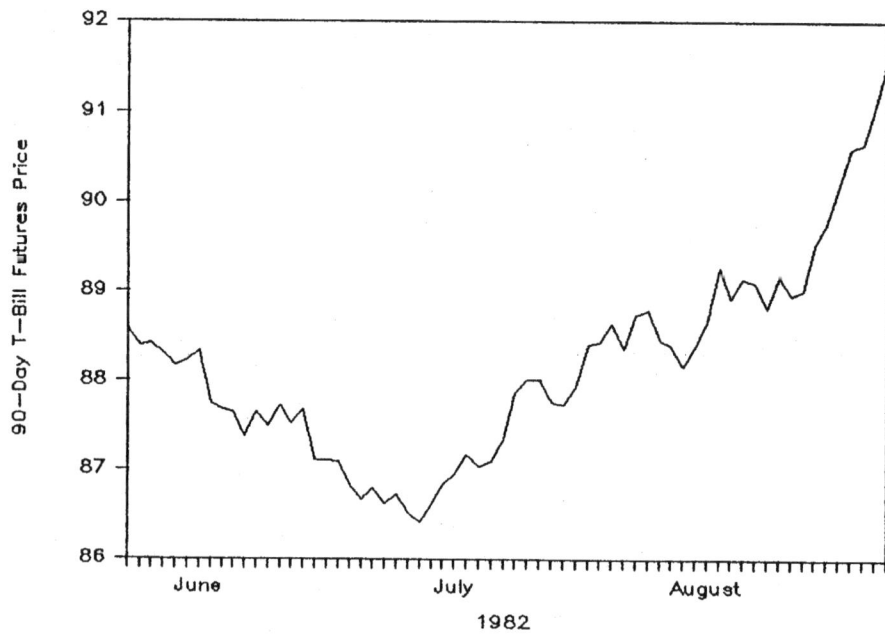

Source: International Monetary Market 1983 Yearbook.

Applications for Financial Futures

Exhibit 5 Peoples Federal Savings Bank

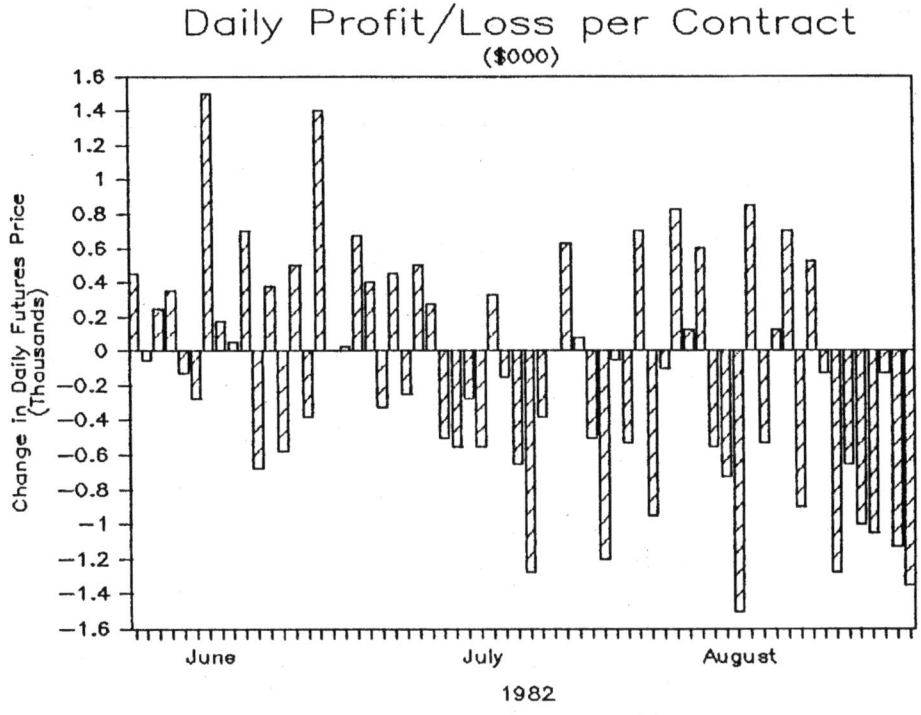

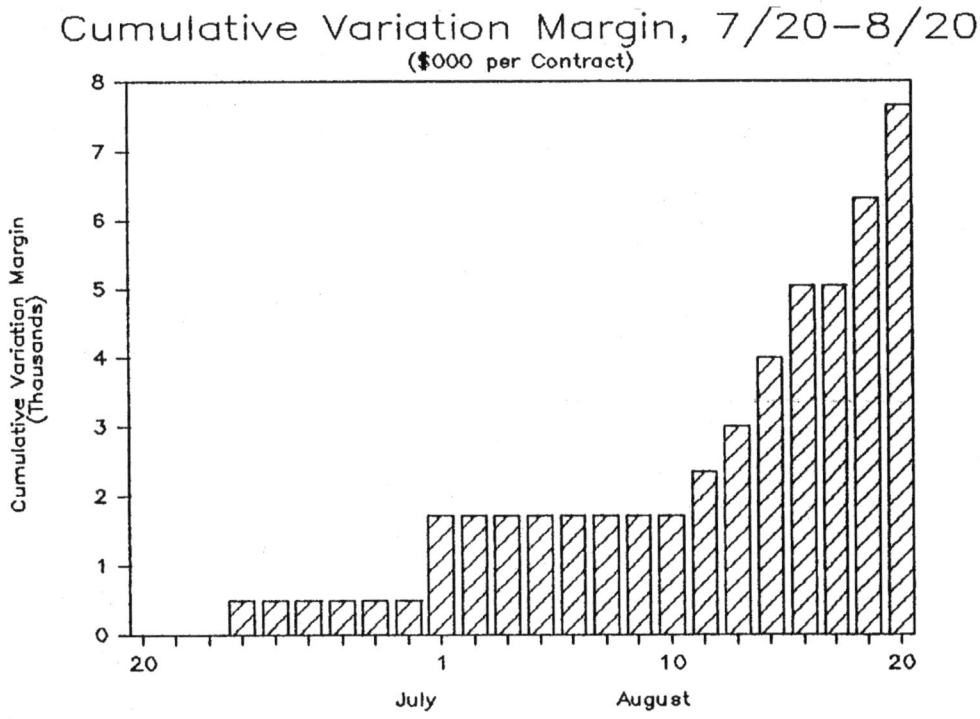

2. Southeast Corporation

On January 6, 1984, Lori Hiratani, treasurer of the Southeast Corporation, reviewed a financial analysis of a plan to build an automated manufacturing facility near Southeast's Atlanta headquarters. Southeast Corporation's management committee had approved construction of the facility late in 1983, and had authorized the issuance of $60 million in long-term debt to finance the project. Although Hiratani considered current borrowing rates to be particularly attractive, she planned to defer issuance of additional debt until the new facility had been completed in August 1984. She believed that completion of the project would improve the company's credit rating, enabling Southeast to secure a Aa rating on the planned $60 million debt issue.

Despite the potential for improvement in the quality of its credit, Hiratani realized that Southeast's total borrowing costs could increase substantially from the current 12.88% Aa rate if long-term interest rates moved against her over the succeeding seven months. In order to lock in the attractive current borrowing rates, Hiratani decided to hedge her August 1984 debt issue by selling short Treasury bond futures contracts.

On January 6, September 1984 T-bond futures prices were quoted at 69-08. Hiratani had determined that this price reflected delivery of the 12% coupon Treasury bond maturing August 1, 2013. This "cheapest-to-deliver" bond was callable after August 1, 2008, and was priced in the cash market at 101-18 (an 11.80% yield). Hiratani estimated the duration of this T-bond at 8.5 years.

The $60 million Southeast debt offering, scheduled to be issued the first week in August, was to carry a maturity of 25 years and sinking fund provisions requiring retirement of 10% of the issue each year beginning in year 20. Assuming the bonds were issued at current coupon levels, the duration of this obligation would equal 7.8 years. As she planned her hedge, Hiratani reviewed a variety of data concerning historical movements in the prices and yields of long Treasury and Aa corporate bonds (see **Exhibits 1** and **2**).

1. How many September 1984 T-bond futures contracts should Lori Hiratani sell short to hedge Southeast's interest rate exposure?

2. What rate will Hiratani "lock in" by initiating this hedge?

3. Does this hedging strategy eliminate Southeast's exposure? If not, what risks remain?

Exhibit 1 Southeast Corporation

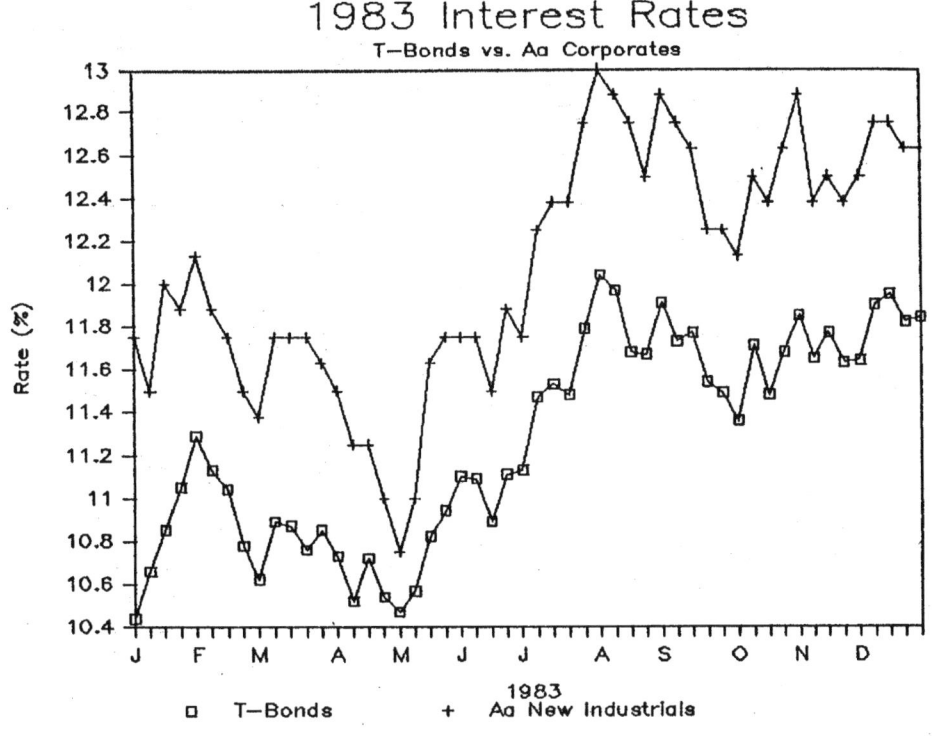

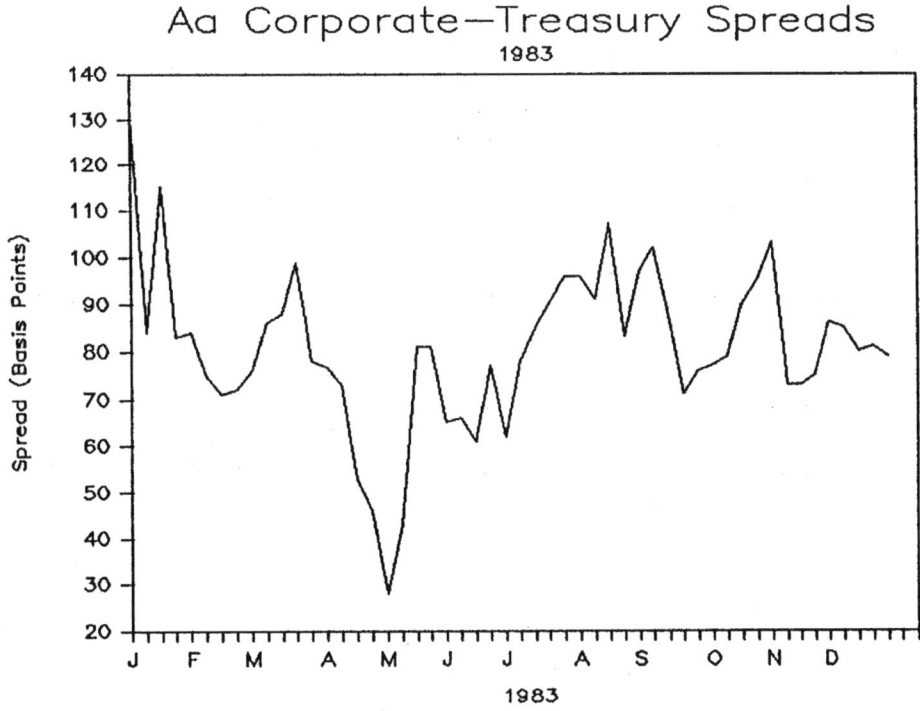

Source: Salomon Brothers, Inc.

Exhibit 2 Southeast Corporation

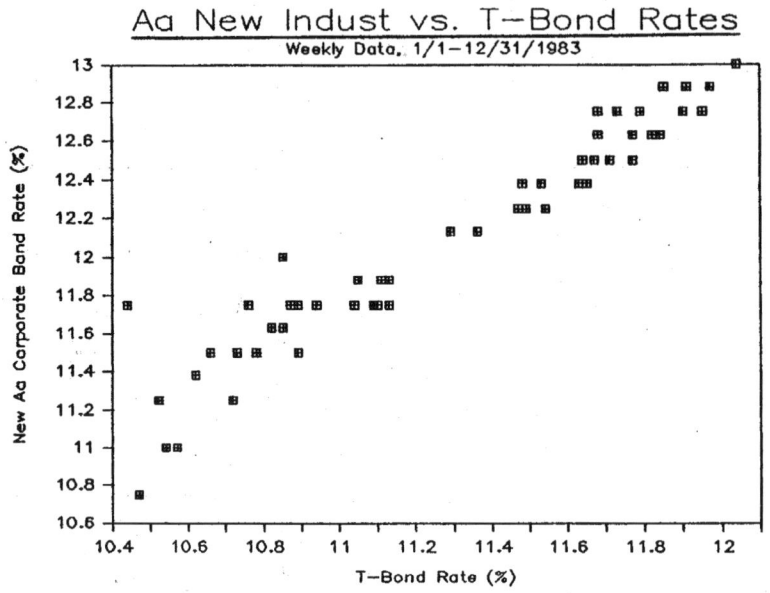

Regression of Aa Industrial Bond Rates on Treasury Bond Rates
Weekly Data: 1/1/83 - 12/31/83

Aa Rate = -.5808 + 1.123 (T-Bond Rate)

Standard Error: (.5341)   (.047)

R^2 = .9184

Source: Salomon Brothers, Inc.

Exhibit 3 Southeast Corporation, Treasury Bill Yields, January 6, 1984

Maturity	Investment Yield (%)
3-Month	9.19%
6-Month	9.61
9-Month	9.75
One Year	10.10

Source: *Wall Street Journal.*

3. Alpha Investors

On July 1, 1985, Jim Roberts felt certain the stock market was in for a correction. The S&P 500 Index had risen 14% since the first of the year, and most analysts were predicting that the market would drop in the third quarter before resuming its climb. Jim, a vice president of Alpha Investors, Inc., managed a $36 million portfolio of NYSE-listed technology and retailing stocks which he expected to outperform the market by a substantial margin over the next three to five years (see **Exhibit 1**).

Although he was anxious to protect the market value of his portfolio, Jim wanted to avoid the large transactions costs required to trade out of equities in anticipation of a market decline. In addition, he believed that liquidation of any significant portion of his current positions could not be achieved without moving the market prices of some of the smaller capitalization stocks in his portfolio. For these reasons, Jim had decided to use S&P 500 stock index futures to hedge his portfolio.

In the course of preparing a hedging strategy, Jim reviewed a Salomon Brothers stock research report entitled "Futures Contracts on Stock Indexes" (Harvard Business School Reprint #8-287-014). Jim was particularly intrigued by the statistical analysis demonstrated in Figure 6, page 9 of the report, and asked Alpha's research department to prepare a similar analysis of price movements in his own portfolio relative to the S&P 500 index (see **Exhibit 2**). By regressing historical price returns on Alpha's portfolio against movements in the market (as measured by the S&P 500 stock index), the research department determined that the beta of Alpha's portfolio was 1.18.

After reviewing the statistical analysis he had requested, Jim was puzzled. "Now that I have compiled all of these statistics, what futures position should I take to hedge my portfolio through the third quarter?"

1. What futures position should Jim take to hedge his portfolio?

2. What risks can Jim eliminate by shorting S&P 500 stock index futures contracts? How effective do you expect his hedge to be? (Try to quantify the effectiveness of Jim's hedge using the methodology described in the Salomon Brothers research report (Appendix 3).)

3. What return can Jim expect to earn during the third quarter of 1985 assuming he adopts your hedging strategy?

Exhibit 1 Alpha Investors' Description of Equity Portfolio at 7/1/85

Security Number	Shares Held	Stock Price ($ per shr)	Market Value ($000)	% of Portfolio Market Value ($000)	Beta	Dividend Yield (%)	Q3 85 Ex-Div Date	Q3 Dividends
1	60,000	$15.125	$907,500	2.5%	1.40	0.00%	------	$0
2	103,500	$48.000	$4,968,000	13.8%	1.05	0.42%	July 19	$5,175
3	87,000	$19.125	$1,663,875	4.6%	1.05	0.00%	------	$0
4	54,000	$14.750	$796,500	2.2%	1.45	1.36%	Aug 12	$2,700
5	111,000	$39.000	$4,329,000	12.0%	1.10	0.51%	Sept 24	$5,550
6	45,750	$24.875	$1,138,031	3.1%	1.40	0.64%	Sept 12	$1,830
7	66,000	$34.250	$2,260,500	6.3%	1.10	0.58%	Sept 30	$3,300
8	82,500	$35.500	$2,928,750	8.1%	1.15	1.35%	Aug 20	$9,900
9	39,000	$16.250	$633,750	1.8%	1.15	2.71%	Sept 24	$4,290
10	73,500	$43.875	$3,224,813	8.9%	1.95	1.23%	Sept 16	$9,923
11	87,000	$17.625	$1,533,375	4.2%	0.75	1.13%	Aug 9	$4,350
12	93,000	$69.500	$6,463,500	17.9%	0.90	4.03%	Aug 5	$65,100
13	52,500	$35.500	$1,863,750	5.2%	1.30	0.00%	------	$0
14	126,000	$27.125	$3,417,750	9.5%	1.40	1.18%	Aug 14	$10,080
Portfolio Totals/Averages			$36,129,094	100.0%	1.18	1.35%		$122,198

Applications for Financial Futures

Exhibit 2 Statistical Analysis of Alpha Investors' Portfolio Versus the S&P 500 Stock Index

I. Analysis of Weekly Price Returns:

S&P 500 = S&P 500 Weekly Price Returns

AIP = Alpha Investors' Portfolio Weekly Price Returns

1) Results of Regression of AIP on S&P 500:

$$\text{AIP} = 0.13 + 1.18 \,(\text{S\&P 500})$$

R-Squared = .690

Correlation Coefficient = .831

2) Summary Statistics:

Average S&P 500	=	+0.22% (Weekly)
Average AIP	=	+0.39% (Weekly)
Standard Deviation of S&P 500	=	2.32% (Weekly)
Standard Deviation of AIP	=	3.29% (Weekly)

II. Comparison of Dividend Yields (at July 1, 1985):

S&P 500	=	4.16%
AIP	=	1.35%

Exhibit 3 Alpha Investors' Price/Yield Quotes on Friday, June 28, 1985

S&P 500 Futures Index Prices:
(Contract Price = 500 Times the Index)

Delivery Date	Open	High	Low	Settle	Open Interest
Sept	194.10	194.35	193.40	193.65	57,485
Dec	197.30	197.35	196.50	196.65	1,168
Mar 86	200.40	200.40	199.70	199.75	123

S&P 500 Stock Index:
(Cash Price)

Open	High	Low	Settle
191.54	191.85	191.04	191.85

T-Bill Rates:
(Investment Yields)

3-Month	7.07%
6-Month	7.41%

Source: *Wall Street Journal*, July 1, 1985.

4. Auto Star

Edith Cooper, treasurer of Auto Star, a U.S.-based importer of automobile parts, paused before phoning Rob Rough, a corporate finance associate at Auto Star's investment bank. Edith was calling Rob to discuss a strategy for hedging Auto Star's exposure on its prime-based, variable rate liabilities. Edith was concerned that Auto Star's extreme leverage and reliance on variable rate financing exposed the company to an unacceptable level of financial risk, and had asked Rob to consider a strategy for hedging Auto Star's interest costs in the financial futures markets.

Auto Star imported auto parts from both Europe and the Far East, marketing products under its own and private labels. Auto Star's products were targeted at the "do-it-yourself" segment of the auto repair market, and were distributed through auto parts and discount stores. Price competition in this market segment, which was dominated by U.S. auto parts manufacturers, was exceptionally keen.

In preparing for her discussion with Rob, Edith had compiled a variety of data relating movements in the prime rate to changes in other short-term interest rates. Because futures contracts on prime-based instruments were not available, Edith realized she would have to cross-hedge her prime rate exposure using T-bill or CD futures contracts. She hoped that Rob could advise her on the construction of such a hedge. She also wanted help in estimating the probable magnitude of variation margin calls on an 18-month hedge. Edith feared that Auto Star would have to secure a new line of credit to finance margin calls on its position. Given the weakness of Auto Star's balance sheet, Edith had been unable to secure additional credit from its lenders in recent months.

"No problem," Edith thought to herself. "Once I hedge Auto Star's rate exposure, our company's financial risk will be reduced to a level even our conservative bankers will find acceptable!"

1. If you were Rob Rough, what advice would you give to Edith Cooper?

Exhibit 1 Auto Star Historical Financial Statements

INCOME STATEMENTS (1979-1981)

	1981	1980	1979
Net sales	$103,140	$93,764	$85,240
Cost of goods sold	64,978	61,884	59,668
Gross margin	$ 38,162	$31,880	$25,572
Selling and administrative expense	23,722	21,566	19,605
Interest expense	5,570	4,501	2,046
Profit before taxes	$ 8,870	$ 5,813	$ 3,921
Taxes	4,080	2,674	1,804
Profit after tax	$4,790	3,139	$2,117

BALANCE SHEET (December 30, 1981)

ASSETS		LIABILITIES	
Cash and securities	$ 3,094	Short-term notes payable	$18,565
Trade receivables (net)	12,377	Current maturities of LTD	1,650
Inventory	23,207	Trade payables	11,861
Other current assets	5,518		
		Total current liabilities	$32,077
Total current assets	$44,196		
		Long-term debt	6,188
Fixed assets	7,375	Deferred taxes	516
		Net Worth	12,789
		Total Liabilities	
Total Assets	$51,570	and Net Worth	$51,570

Exhibit 2 Auto Star

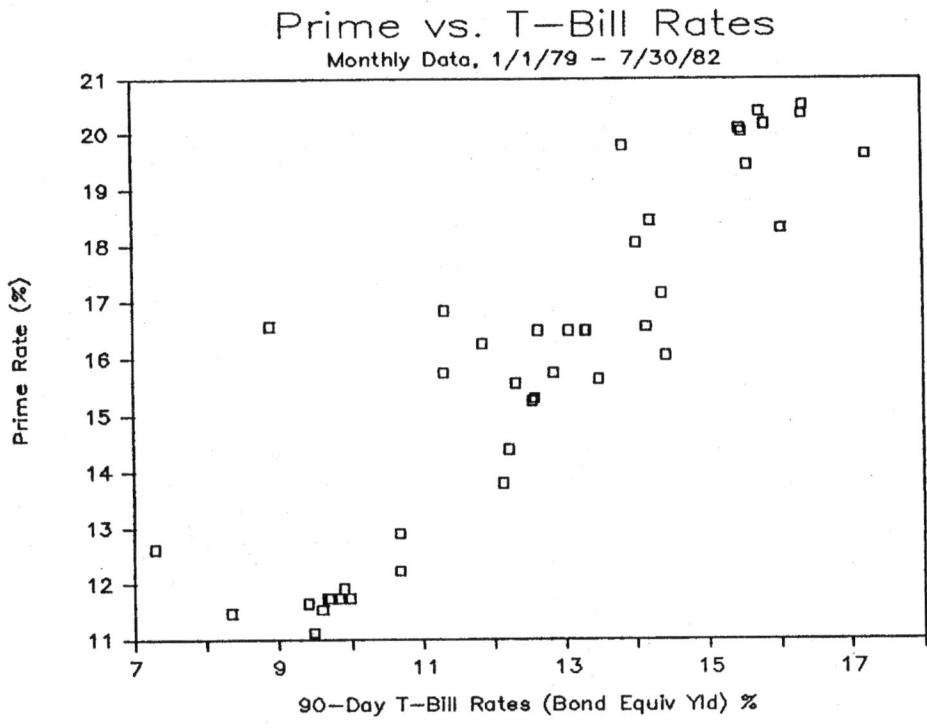

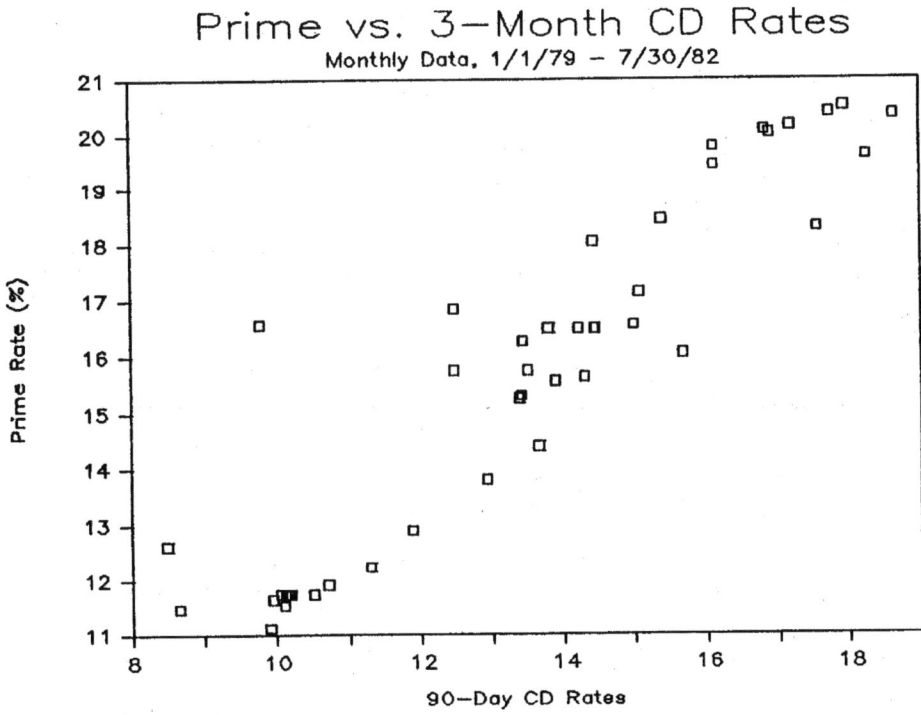

Source: Federal Reserve

Exhibit 3 Auto Star

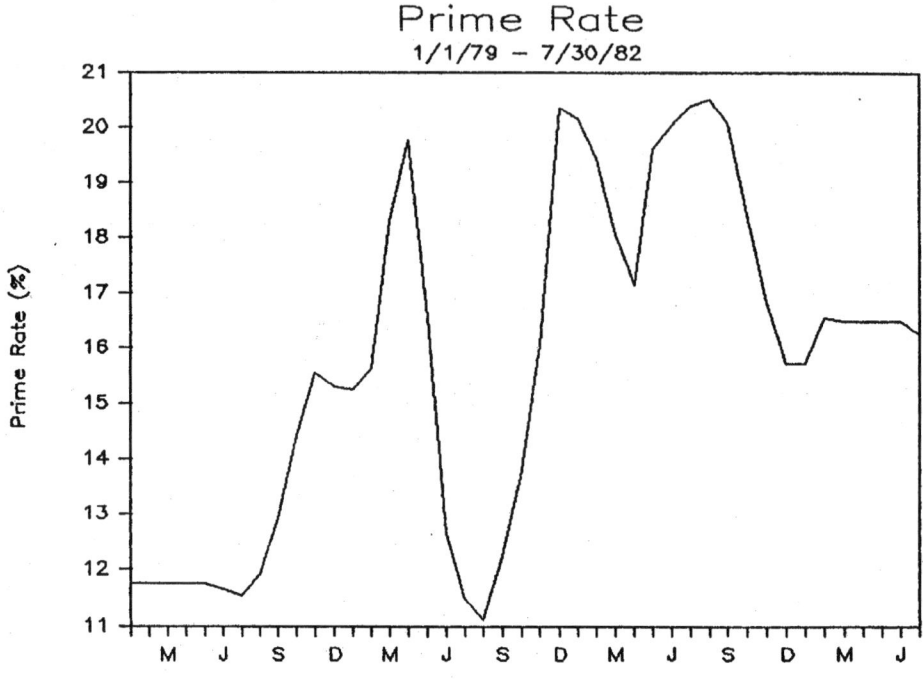

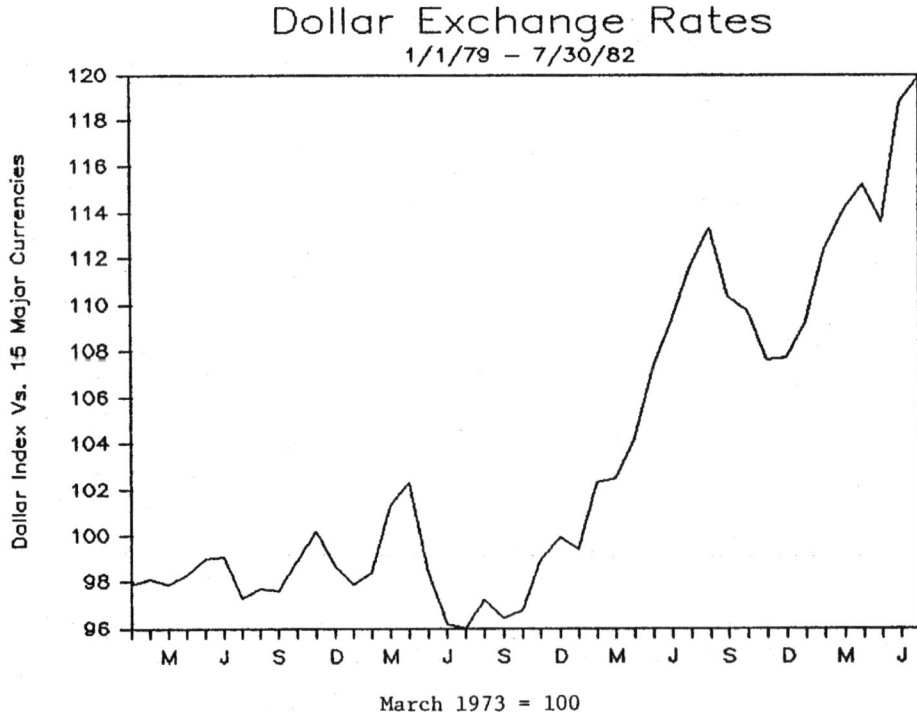

Sources: Federal Reserve, Morgan Guaranty.

Note: This index measures the dollar's trade-weighted average appreciation or depreciation against the currencies of 15 other major countries.

Applications for Financial Futures 286-109

5. Stock Index Futures Arbitrage

On February 26, 1986, Jim Lucey, a program trader at a New York Stock Exchange member firm, studied the pricing of futures contracts written on the Major Market Index (MMI). The MMI, a price-weighted stock index designed to measure the market performance of major U.S. industrial corporations, tracked movements in the prices of 20 blue chip stocks (see **Exhibit 1**). Unlike the Standard & Poor's 500 and other market capitalization-weighted indices, the MMI was affected equally by a price change in any one of its component stocks.

Jim regularly monitored the values of major stock indices and stock index futures in search of index-futures arbitrage opportunities. Although the efficiency of index futures pricing had improved since the initiation of trading in stock index futures contracts in 1982, index futures prices at times diverged significantly from their theoretical values. Such pricing anomalies were usually attributed to the activities of speculators using the futures markets to anticipate major moves in the stock market.

As Jim considered his strategy, he estimated the transaction costs associated with an MMI arbitrage. Transacting for his firm's account, Jim would incur no commission expenses but would be exposed to the market impact of buying/selling the MMI. Although the round-trip market impact of implementing an S&P 500 index-futures arbitrage often totaled 0.5%, Jim believed that transactions in the 20 large-capitalization stocks included in the MMI could be executed with less than 0.25% market impact. Jim's stock purchases would be subject to 10% margin restrictions, and his firm's cost of borrowing was approximately 8.0%.

At mid-morning on February 26 the March 86 MMI futures, which were to expire on March 21, were priced at 313.55, while the cash index stood at 311.74. One-month Treasuries were yielding 6.8%.

1. What is the theoretical price of the MMI March '86 futures contract?

2. Assume that Jim is subject to a $5,000,000 position limit. What position should he take to exploit the mispricing of the March '86 MMI futures?

3. What rate of return can Jim expect to earn on his position?

4. Who, in addition to securities dealers, would you expect to engage in index-futures arbitrage?

5. Why do index futures often trade at a premium or discount to their theoretical values? How do you expect the pricing efficiency of broader market index futures, like the S&P 500, to compare to the pricing of MMI futures?

Exhibit 1 Stock Index Futures Arbitrage, Major Market Index Profile

Component Stocks (20)	Stock Price at 2/25/86	Dividends to be Paid Through 3/21/86
American Express	64	
AT&T	22 1/2	
Chevron	37 7/8	
Coca-Cola	92	$0.78
Dow Chemical	48 3/4	
Du Pont	70 1/2	
Eastman Kodak	55	
Exxon	54 7/8	
General Electric	75 1/2	0.58
General Motors	78 1/4	
IBM	158 1/8	
International Paper	57	
Johnson & Johnson	48 3/8	
Merck	150 3/4	0.90
3M	97 1/4	
Mobil Oil	30 1/8	
Philip Morris	101 1/8	1.15
Procter & Gamble	67	
Sears	42 7/8	
U.S. Steel	22 5/8	
Total	$1,374.50	$3.41

Source: Business Week.

Exhibit 2 Stock Index Futures Arbitrage, Stock Index Futures Prices (2/25/86)

```
MAJOR MARKET INDEX FUTURES (CBT)
($250 x Index number)
```

Season			Daily				
High	Low		High	Low	Close	Chg.	Open Interest
315 1/2	271	Mar	314	310 7/8	312 1/2	+1/8	268
316 1/2	288	Apr	315	312 1/2	313 3/4	+1/8	35
318 1/2	316	Jun	-	-	315 5/8	+3/8	3

Cash Index 311.71, up .34.
Tue.'s sales 6,429.
Tue.'s open interest 4,859, up 4,564.

```
S&P 500 STOCK INDEX FUTURES (CME)
($500 x Index number)
```

Season			Daily				
High	Low		High	Low	Close	Chg.	Open Interest
226.70	182.30	Mar	225.90	223.35	224.65	+.35	61,340
229.55	183.90	Jun	228.80	226.35	227.55	+.35	17,852
231.50	187.00	Sep	230.40	228.80	230.25	+.35	1,628
234.50	178.40	Dec	233.40	231.95	233.25	+.55	26

Cash Index 224.04, up .25.
Est. sales 91,776. Tue.'s sales 85,988.
Tue.'s open interest 80,846, up 911.

Source: *Wall Street Journal*, February 26, 1986.

Exhibit 3 Stock Index Futures Arbitrage, Price/Basis[a] Trends: March 1986 Major Market Index Futures (9/9/85–2/20/86)

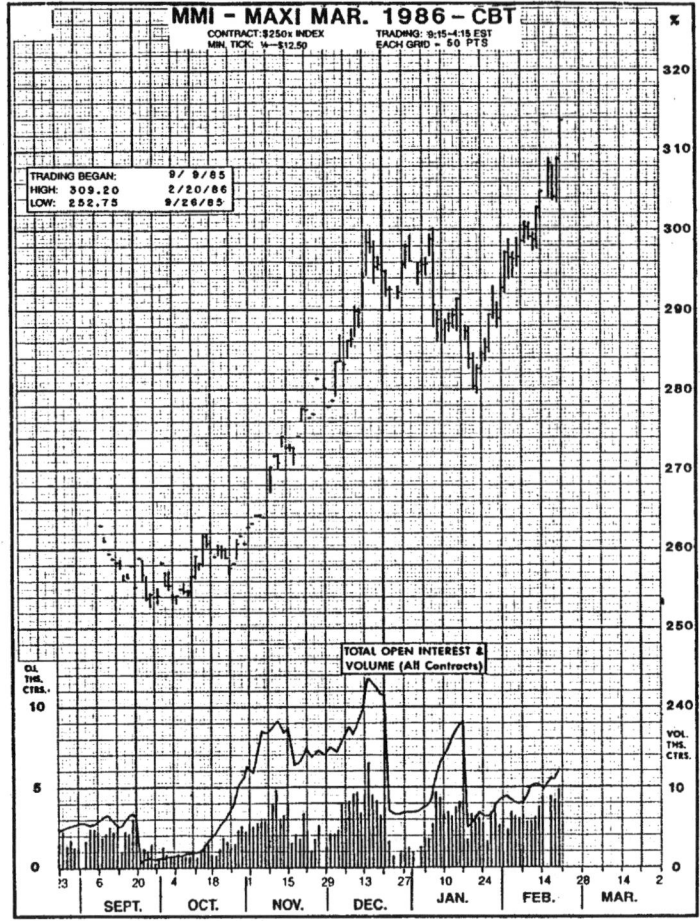

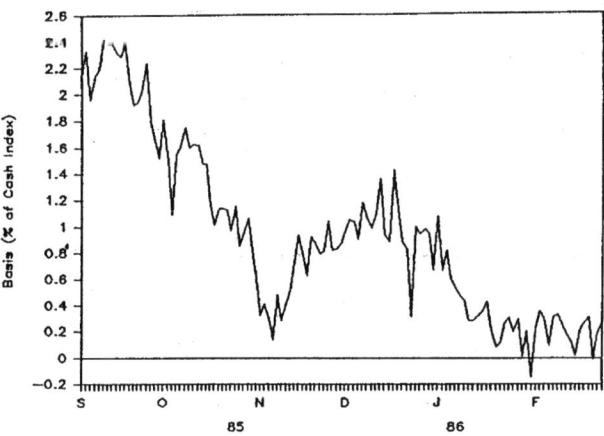

Source: Commodity Research Bureau.

[a] Basis=futures price-cash index. In this analysis, the basis is expressed as a percentage of the cash index value.

Exhibit 4 Stock Index Futures Arbitrage, Price/Basis[a] Trends: March 1986 S&P 500 Index Futures (9/1/85—2/20/86)

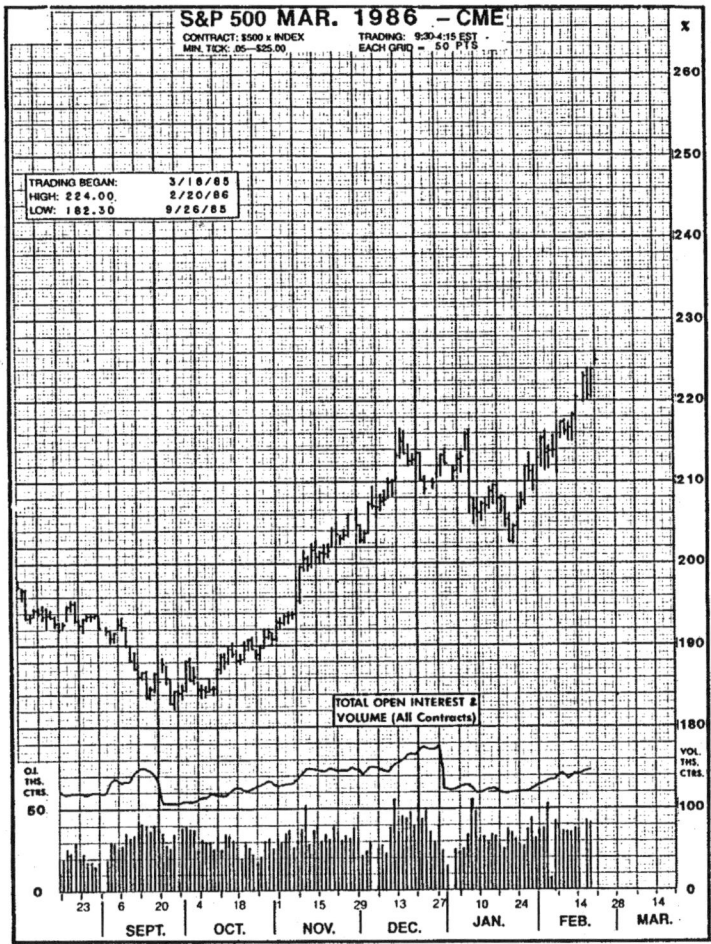

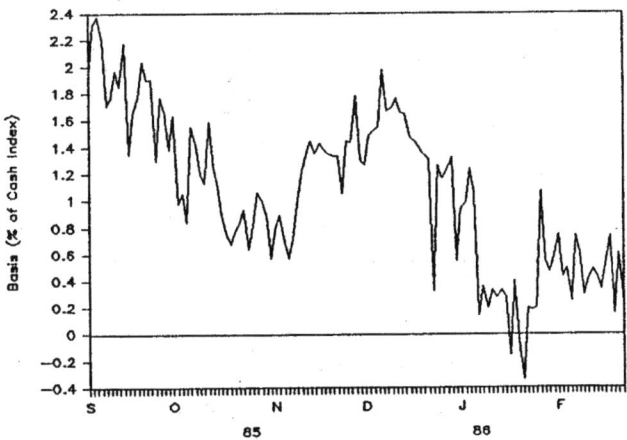

Source: Commodity Research Bureau.

[a] Basis=futures price-cash index. In this analysis, the basis is expressed as a percentage of the cash index value.

9-203-035
REV: JANUARY 26, 2004

BENJAMIN C. ESTY
ALDO M. SESIA, JR.

Basel II: Assessing the Default and Loss Characteristics of Project Finance Loans (A)

> *The Basel II Accord poses a major threat to the project finance industry. It has the potential to drive banks out of the business of project finance, and could dramatically curtail lending in both developed and emerging markets.*
>
> —Chris Beale, Managing Director and Global Head of Project & Structured Trade Finance, Citigroup

On August 23, 2002, the global heads of the project finance business units at ABN AMRO, Citigroup, Deutsche Bank, and Société Générale sent a letter to the Basel Committee's Models Task Force in response to the committee's assertion that project finance loans were significantly riskier than corporate loans and, therefore, warranted higher capital requirements. Nearing finalization of a new capital accord, the committee planned to impose higher risk weights on project finance loans—risk weights that would, in some cases, double or triple the capital requirements on project finance loans. The executives feared the new capital standards would have a devastating effect on project finance lending by making loan spreads uneconomic to potential borrowers and by driving business to nonbank competitors that were not subject to the same capital requirements.

To challenge the proposal, the four banks joined forces and hired Standard & Poor's Risk Solutions to analyze the default and loss characteristics of their combined project loan portfolios. The consortium had now completed the study's first two phases—assessing the historical loss given default (LGD) and the probability of loan default (PD)—and was including the results in its letter to the committee. The results, consortium members believed, proved that project finance loans were less risky than most corporate loans. They wondered, however, if the results would convince the committee to lower the proposed risk weights on project loans.

The Basel Committee

The Bank for International Settlements (BIS), headquartered in Basel, Switzerland, served as a bank for central banks and helped set international monetary policy. In 1975, the central bank

---

Professor Benjamin C. Esty and Research Associate Aldo M. Sesia, Jr. prepared this case. HBS cases are developed solely as the basis for class discussion. Cases are not intended to serve as endorsements, sources of primary data, or illustrations of effective or ineffective management.

Copyright © 2002 President and Fellows of Harvard College. To order copies or request permission to reproduce materials, call 1-800-545-7685, write Harvard Business School Publishing, Boston, MA 02163, or go to http://www.hbsp.harvard.edu. No part of this publication may be reproduced, stored in a retrieval system, used in a spreadsheet, or transmitted in any form or by any means—electronic, mechanical, photocopying, recording, or otherwise—without the permission of Harvard Business School.

governors of the G-10 countries[a] convened to form the Basel Committee on Banking Supervision. Although the committee had no supranational authority, it articulated banking standards and guidelines with the goal of closing gaps in international supervisory coverage. As part of its responsibilities, the committee developed capital adequacy standards for international banks, which served as guidelines for national bank regulators. Prior to the committee's introduction of international capital standards, national regulators established minimum capital requirements using simple capital ratios (e.g., net worth to on-balance sheet assets). In the United States, for example, regulators set the requirement for primary capital at 5.5% of total assets.

The 1988 Capital Accord (Basel I)

The Basel Committee published its first report on capital adequacy in 1988. Called the 1988 Capital Accord (Basel I), the report highlighted "dangerously low" capital levels at the world's largest banks and proposed the creation of uniform minimum capital standards. By setting minimum capital standards, the 1988 Accord protected bank owners, depositors, creditors, and deposit insurers (i.e., governments) against financial distress. The committee chose 8% as the target capital ratio (net worth to assets) though the actual amount of capital required varied as a function of a bank's asset portfolio. The Basel framework identified five broad asset categories and assigned risk weights of 0%, 10%, 20%, 50%, and 100% to them. Whereas cash had a risk weight of 0%, residential mortgages had a risk weight of 50%. Project finance and all corporate loans fell in the highest risk category with a risk weight of 100%. Thus, a bank with a $100 million project finance loan needed to hold $8 million of capital (=$100 million loan x 100% risk weight x 8% target capital ratio). National regulators adopted the accord and required banks to implement it by 1992. Simplicity, the framework's strength, was also its greatest weakness. Using five categories simplified implementation but ignored important differences between loans within a given asset category.

The New Basel Capital Accord (Basel II)

In June 1999, the Basel Committee announced plans to revise the capital standards and described its objectives this way:

> The new framework intends to provide approaches which are both more comprehensive and more sensitive to risks than the 1988 Accord, while maintaining the overall level of regulatory capital. Capital requirements that are more in line with underlying risks will allow banks to manage their businesses more efficiently. ... The Committee believes the benefits of a regime in which capital is aligned more closely to risk significantly exceed the costs, with the result that the banking system should be safer, sounder, and more efficient.[1]

The new regulatory framework consisted of three pillars. Pillar 1 (Minimum Capital Requirements) maintained the same definition of regulatory capital and the 8% target capital ratio. Pillar 2 (Supervisory Review) called for increased regulatory oversight. Pillar 3 (Market Discipline) outlined requirements for increased bank disclosure. The committee hoped to finalize the new accord by the end of 2002 and implement it by 2005.

The new proposal also focused on individual asset classes and not on a bank's entire asset portfolio or its integrated balance sheet (i.e., the combination of assets and liabilities). Rather than

---

[a] The Group of Ten (G-10) countries includes Belgium, Canada, France, Germany, Italy, Japan, Luxembourg, the Netherlands, Spain, Sweden, Switzerland, the United Kingdom, and the United States.

using just a few broad asset classes, however, the new proposal set capital requirements based on credit risk within asset classes using one of two approaches. Under the *standardized* approach, banks would use the ratings on their borrowers or loans, supplied by credit rating agencies approved by regulators, with risk weights set by the Basel Committee to determine the minimum amount of capital they needed to hold. If the borrowers or loans were unrated, banks would have to use 100% risk weights. In contrast, under the *internal ratings based* (IRB) approach, banks would classify their loans into risk categories using their own internal data provided they could demonstrate they had accurate historical default and recovery data. Banks with PD data only, would use the *foundation* IRB approach in conjunction with supervisory estimates of LGD to determine their capital charges.[b] Banks with PD and LGD data would use the *advanced* IRB approach. In both cases, the capital requirements would be based on a framework established by the regulators, which would define the relationship between PD, LGD, and risk weights. In most cases, banks using the IRB approaches would have equal or lower capital requirements than banks using the standardized approach.

Although the IRB approaches implied there would be different standards at different banks, the committee favored the internal approaches because they incorporated a bank's specific risk profile, loan loss experience, and risk-mitigation techniques. By incorporating this information into the capital allocation process, the committee hoped to improve safety, soundness, and efficiency. Based on early feedback from the banks, the committee estimated the new accord would increase total industry capital by 14% (see **Exhibit 1**).

Besides setting capital based on subcategories of asset risk, the new accord treated project finance as an asset class distinct from corporate lending. Although the use of project finance dated back to the 1930s, if not earlier, it was a relatively small business until the 1990s, when it began to grow rapidly. By 2000, total project-financed investment exceeded $200 billion annually (see **Exhibit 2**). Given this growth, the Basel Committee's Models Task Force (MTF), formed to design the accord's IRB approaches, decided that project finance would be classified as a form of "specialized lending." Generally speaking, specialized lending involved loans secured by an asset's cash flow rather than by a corporate balance sheet and earnings (e.g., income-producing real estate). The MTF believed specialized lending was riskier than corporate lending and, therefore, warranted higher risk weights:

> First, such loans possess unique loss distribution and risk characteristics. In particular, given the source of repayment, the exposures exhibit greater risk volatility—in times of distress banks are likely to be faced with both high default rates and high loss rates. . . . MTF's dialogue with the industry also highlighted that historical loan performance data for specialized lending exposures are scarce. Many banks therefore face difficulties in establishing credible and reliable estimates of key risk factors (including probability of default), which can be adequately validated by both the bank and its supervisor. As a result, there is no common industry standard for a rigorous, empirical, and risk-sensitive approach to economic capital estimations for specialized lending exposures.[2]

In January 2002, the Basel Committee provided further details on how project finance would be treated under the new accord. Under the standardized approach and the advanced IRB approach, the risk weights for project loans would be the same as the risk weights for corporate loans with similar ratings and LGD estimates. However, the MTF said project loans would have higher risk

---

[b] Essentially, the Basel Committee wanted banks to hold enough (regulatory) capital to cover their expected loss (EL) and unexpected loss (UL). EL was equal to PD multiplied by LGD multiplied by EAD, where PD and LGD were percentages, and EAD (exposure at default) was the loan's outstanding loan amount plus lending commitments. UL represented the volatility of EL.

weights than corporate loans under the foundation IRB approach because supervisory estimates of LGD for project loans were likely to be higher than LGD estimates for corporate loans. Under the foundation IRB approach, banks would classify project finance loans into four categories (strong, fair, weak, or default) and use risk weights ranging from 75% to 750% set by the Basel Committee (see **Exhibit 3**). Given this proposal, a bank using the foundation IRB approach with a $100 million project finance loan rated "fair" would have to hold an incremental $4 million of capital under the new accord [= (150% Basel II risk weight – 100% Basel I risk weight) x $100 million x 8%]. Assuming a bank required a 20% pretax return on equity (ROE), the higher capital charge would add approximately 80 basis points to the price of the loan [= ($4 million x 20%)/ $100 million], ignoring the benefits of using less debt to fund the loan.[c] While all banks used significantly more sophisticated internal capital allocation systems—most of these systems were based on some notion of risk-adjusted return on capital (RAROC, pronounced "ray rock")—the end result was the same: spreads on low-rated project finance loans would have to increase. (**Exhibit 4** shows typical terms for a project finance loan.) Because sub-investment grade loans (BB+ and below) comprised 50% to 65% of the average bank's project loan portfolio, bankers anticipated higher capital requirements for project loans under Basel II. The Basel committee predicted that total capital for project loans would increase by 22% (see **Exhibit 1**).

Under the new accord, banks that opted to use the IRB approaches for their corporate loans would also be required to use the IRB approaches for their project loans. Banks that had historical data for their corporate loans were likely to choose the IRB approaches because they would, in most cases, reduce their capital requirements. Consequently, these banks would be obligated to use the IRB approaches for their project finance loans as well. In the event a bank did not have sufficient historical data for its project loans, it would be given a transition period to build the necessary internal systems to report the necessary data. In the interim, the bank would slot its project loans into supervisory categories using Basel Committee guidelines and apply risk weights similar to the foundation IRB approach.

Industry Reaction to Basel II

Project finance bankers reacted immediately to the MTF proposal. For example, Chris Beale, managing director and global head of project finance at Citigroup, said:

> As I read the proposal, alarm bells began to go off. We won't be able to price loans high enough to earn an acceptable return on capital, which means the new accord has the potential to put us out of business. Without a doubt, banks' interest in emerging market projects will evaporate, while here in the U.S. borrowers will either look to corporate finance solutions or forgo their investments. The committee's key assumption—the idea that project loans are significantly riskier than corporate loans—doesn't match my personal experience, nor does it reflect the historical performance of Citigroup's project loan portfolio.

Across town at Deutsche Bank's New York office, Managing Director Sandra Bell echoed Beale's reaction:

> The Models Task Force views project finance as very risky due to the perception that the probability of default is high and that it is highly [positively] correlated with loss given default. We don't believe either perception is correct and worry that the resulting capital

---

[c] Target returns, or target returns net of funding costs, depend on many factors such as asset risk, maturity (tenor), capitalization, and current interest rates.

requirements will force us to increase our loan spreads. In a market where loan pricing is important, we won't be able to price competitively with other sources of capital that are not subject to the new Basel Accord. Furthermore, the proposed changes may preclude smaller banks from participating in the syndicated loan market, thereby limiting the borrowing capacity for any single project, as the remaining project lenders won't be willing to take larger, more risky hold positions.

At ABN AMRO in Amsterdam, Managing Director Jan Prins remarked:

> The Models Task Force has incorrectly assumed that project loans are riskier than corporate loans, but this is understandable given that many projects involve greenfield assets and nonrecourse lending. Moreover, the higher margins on project loans hint at greater risk. The MTF may also point to anecdotal evidence to justify their position: that is, high-profile defaults such as Eurotunnel, EuroDisney, and Iridium. But for each of these defaults, there are hundreds of successful deals that you never hear about. When you factor in all those loans, the track record is really quite impressive.

Despite the initial opposition, the Basel Committee seemed intent on establishing higher capital charges for project loans. However, some project financiers believed they could persuade the committee to do otherwise. Beale, for instance, saw the committee's request for feedback as a "call to arms." As he contemplated various responses, he had to face one reality: although most banks had long-term statistics on loan losses, few tracked the performance of project finance loans as a distinct asset class for more than a few years. Furthermore, at least at Citigroup, the reporting systems deleted loans that were prepaid or fully repaid, making it more difficult to document loan performance over the long run. Moody's Investor Service, having analyzed many bank portfolios and its own internal files, recognized this challenge:

> We believe that devising an accurate IRB approach for project finance lending is currently difficult due to one key factor: a lack of historical probability of default and loss given default data.... Without such data, it is difficult for any lending institution to demonstrate the accuracy of risk weights applied to a particular transaction.... We believe that it is currently difficult to verify whether many lending institutions can accurately predict default or losses for a project finance loan.[3]

Yet Beale remained guardedly optimistic, in part because banks were required to file detailed data on loan delinquencies and defaults with their national regulators. There was also the possibility that recent attempts to securitize project finance loans might have generated some useful data. Securitization of project loans began in 1998 when Credit Suisse First Boston issued the first collateralized debt obligation (CDO).[d] Three years later, Citigroup issued a $350 million CDO backed by 25 project loans, and other banks were trying to structure similar deals. To establish capital structures for their CDOs, particularly the size of the "first-loss" tranche, banks turned to the rating agencies to estimate the PD and LGD for their portfolios.

Despite the existence of some limited data, Beale knew it would be difficult to assemble convincing evidence, especially given the short time frame—he believed the committee wanted to finalize the new accord by March 2002. Nevertheless, he believed a quantitative study was the only way to convince the committee to change the current proposal. He hurriedly placed telephone calls to counterparts at 12 other banks, hoping they would join forces in such a study. He did not ask all

---

[d] A collateralized debt obligation is a form of asset securitization in which a portfolio of project loans is placed in a trust. Shares of the trust are then sold to investors across a range of tranches with different loss positions. Collateralized debt obligations provide capital reserve relief, create balance sheet liquidity, and allow lenders to make new loans.

of the top project finance lenders to participate, but he did contact leading banks from a wide range of countries to build a global database and to create information that would interest not only the Basel Committee but also various national regulators. He did not, for example, contact the International Finance Corporation (IFC), a member of the World Bank Group. He felt its portfolio of emerging market loans would have a different risk profile because the IFC sometimes made loans for policy reasons (e.g., to develop economies) rather than for purely commercial reasons.

Commenting on the invitation to participate in a loan loss study, Beale said:

> Some bankers declined to participate in the study because they felt it would not benefit their banks specifically. While it is true that we [Citigroup] will likely qualify for the advanced IRB approach with or without the study, the study will help us, and the industry, on two fronts. First, we hope to convince the Basel Committee to lower the risk weights altogether, which will reduce our capital requirements. Second, many smaller banks that participate in our loan syndicates will not qualify for the advanced IRB approach. These banks will have to use the foundation approach and, therefore, face higher capital charges. We are doing the study to benefit these smaller banks and as a way to protect the viability of our loan syndication business.

Despite these arguments, bankers declined to participate for many reasons: they did not perceive Basel II as a serious threat, they were already preparing their own replies to the Basel Committee, or they did not believe there was enough time to collect the data and respond to the committee.

The Four Bank Consortium

In January 2002, four banks—ABN AMRO, Citigroup, Deutsche Bank, and Société Générale—agreed to collaborate on a loan loss study. Each bank, headquartered in a different G-10 country, was one of the top 10 project finance loan arrangers in 2001. Combined, they had originated over 25% of all project loans in 2001 (see **Exhibits 5a** and **5b**). At their first meeting, they agreed on two objectives: first, to convince the Basel Committee to reduce the risk weights for project finance loans; and second, to build a database that participating banks (e.g. consortium members) could use to estimate PD and LGD so they would qualify for the advanced IRB approach.

To conduct the analysis, the consortium approached Risk Solutions—a division of Standard & Poor's Corporation that provided customized credit analysis, models, and data to help clients manage risk. David Keisman, a managing director, explained.

> We are ideally suited to conduct the project finance loan loss study. First, having worked with corporate debt for years, we have the expertise and the experience to analyze loan losses. Second, given the collaborative nature of the project, we can provide independence and objectivity. And third, as a separate division of Standard & Poor's, our analysis and findings will be independent of the rating agency. If the study results are favorable, the consortium can show them to the Basel Committee, to their national regulators, and to the rating agencies. If not, they don't have to show anyone. Our only concern is whether the banks can get us the data we need to conduct the analysis.

The consortium broke the study into three phases and set deadlines for each one, as follows: (Phase 1) analyze LGD by March 2002; (Phase 2) analyze PD by July 2002; and (Phase 3) repeat the process with six to ten additional banks by March 2003. The consortium decided to analyze LGD first because there would be fewer defaults than loans to analyze by the March deadline (the PD analysis required Risk Solutions to analyze all loans) and because the consortium was primarily concerned with changing the committee's perception that defaults on project finance loans resulted in greater losses than defaults on corporate loans. Phase 2 was needed to estimate EL while Phase 3 was needed to bolster the study's statistical power. Before collecting any data, however, the consortium had to define project finance and determine what constituted a default to ensure consistency in data collection across the banks. Though project finance had generally accepted characteristics (e.g., repayment occurred through project cash flow), nuances in loan characteristics made consistent identification of project finance loans improbable. Prins explained the challenge:

> Conceptually, project finance is very simple. It normally involves a sizeable capital investment that is financed on the merits of the asset itself. A project company is not a going concern, but rather a self-liquidating entity. The project's cash flow services its debt and provides, ideally, a good return on investment for the sponsors. In practice, however, defining a project loan is much more difficult. Basel II assumes a clear distinction between project and corporate loans, but a clear distinction doesn't really exist in practice because many loans have characteristics of both. For example, the highly structured deals in the telecom industry, the recent portfolio financings in the power industry, and the loans to project holding companies like AES highlight the many gray areas between corporate and project finance.

After much discussion, the consortium adopted the following definition for project finance:

> A project company is a group of agreements and contracts between lenders, project sponsors, and other interested parties that creates a form of business organization that will issue a finite amount of debt on inception; will operate in a focused line of business; and, will ask that lenders look only to a specific asset to generate cash flow as the sole source of principal and interest payments and collateral.[4]

The consortium then tried to define what constituted a loan default. Nathan Fox, an assistant vice president at Citigroup, explained:

> If you use a broad definition like technical defaults (e.g., the borrower violates a covenant by failing to maintain credit ratios or missing performance milestones), then a large percent of our portfolio has experienced a default. But we view these types of defaults as one of the advantages of project lending. They serve as an early warning device, a tripwire, which forces borrowers to address faltering business plans and correct problems before they become too serious. In this study, we are interested in payment default (i.e., failure to pay on time and in full), but we recognize the importance of broader definitions.

Deutsche Bank's Bell elaborated:

> The Models Task Force has taken the concept of restructuring in the project finance area as a negative. On the contrary, those of us who practice this every day view restructuring as a basis for ensuring ultimate repayment and recovery. . . . Covenant packages are deliberately designed to allow a lot of things to happen early, providing the opportunity for projects to restructure. . . . [In] the project finance world, restructuring is associated with full recovery and often includes enhanced coverage and security. And that to me is a big distinction not recognized by the committee's process.[5]

The consortium eventually adopted a broader definition of default consistent with Standard & Poor's definition, though its members realized that a broader definition would result in higher default rates yet lower LGD estimates. According to the consortium's definition, a default occurred if:

... a borrower was unable to make a contractually scheduled payment of principal and/or interest. This would include bankruptcies that disrupt payments, including default and cure within the grace period, consensual restructuring, amendment of the credit facility's repayment terms, and/or refinancing of the facility with the original lenders in order to give the borrower more time to repay the loan.

Phase 1—Recovery Rates (Loss Given Default)

The first part of the analysis determined recovery rates for defaulted loans. Risk Solutions created a data template for the banks and asked them to describe each defaulted loan's original terms, cash flow history, default date, and recovery amounts. Each bank appointed a study leader to gather the necessary information. With help from colleagues around the world, they collected and reviewed internal bank files. In some cases, merger activity and reorganizations complicated the process. For example, in 1999, Deutsche Bank acquired Bankers Trust, which two years earlier had acquired Alex. Brown & Sons. In the meantime, Risk Solutions searched public records and provided the banks with a list of likely defaults.

The four banks turned in Phase I data during February 2002. Although Risk Solutions was limited in its ability to verify specific facts because it did not have direct access to company records, it was able to crosscheck information to ensure consistency across the banks. The fact that most project loans were syndicated made this task significantly easier because multiple banks held positions in the same loans. Conflicting classifications and missing data forced Risk Solutions to make several, albeit conservative, assumptions. After reviewing the data, Risk Solutions calculated recovery rates. In present value terms, the recovery rate equaled the amount of the default settlement divided by the sum of the loan principal at default plus accrued interest plus interest penalties. For example, if a bank recovered $97 million on a loan with $98 million of principal due at default plus $2 million of accrued interest and penalties, it had a recovery rate of 97% (= $97 million/$100 million) and an LGD of 3% (= 100% – 97%). The calculation did not include expenses incurred to recover amounts owed.

The four banks identified 43 defaults across a range of regions and industries (see **Exhibit 6**). The mean recovery rate for project loans was 75%; the median was 100% (see **Exhibits 7a** and **7b**). From its existing database, Risk Solutions compared project loans against four types of corporate debt—leveraged loans,[e] secured debt, senior debt, and senior unsecured debt. Although there were more observations for the various types of corporate debt, project loans exhibited higher average recovery rates than all but the leveraged loans.

Risk Solutions compared the distribution of project finance recovery rates with the distributions of recovery rates from the various types of corporate debt using three statistical tests: the Kolmogorov-Smirnov Two-Sample Test, the Wilcoxon Rank Sum Test, and the Kruskal-Wallis Test (see **Appendix A** for more information on the statistical tests). Based on the results, Risk Solutions concluded that the performance of project finance was most similar to the performance of leveraged loans. Risk Solutions then tested the project loans against two subcategories of leveraged loans and found they performed more like senior or *pari passu* leveraged loans (LL Rank 1) than subordinated leveraged loans (LL Rank 2).

---

[e] Leveraged loans include senior debt obligations rated BB+/Ba or lower and all unrated debt as long as the price spreads are Libor plus 150 basis points (bps) or more. Investment grade debt, real estate, securitization vehicles, and traditional project finance are not considered leveraged loans. Source: Loan Pricing Corporation, <http://www.loanpricing.com/>.

Basel II: Assessing the Default and Loss Characteristics of Project Finance Loans (A)

The results essentially confirmed what the bankers had originally asserted. Beale explained:

> When I saw the results, I felt vindicated. Although we lend without the benefit of recourse to diversified corporate operations, project loans are less risky than comparably rated corporate loans. While there are many reasons for this outcome—better security, contractual mitigation of key risks, etc.—I believe the primary reasons are better information and greater transparency. In project finance you get complete access to project data and can analyze the impact of every input and output. You just can't do that in corporate lending.

On March 18, 2002, the consortium members sent a letter describing the results to the Basel Committee and to their own national bank regulators. The consortium wrote:

> The data suggests project finance loans have a significantly better LGD profile than claims on corporates. Indeed, we believe this data supports our proposal that project finance loans should receive more favorable regulatory treatment than claims on corporates across the full credit spectrum.... Based on the preliminary findings ... project finance loans should require approximately half as much capital as claims on corporates under the IRB approach.[6]

The letter not only proposed reduced risk weights for project loans (see **Exhibit 3**), it also listed 11 reasons why project finance loans were likely to outperform corporate loans (see **Exhibit 8**). Jay Worenklein, global head of project finance at Société Générale, elaborated:

> The portfolio performance of most of the major finance banks demonstrates that in crisis situations ... banks have much higher recoveries on their project finance loans than on corporate loans. This is because of the combination of the well-structured and secured nature of most projects, the amount of equity underlying the project debt, the need for the output of the project, the sponsorship of projects by companies with a long-term commitment to their industries and to the countries involved, the careful analysis of downside scenarios relating to commodity pricing, and other factors.[7]

Phase 2—Probability of Default

With time running out, the consortium quickly turned to the second phase, the PD analysis. The consortium's pooled portfolio consisted of 759 facilities and included loans from a broad range of industrial sectors and geographic locations (see **Exhibits 9** and **10**). Risk Solutions formed static pools at the beginning of each year to calculate *portfolio* default rates over time (see **Appendix B** for an explanation of this methodology). Static pool analysis differed from mortality analysis, in which the rating agencies calculated *loan* default rates from origination to maturity.

Risk Solutions first analyzed the PD with default broadly defined, as it had been in Phase I. It also conducted the analysis with PD narrowly defined (i.e., excluding restructured loans with no accounting loss but with changes to amortization or maturity and defaulted loans where the borrower made payments during the cure period). Risk Solutions then compared the consortium's two PD rates with default rates on corporate loans. The definition of a corporate loan default was most similar, but not identical, to the broad default definition used for project finance loans.

The analysis suggested that project finance loans had a lower probability of default than corporate loans. The 10-year cumulative PD for project loans was 7.63% under the broader definition of default compared with 9.38% for that of corporate loans (see **Exhibit 11**). According to Risk Solutions, this result meant that project loans performed like corporate credits rated BBB- to BB, although project loans had a higher recovery rate (75% for project loans versus approximately 50% for corporate loans). Using the narrower definition of default resulted in 19 defaults (compared with 43 using the broad definition). Project loans had a PD of 3.68% and an LGD of 56%, similar to the rates of BBB+/BBB corporate loans.

With the PD results in hand, the consortium sent a second letter to the Basel Committee on August 23, 2002. The letter stated, "This data indicates project finance loans perform better than claims on corporates, regardless of the definition of default; under a broad definition LGDs are low and PDs are average, while under a narrow definition LGDs are average and PDs are low."[8]

The IPFA and IFC Respond to Basel

In addition to the consortium, other banks and related parties responded to the Basel Committee's request for feedback. In fact, the committee received hundreds of responses on its original proposal. The International Project Finance Association (IPFA), an industry trade group, presented a working paper to the committee signed by 21 project sponsors and banks. It stated:

> An important point that IPFA would like to raise is that project finance loans enjoy a much better Loss Given Default history than Corporate Finance. ... Based on this the proposed regulatory structure needs to be amended with terms more favourable to project finance. ... Whilst IPFA recognizes the importance of ensuring that financial institutions maintain sound balance sheets it hopes that the new regulatory framework ... will not impede lenders' ability to participate in project finance lending because of a disproportionate level of regulatory capital.[9]

The IFC, responsible for promoting private sector investment in developing countries, sent data on its portfolio of project loans to the Basel Committee. The IFC's portfolio of project loans had experienced a 2.1% loss rate compared with a 3.1% loss rate for all loans in its 45-year history (see **Exhibit 12**). In a letter to the committee, Suellen Lazarus, director of syndication and international securities, commented:

> In our view the specialized lending paper does not give sufficient recognition to the numerous risk mitigants that are put in place for any typical project finance transaction. By failing to do so, the proposed regulatory framework on Specialized Lending jeopardizes long-term financing for investors seeking access for their substantial long-term capital investments throughout the world, and particularly in emerging markets. ... We strongly recommend that project finance not be included in Specialized Lending as separate from corporate lending.[10]

Lazarus also acknowledged the challenges facing the Basel Committee:

> Project finance lending is a small component of the business of most banks. For this reason, relative to its far-reaching impact, the proposal has not been at the top of most banks' Basel II agendas. ... The Basel Committee has before it an enormous task. Its members have been impressive in their openness to ideas and patience in listening to divergent views. They are grappling with highly technical issues that are not simply resolved, and yet there is the need to reduce complexity. At the same time, they are not commercial bankers and often have limited experience with the range of products they must regulate. There are few people who would want this responsibility on their shoulders.[11]

Conclusion

Having completed the first two phases of the loan loss study, consortium members had to decide what to do next. James Berner, an associate at Deutsche Bank, said:

> At this point, I think the difficult work is done. All four banks have collected historical data, Risk Solutions has analyzed it, and we have reported the results to the Basel Committee. The results are fairly clear: project finance loans are not riskier than comparably rated corporate loans either from an LGD or PD perspective. We hope this information will convince the Models Task Force to change their original position and adopt risk weights that are equal to, if not more favorable than, the risk weights for corporate loans. In the meantime, we should try to add more banks to the study to strengthen its validity and continue to collect loan performance data for our own internal purposes.

Keisman, of Standard & Poor's Risk Solutions, concurred:

> Although the results are strong, there is a need for additional analysis. We currently have data covering approximately 25% of project loan origination. I'd like to see that number closer to 50%, and I'd like to see broader geographic coverage with banks from Asia, South America, and Australia. On a more practical level, the goal is to get to the point where the addition of an incremental bank does not change the overall results. We'd also like to analyze the relationships among loan characteristics, credit behavior, and loan performance.

In keeping with the original plan, the consortium sent letters inviting other banks to join it. While it received some expressions of interest, no other banks had yet agreed to participate in the study. One project finance banker, not involved with the consortium, conceded that project finance loans would become pricier under Basel II, but he was not convinced Basel II would have a dramatic effect on the industry. Another banker believed the industry would feel "an initial jolt" but did not believe Basel II would drive borrowers to non-bank lenders. Beale, Bell, Prins, and Worenklein, the global heads of project finance at the consortium's member banks, were less sanguine about the future under Basel II. They believed it had the potential to inflict serious damage on the industry and hoped the loan loss study would avert such a scenario.

Exhibit 1 The Impact of Basel II on Banking Industry Capital

Asset Class	Percent of Total Capital Under Current Capital Requirements	Basel II[a] Percentage Change in Required Capital by Asset Class	Change in Required Capital as a Percent of Current Total Capital Required for All Assets
Corporate	61%	22%	14%
Sovereign	1	238	3
Interbank	8	49	4
Retail	24	(28)	(7)
Securitization	1	108	1
Equity	3	(17)	0
Project Finance	2	22	0
Total	100%		
Total increase in capital			14%

Source: "Results of the Second Quantitative Study," Basel Committee on Banking Supervision, November 5, 2001, p. 5.

[a] Percentage increase is based on the foundation IRB approach.

Exhibit 2 Project Finance Investment Growth and Debt Type (1994–2001)

	Total Project-Financed Investment (US$ billion)								
	1994	1995	1996	1997	1998	1999	2000	2001	5-Year CAGR
Bank loans	$13.7	$23.3	$42.8	$67.4	$56.7	$72.4	$110.9	$108.5	20%
Bonds	4.0	3.8	4.8	7.5	9.8	20.0	20.8	25.0	39
Total Project Lending	17.7	27.1	47.6	74.9	66.5	92.4	131.7	133.5	23
Year-to-Year Change in Lending		53%	76%	57%	-11%	39%	43%	1%	
MLA/BLA development agencies [a]	11.3	17.6	19.0	21.9	18.5	16.6	17.7	18.8	0
Equity Financing (estimate) [b]	12.4	19.2	28.5	41.5	36.4	46.7	64.0	65.2	18
Total Private Sector Investment (including debt and equity)	$41.4	$63.9	$95.1	$138.3	$121.4	$155.7	$213.4	$217.5	18%

	Percent of Lending by Type of Debt							
	1994	1995	1996	1997	1998	1999	2000	2001
Bank loans	77%	86%	90%	90%	85%	78%	84%	81%
Bonds	23	14	10	10	15	22	16	19
Total	100%	100%	100%	100%	100%	100%	100%	100%

	Number of Projects							
	1994	1995	1996	1997	1998	1999	2000	2001
Number of projects:								
With bank loan financing	NA	NA	341	407	419	559	594	314
With bond financing	NA	22	19	25	43	78	86	79

Source: Adapted from *Project Finance International* (London, U.K.: IFR Publishing, 3/2/95, 2/28/96, 1/29/97, 1/28/98, 1/27/99, 1/26/00, 1/24/01, and 1/23/02).

[a] Private sector investment made by bilateral development agencies (BLAs), multilateral development agencies (MLAs), export credit agencies (ECAs), and export financing institutions. Adapted from "The Private Sector Financing Activities of International Financial Institutions: 1991–1997," IFC, January 1998. The numbers for 1994 and 2001 are casewriter estimates. Some of the reported total is for guarantees; we assume 75% of the total is for equity and debt investments.

[b] Assuming a total debt/total capitalization ratio of 70%.

Exhibit 3 Proposed Risk Weights for Corporate and Project Loans (Foundation IRB Approach)

			Risk Weights for Project Finance Loans		
Supervisory Rating Category	Probability of Default	Risk Weights for Corporate Finance Loans Basel Committee Proposal[a]	Basel Committee Supervisory Categorization	Basel Committee Proposal (Jan. 2002)	Consortium Proposal (Mar. 2002)
AAA to A-	0.03–0.09%	19–35%	Strong	75%	10–18%
BBB+ to BBB-	0.25	55	Strong	75	28
BB+	0.75	90	Fair	150	46
BB	1.00	100	Fair	150	50
BB-	2.00	130	Fair	150	65
B+	3.00	150	Fair	150	75
B to C	5–20.00	186–376	Weak	300	93–188
Default[b]	N/A	625	Default	750	313

Source: Four Bank Consortium memorandum to the Basel Committee and national regulators, March 18, 2002, p. 2.

[a] Assumes an LGD of 45% to 50% (casewriter interpretation of the Basel Committee's position).

[b] Loan ratings can migrate to the default category over time.

Exhibit 4 Returns on Project Finance Loans

Origination Returns		
Participation/Underwriting Fees	25–75bp	Assumes loan is fully drawn (no commitment fees)
Administrative Expense	25–75bp	Credit review and underwriting expenses
Ongoing Returns		
Interest Rates (3-month Libor)	5.00%	Recent historical average
Spread (Interest Income)	Libor + 180bp	
Interest Expense	Libor	
Operating (Noninterest) Expense	10bp	
Expected Loan Loss	??	= (Probability of Default * Loss Given Default)
Desired Pretax Return on Equity (ROE)	20%	
Loan Terms		
Average Size ($ millions)	$175	Median = $70
Average Maturity (years)	8.6	Median = 8.0
Syndicate Structure		
Total number of banks	14	
Number of arranging banks	11	
Number of participating banks	3	

Source: Casewriter estimates and data contained in S. Kleimeier and W. Megginson, "Are Project Finance Loans Different From Other Syndicated Credits?" *Journal of Applied Corporate Finance* 13, Spring 2000: 75–87.

Exhibit 5a Volume of Syndicated Loans Arranged by Consortium Members (US$ millions)

	1997	1998	1999	2000	2001	Total
Citigroup	$2,913	$2,514	$5,897	$11,927	$15,512	$38,763
ABN AMRO	4,512	2,350	2,302	7,875	4,019	21,058
Société Générale	754	1,998	3,218	9,616	5,301	20,887
Deutsche Bank	3,315	4,091	3,045	6,487	3,623	20,561
Subtotal	11,494	10,953	14,462	35,905	28,455	101,269
Total Market	67,425	56,651	72,392	110,885	108,478	415,831
% of Total Market	17.0%	19.3%	20.0%	32.4%	26.2%	24.4%

Source: Four Bank Consortium memorandum to the Basel Committee and national regulators, March 18, 2002, p. 6.

Exhibit 5b Global Lead Arrangers—Bank Loans (US$ millions)

2001 Rank	Name	2000 Rank	Number of Issues in 2001	Amount Underwritten in 2001	Percent of Total Lending in 2001
1	**Citigroup**	1	54	$15,512	14.3%
2	WestLB	7	27	8,235	7.6
3	BNP Paribas SA	9	21	6,429	5.9
4	**Société Générale**	2	17	5,301	4.9
5	CSFB	6	8	4,742	4.4
6	JP Morgan	5	18	4,333	4.0
7	Dresdner Kleinwort Wasserstein	11	17	4,038	3.7
8	**ABN AMRO**	4	19	4,019	3.7
9	**Deutsche Bank**	8	14	3,623	3.3
10	Barclays	10	18	3,612	3.3
11	Mizuho Financial Group	14	20	3,187	2.9
12	IntesaBci	24	5	2,621	2.4
13	Bank of America	3	13	2,282	2.1
14	Credit Lyonnais	17	12	2,019	1.9
15	Royal Bank of Scotland	28	16	1,911	1.8
	Other banks			36,614	33.8
	Total Market			**$108,478**	**100.0%**

Source: Adapted from *Project Finance International*, January 24, 2001 and January 23, 2002.

Exhibit 6 Distribution of Defaulted Loan Facilities by Region and Sector

Region	Number of Facilities	Percent of Total	Sector	Number of Facilities	Percent of Total
North America	18	41.9%	Power	9	20.9%
Europe	8	18.6	Oil & Gas	8	18.6
Asia Pacific	6	14.0	Infrastructure	7	16.3
Latin America	6	14.0	Metals & Mining	6	14.0
Other (incl. Africa)	5	11.6	Telecom	6	14.0
			Other	7	16.3
Total	43	100.0%	Total	43	100.0%

Source: Adapted from "Project Finance Recovery Study," Standard & Poor's Risk Solutions, March 18, 2002, p. 9.

Exhibit 7a Descriptive Statistics on Recovery Rates by Asset Type

Asset Type	Number of Observations	Mean	Median	Standard Deviation	Maximum[a]	Minimum	Kolmogorov-Smirnov Test[b]	Rank Sum Test[b]	Kruskal-Wallis Statistic[c]
Project Finance	43	75.39%	100.00%	34.90%	100.00%	0%			
Leveraged Loans[d]	203	78.03	98.26	29.56	151.01	0	1	0	0.7424
Secured Debt	339	68.85	78.86	32.68	111.49	0	1	0	0.0829
Senior Debt	844	67.33	78.05	34.19	125.23	0	1	0	0.0567
Senior Unsecured	311	46.20	40.38	36.27	125.23	0	1	1	0.0000

Exhibit 7b Descriptive Statistics on Recovery Rates—Project Finance vs. Leveraged Loans

Asset Type	Number of Observations	Mean	Median	Standard Deviation	Maximum[a]	Minimum	Kolmogorov-Smirnov Test[b]	Rank Sum Test[b]	Kruskal-Wallis Statistic[c]
Project Finance	43	75.39%	100.00%	34.90%	100.00%	0%			
Leveraged Loans[d]	203	78.03	98.26	29.56	151.01	0	1	0	0.7424
LL Rank 1[e]	182	81.66	100.00	26.55	151.01	0	1	0	0.8574
LL Rank 2[f]	19	51.29	50.85	34.33	104.36	0	1	1	0.0074
Not Classified	2	n/a	n/a	n/a	n/a	n/a	n/a	n/a	n/a

Source: Adapted from "Project Finance Recovery Study," Standard & Poor's Risk Solutions, March 18, 2002, pp. 12 and 15.

[a] Recovery rates greater than 100% can occur when a bank receives equity as part of a loan restructuring and the equity subsequently appreciates. Defaults with recoveries greater than 100% account for less than 1% of the total number of observations.

[b] A value of 1 indicates the distribution of recovery rates for this type of loan is significantly different from the distribution for project finance loans.

[c] A value near 0 indicates that the distribution for this type of loan is significantly different from the distribution for project finance loans.

[d] Leveraged loans contain secured and unsecured corporate loans of companies with over $50 million in debt at the time of default.

[e] Leveraged loans of Rank 1 are senior or *pari passu* with other existing debt.

[f] Leveraged loans of Rank 2 are subordinate to other existing debt.

Exhibit 8   Reasons Why Project Finance Loans Outperform Corporate Finance Loans

Reason	Explanation
1. Control of Collateral	Perfected first priority liens on and pledges of the project's collateral (including shares, assets, and material contracts) preserve exclusive access to repayments from a liquidation of the project or for negotiating purposes with sponsors and other lenders.
2. Strong Sponsors	Involvement of deep-pocket partners with vested interest in the projects, including central governments, sponsors, contractors, insurers, suppliers, off-takers, etc. These parties often have key stakes in the success of the project.
3. Covenant Triggers	Step-in rights and covenant triggers that serve as "early warnings" to banks to renegotiate a structure before the borrower's credit quality deteriorates beyond a curable point. While corporate loans also have these features, project finance loans are structured deliberately with tighter covenants to trigger a renegotiation of loan terms before any significant credit deterioration occurs.
4. Sponsor Interests	Sponsors often act as counterparties in the projects, giving them vested interests in the success of the project. While not contractually obligated to support a project, these groups are frequently willing to inject equity into a troubled project.
5. Restrictions	Restrictions on facility drawdowns, use of proceeds, and mandatory payments in favor of the lenders.
6. Sponsor Incentives	Contractual obligations, penalties, and remedies to influence the activities of the sponsors in favor of the lenders.
7. Cash Flow Protections	Offshore and debt service accounts to mitigate cash flow volatility where appropriate.
8. Debt Limits	Prohibition on additional indebtedness, which, when combined with the typically steady or increasing cash flows of projects, increases debt service coverages over time.
9. Transparency	Transparency of the project's performance due to its single-asset nature. In contrast, corporate borrowers frequently have diverse streams of revenues, complicated subsidiary structures and accounting treatments, and cash flow streams that are difficult to analyze.
10. Project Independence	The essential commercial value of projects allows them to survive the bankruptcy or credit deterioration of a sponsor, supplier, contractor, etc. This ability is due to the inherent independent viability of the project's value and cash flow.
11. Loan Syndication	The syndication of project financing loans encourages conservative structures that appeal to a broad retail market, limits the possibility of unsophisticated banks being able to offer aggressive bilateral loans, and ensures that all lenders benefit from a controlled recovery process in a default situation irrespective of the size or importance of their respective participations.

Source: Four Bank Consortium memorandum to the Basel Committee and national regulators, March 18, 2002, pp. 3–4.

Exhibit 9 Distribution of Project Finance Facilities by Year of Origination

Year of Origination	Number of Facilities	Percent of Total
1988	6	0.8%
1989	11	1.5
1990	13	1.7
1991	13	1.7
1992	15	2.0
1993	23	3.0
1994	88	11.6
1995	60	7.9
1996	63	8.3
1997	99	13.0
1998	98	12.9
1999	106	14.0
2000	99	13.0
2001	65	8.6
Total	759	100.0%

Source: Adapted from "Project Finance Default Study," Standard & Poor's Risk Solutions, July 18, 2002, p. 7.

Exhibit 10 Description of the Project Finance Loan Sample

Region	Power	Oil, Gas & Petrochem.	Infra-structure	Metals & Mining	Media & Telecom	Other	Total	Percent of Total
North America	128	22	8	6	30	10	204	26.9%
Europe	50	16	41	9	61	14	191	25.2
Asia Pacific	62	42	17	16	17	23	177	23.3
Latin America	48	25	1	15	29	8	126	16.6
Africa	9	26	1	15	10	0	61	8.0
Total	297	131	68	61	147	55	759	100.0%
Percent of Total	39.1%	17.3%	9.0%	8.0%	19.4%	7.2%	100.0%	

Source: Adapted from "Project Finance Default Study," Standard & Poor's Risk Solutions, July 18, 2002, p. 7.

Exhibit 11 Default Rates on Project Finance and Corporate Finance Loans

| | Project Finance Loans | | | | Corporate Finance Loans | |
| | Default—Broadly Defined[a] | | Default—Narrowly Defined[b] | | Default—Broadly Defined[a] | |
Year	Weighted Avg. Marginal Default Rates[c]	Cumulative Average Default Rate[d]	Weighted Avg. Marginal Default Rates[c]	Cumulative Average Default Rate[d]	Weighted Avg. Marginal Default Rates[c]	Cumulative Average Default Rate[d]
1	1.52%	1.52%	0.63%	0.63%	1.49%	1.49%
2	1.61	3.13	0.69	1.32	1.49	2.98
3	1.27	4.40	0.59	1.91	1.32	4.30
4	1.19	5.58	0.54	2.46	1.08	5.38
5	1.07	6.65	0.53	2.99	0.90	6.27
6	0.44	7.09	0.14	3.14	0.79	7.06
7	0.21	7.30	0.21	3.35	0.69	7.75
8	0.33	7.63	0.33	3.68	0.59	8.34
9	0.00	7.63	0.00	3.68	0.54	8.87
10	0.00	7.63	0.00	3.68	0.51	9.38

Source: Adapted from "Project Finance Default Study," Standard & Poor's Risk Solutions, July 18, 2002, pp. 10–13.

[a] Borrower was unable to make a contractually scheduled payment of principal and/or interest. This includes bankruptcies that disrupt payment, including default and cure within the grace period, consensual restructuring, amendment of the credit facility's repayment terms, and/or refinancing of the facility with the original lenders in order to give the borrower more time to repay.

[b] Excludes loans restructured, with no accounting loss, but with change of amortization or extension of maturity, and defaulted loans paid during the cure period.

[c] The weighted average of all static pool defaults in years 1, 2, etc.

[d] Sum of weighted average marginal default rates.

Exhibit 12 International Finance Corporation Portfolio Performance: 1956–2001

	Number of Projects	Total Distributions (Millions)	Average Loan Amount (Millions)	Net Losses (Millions)	Net Loss Rate
All Closed A & C Loans[a]	1,175	$9,250	$7.87	$284	3.07%
Project Finance Portfolio	675	$5,826	$8.63	$123	2.11%

Source: Adapted from letter from Suellen Lazarus, International Finance Corporation's director of Syndications and International Securities Department, to Daniele Nouy, Secretary-General of the Basel Committee on Banking Supervision, November 16, 2001, Attachment 1. Available from <www.ifc.org/syndications/>.

[a] Loans are fixed and variable rate loans for International Finance Corporation's own account to private sector projects in developing countries; C-loans are a full range of quasi-equity products including convertible debt that impose a fixed repayment schedule also to private sector projects in developing countries.

Appendix A
Description of Statistical Tests

	Wilcoxon Rank Sum Test (Mann-Whitney Test)	Kruskal-Wallis Test	Kolmogorov-Smirnov Two-Sample Test
Definition	A nonparametric test used to compare two independent (unpaired) groups of sampled data.	A nonparametric test used to compare N-independent groups of sampled data (typically N ! 3; when N = 2, this test is approximately equal to the Wilcoxon Rank Sum Test).	A nonparametric test used to compare two independent groups of sampled data.
Test Procedure	Uses the average ranks of the data rather than their raw values to determine whether the two samples come from identical populations. Greater differences between the average ranks indicate the samples come from different populations.	Uses the average ranks of the data rather than their raw values to determine whether the two samples come from identical populations. Greater differences between the average ranks indicate the samples come from different populations.	Uses the empirical distribution functions to test whether two sample distributions are identical. Calculates the maximum distance between the cumulative distribution functions. Greater distances indicate different sample populations.
Test Statistic Distribution	Standardized normal	Chi-square with N-1 degrees of freedom	A specialized distribution
Key Assumptions	Samples are independent	Samples are independent	Samples are independent and reasonably large (>30 observations); underlying distributions are continuous.
Equivalent Parametric Test	T-test	Analysis of variance (ANOVA)	Chi-square goodness-of-fit test

Source: Casewriter descriptions.

Definitions:

Parametric tests: When statistics are calculated under the assumption that the data follow some common distribution such as a normal (Gaussian) distribution. In this case, we can use the properties of the underlying distribution to assist in developing significance tests. Tests that do not make assumptions about the underlying population distribution are known as nonparametric or "distribution-free" tests.

Paired data: Paired data typically arise from repeated measurements on the same subject (i.e., before and after some kind of intervention) or if the subjects are matched (paired) based on some other criteria before the data are collected.

Rank: An ordinal number assigned to data after it has been arranged from the smallest to the largest (e.g., the smallest value is assigned a 1).

Appendix B
Standard & Poor's Probability of Default Methodology

Portfolio Analysis (Static pools by year)

Year	Total # Loans in Prior Year's Portfolio	# Loans Removed from Prior Year's Portfolio Due to: Default	# Loans Removed from Prior Year's Portfolio Due to: Repayment	# New Loans Added to Portfolio	Total # Loans in Current Year's Portfolio	Number of Defaults (origination year, default year) Year 1	Year 2	Year 3
1990	0	0	0	100	100	$2_{90,90}$	$4_{90,91}$	$5_{90,92}$
1991	100	2	0	100	198	$3_{91,91} + 4_{90,91}$	$6_{91,92} + 5_{90,92}$	
1992	198	7	2	100	289	$1_{92,92} + 6_{91,92} + 5_{90,92}$		

Marginal Probability of Default Analysis

Year	Year 1	Year 2	Year 3
1990	=(2/100) =0.020	=(4/100) =0.040	=(5/100) =0.050
1991	=(3+4)/(198) =0.035	=(6+5)/(198) =0.056	
1992	=(1+6+5)/(289) =0.042		
Weighted Average Marginal Default Rates	=(2+3+4+1+6+5)/(100+198+289) =**0.036**	=(4+6+5)/(100+198) =**0.050**	=(5)/(100) =**0.050**

Cumulative Probability of Default Analysis

	Year 1	Year 2	Year 3
Cumulative Average Default Rates	=**0.036**	=(0.036+0.050) =**0.086**	=(0.086+0.050) =0.136

Source: Casewriter analysis.

Endnotes

[1] "The New Basel Capital Accord: An Explanatory Note," Secretariat of the Basel Committee on Banking Supervision, June 2001, p. 2.

[2] "Working Paper on the Internal Ratings-Based Approach to Specialised Lending," Basel Committee on Banking Supervision, October 2001, p. 1.

[3] Moody's Response to the Basel Committee Proposal on an Internal Rating-Based Capital Adequacy Approach for Project Finance, May 2001, p. 43.

[4] "Project Finance Recovery Study," Standard & Poor's Risk Solutions, March 2002, p. 5.

[5] "React or Die," *ProjectFinance Magazine*, February 2002, p. 42.

[6] Four Bank Consortium letter to national regulators and the Basel Committee on Banking Supervision Models Task Force on Specialised Lending, March 18, 2002, pp. 1–2.

[7] "React or Die," *ProjectFinance Magazine*, February 2002, p. 42.

[8] Four Bank Consortium letter to national regulators and the Basel Committee on Banking Supervision Models Task Force, August 23, 2002, p. 2.

[9] "IPFA Response to Basel Committee's Proposals (Basel II)," The International Project Finance Association, February 2001, pp. 2–3.

[10] IFC letter from Suellen Lambert Lazarus to the Secretary-General of the Basel Committee on Banking Supervision, November 16, 2001, p. 2. Source: International Finance Corporation, <http://www.ifc.org/syndications>.

[11] Suellen Lambert, "Basel II: The Project Blocker?" *Strategic Direct Investor*, March/April 2002, pp. 53–55.

HARVARD | BUSINESS | SCHOOL

9-204-094
JANUARY 27, 2004

BENJAMIN C. ESTY
ALDO SESIA, JR.

Basel II: Assessing the Default and Loss Characteristics of Project Finance Loans (B)

Introduction

The Basel Committee on Banking Supervision released the third draft of its new proposed capital accord on April 29, 2003, and asked banks to review the proposal and provide comments by July 31, 2003. As a response to the request, members of the project finance units at ABN AMRO, Citigroup, Deutsche Bank, and Société Générale were busy completing Phase 3 of their joint study on the historical performance of project finance loans. Since January 2002, the four banks had been working together to study the default and loss characteristics of their project finance loan portfolios. They had completed Phase 1, an analysis of Loss Given Default (LGD), in March 2002, and Phase 2, an analysis of probability of default (PD), in August 2002, and had sent their findings to the Basel Committee.

Largely through the consortium's efforts, the Basel Committee had decided that the capital requirements for project finance loans using the standardized approach or either the *foundation* or *advanced* internal ratings based (IRB) approach would be the same as for corporate loans. This represented a change from the Basel Committee's second draft of the accord, which had established higher risk weights for project finance using the *foundation* IRB approach. Although the consortium had recommended that project finance loans have lower risk weights than corporate loans, the committee's decision to use the same risk weight framework was a major triumph for the consortium. The goal of Phase 3 was to include additional banks and add additional data from 2002 to bolster the study's statistical power.

As of July 2003, eight additional banks had joined the consortium and provided data, bringing the total number of banks in the study with data to 12. The 12 participating banks arranged 34% of the project loans during 2002 (see **Exhibit 1**). Standard & Poor's (S&P) Risk Solutions, which collected and analyzed the data for the banks, reviewed loans from January 1, 1988 to December 31, 2002. The total number of loans in the Phase 3 study sample was 1,955—up from 759 loans in Phase 2 (see **Exhibit 2** for breakdown of loans by geographic region and industrial sector). The consortium wanted to use the results from Phase 3 in their response to the Basel Committee.

Professor Benjamin C. Esty and Research Associate Aldo Sesia, Jr. prepared this case. HBS cases are developed solely as the basis for class discussion. Cases are not intended to serve as endorsements, sources of primary data, or illustrations of effective or ineffective management.

Copyright © 2004 President and Fellows of Harvard College. To order copies or request permission to reproduce materials, call 1-800-545-7685, write Harvard Business School Publishing, Boston, MA 02163, or go to http://www.hbsp.harvard.edu. No part of this publication may be reproduced, stored in a retrieval system, used in a spreadsheet, or transmitted in any form or by any means—electronic, mechanical, photocopying, recording, or otherwise—without the permission of Harvard Business School.

Chris Beale, managing director and global head of project and structured trade finance at Citigroup, explained the significance of the larger sample:

> Our small, four-bank study has been extremely influential. It gave the Basel Committee actual default and loss data, and provided them with a rationale for lowering the capital requirements on project loans, or at least setting them in parallel with corporate loans. But the 12-bank study significantly enhances our position. It confirms our earlier findings and supports our original case that project loans are not riskier than corporate loans.

Phase 3 Results

Probability of Default (PD)

The banks reported 123 defaults, up from 43 in Phase 2, using the following broad definition of default:

> Borrower was unable to make a contractually scheduled payment of principal and/or interest. This would include bankruptcies that disrupt payments, including default and cure within the grace period, consensual restructuring, amendment of the credit facility's repayment terms, and/or refinancing of the facility with the original lenders in order to give the borrower more time to repay the loan.

The 10-year cumulative average probability of default was 13.3% compared to 7.63% in Phase 2.[a] The recent crises in the power and telecom sectors were largely to blame for the increase. In fact, industry analysts agreed that 2002 was one of the worst years ever for the project finance industry. However, it was important for the study to cover a full business cycle, which made the 2002 data especially important from a regulatory perspective. As a point of comparison, the 10-year cumulative average default rate on corporate loans with 2002 loan data was 10.64%, up from 9.38% with data through 2001 only (see **Exhibit 3** for details). Essentially, project finance loans performed like low investment grade loans when it came to default rates.

Recovery Rate (Loss Given Default—LGD)

In present value terms, the recovery rate equaled the amount of the default settlement divided by the sum of the loan principal at default plus accrued interest and interest penalties. The calculation excluded any additional costs or revenues related to restructuring or terminating the loan (e.g., legal and other expenses offset by extra fees and higher default interest rates). For purposes of the study, the banks defined emergence from default (i.e., what the bank received and when it received it) as: repayment of overdue interest, restructuring with no subsequent default, restructuring with the bank being taken out of the deal, material restructuring, and liquidation

Of the 123 loan defaults reported in Phase 3, 83 facilities, representing 76 projects, had emerged from default. The average recovery rate was 75.3%—approximately the same rate as reported in Phase 1. Moreover, each participating bank had an average recovery rate in excess of 50%. The

---

[a] Standard & Poor's Risk Management formed static pools at the beginning of each year to calculate portfolio default rates over time. A static pool was formed on the first day of each year covered by the study and followed from that point forward. The pools were static in the sense that their membership remained constant over time. Static pool analysis differed from mortality analysis in which the rating agencies calculated loan default rates from origination to maturity.

median recovery rate was 100%, the same rate as reported in Phase 1. The consortium and S&P Risk Solutions concluded that 75% seemed to be a fair representation of the average recovery rate for project finance loans. (See **Exhibit 4** for comparison of project finance recovery rates versus other types of debt.)

Conclusion

By most accounts, 2002 was a challenging year in the banking industry given the global economic downturn. Yet, despite including data from this difficult period—loans from the hardest hit sectors (power and telecom) and geographies (U.S. and Argentina)—the study showed that project finance loans were solid credits with high recovery rates.

Buoyed by the Phase 3 study results, the global heads of project finance at ABN AMRO, Citigroup, Deutsche Bank, and Société Générale sent a letter to the Basel Committee on July 28, 2003. The bankers wanted to use their study—a seminal analysis of project finance loan performance—to further inform the Basel Committee about the default and loss characteristics of project loans; the Committee planned to finalize the new capital guidelines by the end of 2003 and implement them by the end of 2006. The consortium recognized that few banks individually had sufficient project finance loan data to qualify them to use the *advanced* IRB approach, which would likely lower their capital requirements. Consequently, having established the first industry database of project loans, the consortium asked the Basel Committee to include the following language to the new Basel Accord:

> Banks using the Advanced IRB approach for PF loans may, to the extent they have insufficient internally-generated data to be statistically significant, use externally-generated data from an industry database, provided the external data represents the PF segment broadly over a period of at least ten years and has been verified by a credible independent external institution. The external data may be adjusted if a bank using the data determines the performance of its own portfolio differs significantly from the external data.

By the end of July 2003, five more banks had agreed to join the consortium, raising the total number of participating banks to 17. S&P Risk Solutions anticipated having the data from these additional banks within a few months, at which point the consortium would represent more than 40% of all project loans by number. In the future, S&P Risk Solutions planned to update the loan database as new banks joined the consortium, and provide annual reports for member banks.

Having completed all three phases of the loan loss study, and provided both data and comments, as requested by the Basel Committee, the bankers now waited for the committee's final draft of the new capital accord. While their efforts to date had largely been successful, they hoped the final draft would provide even more favorable treatment for project loans. Given the study, the idea that project loans were strong credits was no longer a stated opinion by interested bankers. Instead, it was a claim supported by hard data.

Exhibit 1 Lead Arranger Ranking for the 12 Consortium Banks—Bank Loans (US$ millions)

2002 Rank	Name	2001 Rank	Number of Issues in 2002	Amount Arranged in 2002	Percent of Total Arranger Market in 2002
1	Citigroup	1	43	$6,248	10.0%
2	Société Générale	4	21	3,589	5.8
3	Royal Bank of Scotland	15	23	3,257	5.2
4	Westdeutsche Landesbank	2	29	2,894	4.7
9	Deutsche Bank	9	12	1,608	2.6
11	ABN AMRO	8	16	1,422	2.3
14	Credit Lyonnais SA	14	13	1,067	1.7
41	ING Group	25	7	425	0.7
43	Dexia	41	9	386	0.6
48	DZ Bank	40	6	310	0.5
86	Deutsche Pfandbrief Hypotheken	—	2	110	0.2
—	Rabobank	56	0	0	0.0
	Consortium Total (12 banks)			**$21,316**	**34.3%**
	Total Bank Loan Market			**$62,172**	**100.0%**

Source: Adapted from *Project Finance International*, January 23, 2002 and January 22, 2003.

Exhibit 2 Breakdown of Project Finance Loan Sample by Geographic Region and Industrial Sector[a]

Region	Power	Media & Telecom	Infra-structure	Oil, Gas & Petrochem.	Metals & Mining	Other	Total
Europe	10%	8%	10%	2%	1%	4%	35%
North America	19	7	3	3	1	1	34
Asia Pacific	4	3	2	3	1	2	15
Latin America	5	2	1	2	2	0	12
Africa	1	0	0	2	1	0	4
Total	39%	20%	16%	12%	6%	7%	100%

Source: Adapted from Standard & Poor's Risk Solutions, July 2003.

[a] The loan sample included 1,955 loans.

Exhibit 3   Probability of Default: Project Loans vs. Corporate Loans

Asset Type	10-Year Cumulative Average Default Rates (%)	
	Through 2002	Through 2001
Project Finance Loans	13.29%	7.63%
Corporate Loans:		
AAA	0.48	
AA	0.85	
A	1.82	
BBB	6.68	
BB	20.82	
B	35.87	
CCC	57.21	
Investment grade	2.72	
Speculative grade	30.07	
All ratings	10.64%	9.38%

Source: Adapted from the following Standard & Poor's documents: Project Finance Default Study (July 18, 2002); Project Finance Default and Recovery Study (July 24, 2003); and Ratings Performance 2002 (February 2003).

Exhibit 4   Recovery Rates on Project Finance Loans vs. Other Types of Debt [a]

Asset Class	Number of Facilities	Recovery Rate		
		Mean	Median [b]	Standard Deviation
Project Finance Loans				
Phase 1 (4 banks)	43	75.39%	100.00%	34.90%
Phase 3 (12 banks)	83	75.23	100.00	n/a
Leveraged Loans [c]	203	78.03	98.26	29.56
Secured Debt	339	68.85	78.86	32.68
Senior Debt	844	67.33	78.05	34.19
Senior Unsecured Debt	311	46.20	40.38	36.27

Source: Adapted from "Project Finance Default and Recovery Study," Standard & Poor's Risk Solutions, July 24, 2003.

[a] For loans that have emerged from default, the recovery rate equals 1 minus the loss rate. Whereas the project finance sample includes loans to December 31, 2002, the other asset classes include results to March 18, 2002 only.

[b] Recovery rates greater than 100% can occur when a bank receives equity as part of a loan restructuring and the equity subsequently appreciates. Defaults with recoveries greater than 100% account for less than 1% of the total number of observations.

[c] Leveraged loans contain secured and unsecured corporate loans from companies with over $50 million in debt at the time of default.

 **Harvard Business School**

9-298-116
April 13, 1998

Cephalon, Inc.

As April 1997 began, J. Kevin Buchi, Chief Financial Officer of Cephalon, Inc., a ten-year old biotechnology firm, considered the commercial prospects for his company's leading experimental drug, the financing needs its success would generate, and the merits of an unusual financing proposal from investment bank SBC Warburg Dillon Reed (SBC). On February 11 of that year, Cephalon had submitted to the Food and Drug Administration (FDA) an application to approve the sale of the drug Myotrophin. On May 8, only a month away, an FDA advisory panel was scheduled to complete a review of Myotrophin and issue its recommendation on the application. A final FDA decision was expected by the end of summer.

While many industry observers were optimistic about the prospects for Myotrophin, the panel's recommendation was uncertain. New drugs routinely failed the FDA's tough review process, and there were questions raised about the sufficiency of Cephalon's scientific data.

In addition to facing uncertainty about FDA approval, Cephalon also had financing concerns. If Myotrophin was approved by the FDA, Cephalon might need $125 million or more to buy back the rights to the drug and continue its development, significantly more than the company had available at the moment. This was of particular concern because financing in the biotechnology industry was at times costly or even unavailable.

As a potential solution to these financing needs, bankers at SBC had proposed a transaction whereby Cephalon would purchase call options on its own stock. While the calls might provide cash just when Cephalon needed it, there was also a chance the options would expire worthless, and Cephalon would lose the premium it had paid for the options. Buchi weighed his potential financing needs, the attractiveness of different financing arrangements including the call options, and the uncertainty of the FDA review process as he considered how to respond to the bank's proposal.

Professor Peter Tufano, Ph.D. candidate Geoffrey Verter, and Charles M. Williams Fellow Markus F. Mullarkey prepared this case as the basis for class discussion rather than to illustrate either effective or ineffective handling of an administrative situation. The authors thank executives at Cephalon, Inc.; SBC Warburg Dillon Reed; Cowen & Co.; Hambrecht & Quist; and UBS Securities for their assistance. This case is based on public information.

Copyright © 1998 by the President and Fellows of Harvard College. To order copies or request permission to reproduce materials, call 1-800-545-7685 or write Harvard Business School Publishing, Boston, MA 02163. No part of this publication may be reproduced, stored in a retrieval system, used in a spreadsheet, or transmitted in any form or by any means—electronic, mechanical, photocopying, recording, or otherwise—without the permission of Harvard Business School.

Cephalon and Myotrophin

Founded in 1987 in West Chester, Pennsylvania, Cephalon, Inc. was a biotechnology firm that focused on treatments for neurological disorders. As of April 1997, the company had no FDA-approved drugs and no commercial sales, but it did have a number of products in various stages of the development pipeline.[1] These products included Provigil, a treatment for narcolepsy, which afflicted an estimated 125,000 Americans, as well as treatments for Alzheimer's disease, stroke and head trauma, and prostate disease. **Exhibit 1** outlines Cephalon's historical financial results.

Cephalon's most advanced product was Myotrophin, a treatment for Amytrophic Lateral Sclerosis (ALS). ALS, also known as Lou Gehrig's disease, was a fatal neurodegenerative disorder that afflicted approximately 25,000 people in the United States and an estimated 75,000 worldwide. As a result of the disease, patients progressively lost control over their muscles over a period of three to five years, and consequently their ability to move, speak, swallow, and breathe. Most patients eventually died of respiratory failure resulting from the decay of respiratory muscle control. The cause of ALS was unknown and there was no known cure. Only one FDA-approved treatment existed, Rhône-Poulenc Rhorer's Rilutek, which extended life for up to three months with some side effects, but did not retard patients' physical deterioration.

Developed over many years at a cost of approximately $180 million, Myotrophin was a proprietary form of human insulin-like growth factor, a protein scientists hypothesized could promote nerve and tissue growth. Cephalon researchers believed Myotrophin encouraged the survival of motor neurons and could slow the onset of physical decline caused by ALS. They also hoped to use the drug to treat a variety of peripheral nervous system disorders characterized by the deterioration of sensory and motor nerves, known collectively as peripheral neuropathies. Analysts estimated the worldwide market for treatments of ALS at over $500 million and the peripheral neuropathy treatment market at over $3 billion.[2]

Cephalon had developed Myotrophin in partnership with Chiron Corporation, a California-based biotechnology firm. While Cephalon had conducted the majority of the preliminary research and clinical testing, Chiron would be responsible for manufacturing Myotrophin, should the drug be approved, including payment of any capital expenditures or net working capital requirements. Upon commercialization, Chiron and Cephalon would divide profits from Myotrophin evenly.

FDA Approval Process

To develop and release Myotrophin commercially, Cephalon had to comply with a rigorous FDA approval process consisting of a series of company-sponsored clinical tests and a formal FDA regulatory review process.[3] The approval process began when a drug manufacturer submitted an Investigational New Drug application (IND) to the FDA that reported the results of the company's non-human research. If the FDA did not disapprove the IND within 30 days, the manufacturer could begin Phase I clinical testing, where the drug would be tested for safety and dosage level on a small, healthy human test group. In Phase II tests, the drug was tested for effectiveness on a small group of

---

[1] Though none of Cephalon's drugs were on the market at the time of the case, the company generated a small amount of revenue by distributing two Bristol-Myers Squibb products: Stadol NS, a pain analgesic, and Serzone, a treatment for depression.

[2] Joyce A Lonergan, David K. Stone, and Felicia L. Reed, Cowen & Co., *Cephalon, Inc.*, February 20, 1997, p. 3; Meg Malloy, Hambrecht & Quist Biotechnology Company Reports, *Cephalon, Inc.*, March 20, 1997, p. 13.

[3] For a summary of the FDA approval process, see Hilary Shane, "The Impact of the Food and Drug Administration's Approval Process on the Market Value of Biotechnology Firms," Wharton School of Business Working Paper, April 1995, and Cephalon, Inc. 10-K, December 1996.

patients. In Phase III clinical testing, double-blind studies were conducted on a larger sample of patients to verify effectiveness and test for adverse reactions.[4] Sometimes, companies combined the phases of clinical testing. During the clinical testing period, manufacturers often maintained close contact with the FDA and received guidance on how to conduct trials.

If the results of these tests were promising, the manufacturer would submit a lengthy New Drug Application (NDA) to the FDA detailing the results of clinical testing and plans for the manufacturing process. The FDA typically appointed an advisory panel consisting of academic specialists to review the application and provide an opinion on the drug's effectiveness and safety. While the advisory panel's opinion was not legally binding, the FDA nearly always followed its recommendation. Because the results of clinical testing often required a significant level of statistical and scientific interpretation, debate over the acceptance of a given drug was often heated.

The final stage of the process was the issuance of the official FDA decision. The FDA could approve, disapprove, or grant conditional approval to an application. Under conditional approval, the FDA indicated that the drug would be approved after minor modifications had been made. In some cases, the FDA required Phase IV post-commercialization clinical testing as a condition for approval. From preliminary research to final FDA approval, the drug commercialization process usually took many years, and costs often ran in the millions of dollars.

The Myotrophin Application

By April 1997, Cephalon had already passed through a number of hurdles in the FDA process to gain approval for Myotrophin, as shown by the timeline below:

Timeline for FDA Approval of Myotrophin

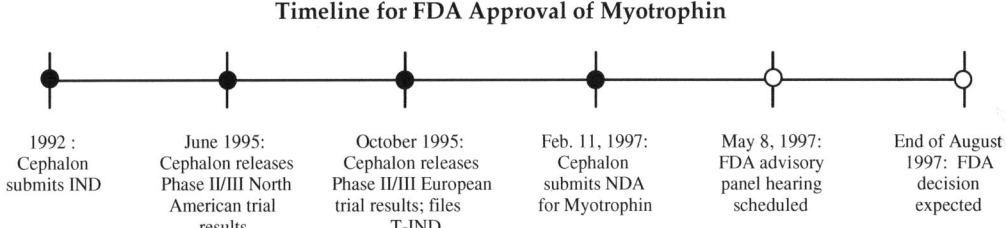

| 1992: Cephalon submits IND | June 1995: Cephalon releases Phase II/III North American trial results | October 1995: Cephalon releases Phase II/III European trial results; files T-IND | Feb. 11, 1997: Cephalon submits NDA for Myotrophin | May 8, 1997: FDA advisory panel hearing scheduled | End of August 1997: FDA decision expected |

Cephalon had submitted an IND in 1992 and proceeded through Phase II and Phase III testing in both North America and Europe.[5] Results from Cephalon's first Phase II/III clinical trial, the "North American trial," showed slowing in the progression of ALS with only minor side effects. The results were considered statistically significant at the 1% level (i.e., they had p-values less than or

---

[4] Usually, two Phase III clinical tests were required for FDA approval.

[5] Cephalon conducted two types of tests to determine the reduction in patients' rates of decline caused by Myotrophin. In both, a patient's degree of ALS affliction was measured over the course of the study, and the rate of change in his or her condition was calculated.

equal to .01).[6] In addition, the research suggested the drug added as much as three months of additional life and, unlike Rilutek, it retarded the deterioration of muscle control so quality of life was sustained during those additional months.

In October 1995, the company announced the results of a second trial, the "European trial," conducted on 183 patients in six European countries. The results of the European tests were mixed, indicating positive results, though ones that were less compelling than those found in the North American trial. In addition, mortality rates were higher for treated patients than for those receiving a placebo, and the statistical results of the European trial were weaker than those of the North American study. On one test, Myotrophin showed a decline in patients' rate of deterioration of 22% (with a p-value of 0.038), whereas the other showed a decline of only 16% (p-values ranged from .04 - .06).

On the basis of these two trials, in October 1995 the company filed a Treatment Investigational New Drug application (T-IND) for Myotrophin to expand patient access to the drug prior to FDA approval. While the FDA approved the T-IND, the advisory panel appointed to evaluate the drug application expressed concerns over the statistical significance of the European data, and some members called for additional clinical testing.

On February 11, 1997, much later than originally expected, Cephalon submitted an NDA for Myotrophin. It elected not to conduct an additional Phase II/III study prior to submission of the NDA, stating that a new study would be expensive and time-consuming, and arguing that the North American and European trials already demonstrated the beneficial effects of Myotrophin in ALS patients.[7] Instead, the company submitted new analyses of the existing data and expressed its willingness to conduct Phase IV post-commercialization studies after approval was granted. An advisory panel meeting was scheduled for May 8, 1997.

Despite reservations about the statistical significance of the European data and concerns over the advisory panel criticisms, a number of industry analysts expressed optimism about the approval of Myotrophin. These analysts considered the European data adequate, and they observed that previous NDAs had been approved on the basis of only one significant study (such as Myotrophin's North American trial) and what they considered weaker evidence. Several observers also considered the application for Myotrophin significantly stronger than the one that had been submitted and approved for Rilutek.

In addition, some analysts believed that humanitarian considerations and political pressures boosted the chances for approval of Myotrophin. ALS was a devastating, fatal disease, and Rilutek, the only commercially available treatment, was, by most accounts, of limited effectiveness. Observers suggested it would be difficult for the FDA to reject a reasonably strong application when no real alternatives existed. In the first quarter of 1997, some analysts' estimates of the probability of FDA approval ran as high as 70 percent.[8]

---

[6] The p-value for a clinical drug test is a measure of the reliability of the test's results. A p-value of .05, for example, indicates a 5% probability that the effects witnessed in the test sample are due to random sampling error, as opposed to clinical effects of the drug being tested. Higher p-values, therefore, indicate less reliable test results. A p-value of .05 or less was quoted by securities analysts as an indication of statistical significance — for example, see Joyce A. Lonergan and David K. Stone, Cowen & Co., *Cephalon, Inc.*, March 1996.

[7] Cephalon 10-K, December 31, 1996.

[8] See Timothy Wilson and Eric Schmidt, UBS Securities Equity Research, *Cephalon Inc.*, May 7, 1997, and Frances Bishopp, "Cephalon, Chiron Submit NDA for Myotrophin," *Bioworld Today*, February 12, 1997.

Financial Decisions

If approved, Myotrophin would be an important source of income for Cephalon. Analyst projections of Myotrophin sales ranged from $30 million in 1997 to over $400 million in 1999, and post-approval Cephalon share price estimates ranged from the mid-thirties to the mid-forties. In contrast, analysts estimated that Cephalon's share price would be in the twelve to twenty dollar range were the FDA to reject the Myotrophin application (see **Exhibit 2**).[9] **Exhibit 3** provides an estimate of the cash flow of Myotrophin based on securities analysts' estimates of the drug's likely revenue and profitability potential if it was approved.

In order to capitalize on the commercial opportunity of Myotrophin if the drug was approved, Cephalon would require additional cash. In addition to the cash flow required to commercialize Myotrophin, FDA approval would spark immediate cash demands on the company because of a contractual arrangement Cephalon had entered into to finance its research on the drug.

Cephalon Clinical Partners, L.P.

In August 1992, in order to fund the development of Myotrophin, Cephalon raised $38.7 million from Cephalon Clinical Partners, L.P. (CCP), a research and development limited partnership organized by Paine Webber.[10] In return for providing research and development funding for Myotrophin, CCP received the exclusive rights to commercialize Myotrophin once it was approved by the FDA. Cephalon retained the right to repurchase the rights from the partnership by making a Milestone Payment and exercising the terms of a contractual Purchase Option.

Interim License In return for a $16 million *Milestone Payment* to be paid upon FDA approval of Myotrophin, Cephalon received an *Interim License* to commercialize Myotrophin in the United States, Canada, and Europe for a limited time that was tied to the timing of Myotrophin's first commercial sale (analyst expectations were that the Interim License would likely expire after two years). During Cephalon's interim license period, the company would make royalty payments on sales of Myotrophin to CCP in an amount equal to 10% of the drug's revenues.

Purchase Option Under the terms of its contract with CCP, Cephalon had the right to purchase the remaining rights to Myotrophin from the partnership upon expiration of the company's interim license. The *Purchase Option* would become available during a 45-day period when the interim license expired, commencing between two and four years after FDA approval, with the exact starting date determined by the timing of Myotrophin's first commercial sale. To exercise its option, Cephalon was required to make a lump-sum payment to CCP of $40.275 million in cash. The company also had the option to exercise the purchase option with $42.369 million in Cephalon stock (a 5% premium to the cash purchase price).[11] In addition, Cephalon would continue making royalty payments to CCP for eleven more years, though the royalty percentage would drop from 10% to 5% after approximately 7 years. If Cephalon did not exercise the Purchase Option, all development and marketing rights in North America and Europe would revert to the partnership at that time

---

[9] A 1995 study found a 4% abnormal return associated with FDA approval of a new product application, and a negative 25% abnormal return associated with FDA rejection of a new product application. See Hilary Shane, "The Impact of the Food and Drug Administration's Approval Process on the Market Value of Biotechnology Firms," Wharton School of Business Working Paper, April 1995.

[10] Cephalon raised $45 million from the partnership; approximately $6 million was paid in offering fees.

[11] If Cephalon chose to exercise with stock, the value of stock would be calculated at the market price of Cephalon shares at the time of the exercise of the Purchase Option

Instead of making payments over the next decade, as called for under the CCP contract, Cephalon managers believed it would be possible to repurchase the CCP rights outright through a one-time tender offer to CCP. In consultation with the brokers who had originally placed the CCP partnership, the managers at Cephalon were confident that a cash tender of $125 million would be sufficient to acquire full rights to manufacture and market Myotrophin without the obligation of royalty payments.[12] While this purchase method would require a great deal of cash up front, it had the advantage that future Myotrophin cash flows would not be diminished by royalty payments.

Were Cephalon to tender for the CCP shares, it could offer shares instead of cash, but it was unclear what value of shares Cephalon would need to deliver. Also, a stock tender might expose Cephalon to the risk of CCP limited partners selling the Cephalon stock immediately following the tender, thereby placing negative price pressure on Cephalon's stock. The brokerage firm that had sold the CCP shares did not actively follow Cephalon with equity analysts or reports, and as a result, managers feared that the sell-off might be substantial.

The tender offer provided certain important accounting benefits regardless of whether it was carried out with cash or stock. Under GAAP rules governing the accounting for purchased research and development projects, the price paid for *unproven* projects was expensed immediately, while the purchase price of *proven* projects was capitalized and amortized over the projected life of the purchased product. In the case of Myotrophin, Cephalon felt that full FDA approval, which would occur at the end of August 1997, would constitute proven status for the drug. Any purchase conducted after that time, such as under the CCP Purchase Option, would give rise to amortized R&D expenses over Myotrophin's commercial life. By tendering for the partnership's rights *before* August, however, Cephalon could expense the purchase price immediately, thereby protecting future firm earnings from potentially large amortization of capitalized R&D.

These various payment options are outlined below:

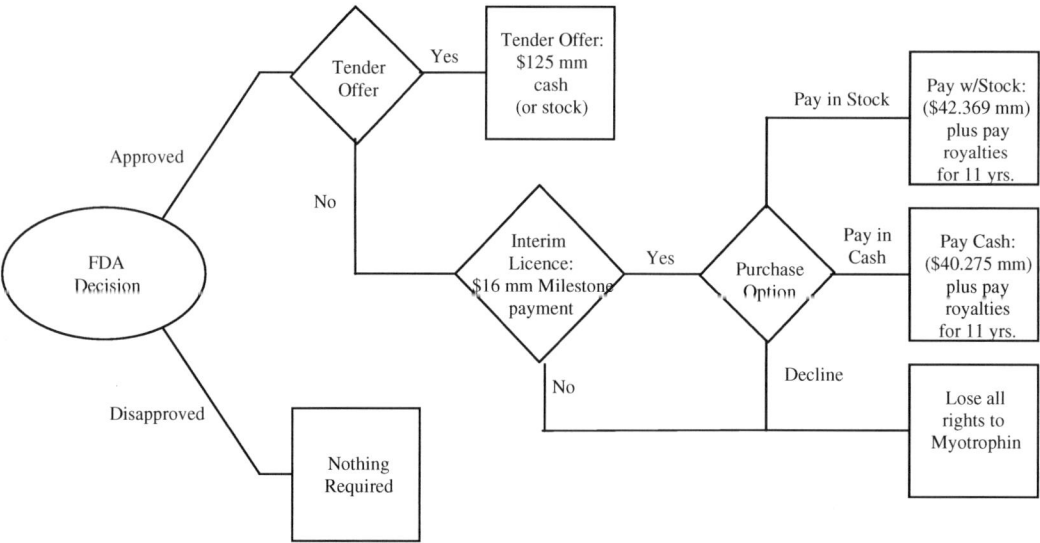

---

[12] In August 1995, a Cephalon tender offer of $50 thousand per unit allowed the company to purchase 67 of the 900 limited partnership interests at a total cost of $3.35 million.

Cephalon, Inc.

Sources of Funding

Because Cephalon's future funding needs were dependent both on the FDA's decision, and on the company's choice with regard to buying back the rights to Myotrophin from CCP, the company's cash needs were uncertain in April 1997. Moreover, the funds required were potentially quite large. In addition to the potential need for as much as $125 million to execute a tender offer, Cephalon might require an additional $25 million in the short-term to commercialize Myotrophin and finance Cephalon's research on drugs other than Myotrophin. These potential cash scenarios are outlined in **Exhibit 4**.

In part, the firm could fund Cephalon's cash needs by drawing down the company's cash balances. As of the end of March 1997, the company had approximately $119 million in cash equivalents and short-term investments that could be liquidated on short notice. Cephalon management was reluctant to reduce these holdings too dramatically, however, as the company had sought to keep cash balances equal to two to three years of projected spending. Buchi noted, "No biotech firm ever went out of business because they had too much cash."

Cephalon could also rely on external funding. In addition to raising money from venture capital sources and the CCP partnership, Cephalon had conducted three public stock offerings between 1993 and 1997, raising a total of approximately $150 million in equity funding (see **Exhibit 5** for details of Cephalon's issues). Raising equity was considered an expensive alternative. Cephalon managers estimated the total "deadweight" cost of equity financing at as much as 16 to 20 percent of the total funds raised in an equity issue, including underwriting fees and expenses of about 6%, underpricing of the issue of 10%, and the impact of the offering on the value of outstanding shares. Also, Cephalon could raise funds in anticipation of the FDA decision, or it could wait until after the panel's recommendation were made. Were it to wait, it could not be certain about the market conditions it would face. Financing in the biotechnology industry oscillated between being easily accessible and formidably expensive, and Buchi had witnessed many periods in which it was particularly difficult for any biotech firm to raise external funds (**Exhibit 6** contains data on industry financing).

Biotechnology firms tended not to issue straight debt instruments, but they did use equity-linked debt issues such as convertible notes. Cephalon had recently completed a $30 million private placement of one-year senior notes. These notes carried a 7% interest rate that increased to 10.75% if the instrument were not converted. The notes were convertible into Cephalon common stock at the option of the holder at a 6% discount to the market price at the time of conversion. Managers estimated the "deadweight" costs of convertible issues to be somewhat smaller than for equity issues. If Myotrophin was approved and the firm decided to proceed with a cash tender offer, the firm might be able to raise an additional $70 to $100 million from the sale of convertibles similar to those that had most recently been issued. However, given the need for $150 million, Cephalon would still require incremental funding.

SBC and the Option Proposal

To meet this incremental need, Cephalon considered a variety of alternative equity structures. One particularly intriguing one was proposed earlier that year by SBC Warburg Dillon Reed (SBC). SBC suggested that Cephalon buy capped call options on its own stock. While a number of companies had entered into derivative transactions on their own stock recently, these transactions were more typically put option sales used in conjunction with stock repurchase plans.[13] SBC's proposal that Cephalon buy calls on its own stock was relatively unique.

Under the terms of SBC's proposal, the bank would sell Cephalon 2.5 million capped call options on Cephalon's own common stock. The options, which would be issued on May 7, 1997, would be European-style, would expire on October 31, 1997, and would carry a strike price of $21.50 per share. The payoff of the calls would be capped. If Cephalon's stock price upon exercise of the call options was greater than $39.50, $39.50 would be used in determining the exercise value of the options. As premium payment for the call options, Cephalon would deliver to SBC 490,000 shares of Cephalon stock on May 8, 1997. Additional details of the proposal are provided in **Exhibit 7**.

The SBC proposal had many attractive features. Given analyst projections of Cephalon's likely stock price in the event of an FDA panel approval (in **Exhibit 2**), Cephalon would likely profit substantially from call options if Myotrophin were approved. Furthermore, the timing of the option payoff, should it occur, would be good for the company. As Buchi described it, the deal was a "backwards insurance policy" in that it paid off when good news occurred.[14] More specifically, the option would pay off right when the company needed cash to commercialize its approved product — and to repurchase the rights to Myotrophin if it decided to do so.

Cephalon's Decision

With the FDA advisory panel's verdict only a month away, Buchi faced difficult decisions. Most immediately, should he accept SBC's proposal and purchase the options? In evaluating the proposal, Buchi needed to consider whether an option transaction was the best way to meet the company's financial needs, and whether SBC's price for the options was fair (historical Cephalon stock prices and volatility, and biotech and interest rate data are provided in **Exhibit 8, Exhibit 9**, and **Exhibit 10**). Even more basically, Buchi had to sort through the alternatives Cephalon would have if Myotrophin were approved. Because different alternatives required varying amounts of cash, the company could face dramatically different funding needs. Buchi had little time to waste.

---

[13] See Chris Innes, Peter B. Blanton, Nomo Nomo-Ongolo, and Cindy Sieden, "Stock Buybacks – Strategy and Tactics," Salomon Brothers, February 1997, and E.S. Browning and Aaron Lucchetti, "More Firms Use Options to Gamble on Their Own Stock," *Wall Street Journal*, May 22, 1997, p. C1.

[14] Walter Hamilton, "Capital Flows," *Investor's Business Daily*, May 5, 1997, p. A1.

Cephalon, Inc. 298-116

Exhibit 1 Cephalon historical financial results — $ thousands

	December 31, 1994	December 31, 1995	December 31, 1996	March 31, 1997 (3 months)
Balance Sheet Data:				
Cash and Equivalents	11,063	6,565	5,671	3,016
Reverse Repurchase Agreements	68,031	23,126	5,207	8,351
Short-term Investments	35,364	148,376	135,970	116,178
Property, Plant, & Equipment (net)	16,961	30,002	22,086	22,044
Other Assets	7,754	13,261	8,957	13,094
Total Assets	**140,173**	**221,330**	**177,891**	**162,683**
Long Term Debt (including current portion)[1]	18,991	25,575	22,138	18,360
Other Liabilities	8,415	15,550	18,427	24,294
Total Liabilities	**27,406**	**41,125**	**40,565**	**27,894**
Common Stock & Additional Paid-in Capital	184,377	286,361	297,114	299,930
Treasury Stock	(69)	(1,487)	(1,778)	(1,970)
Accumulated Deficit	(71,679)	(104,682)	(157,967)	(173,097)
Cumulative Translation Adjustment	—	13	(43)	(74)
Total Shareholders' Equity	**112,767**	**180,205**	**137,326**	**124,789**
Income Statement Data:				
Total Revenues	21,681	46,999	21,366	5,628
Research & Development Expenses	(51,613)	(73,994)	(62,096)	(13,177)
SG&A Expenses	(9,180)	(15,762)	(28,605)	(8,697)
Operating Income (Loss)	(39,112)	(42,757)	(69,335)	(16,246)
Interest Income	4,473	12,866	8,491	1,617
Interest Expense	(1,426)	(3,112)	(2,286)	(501)
Gain on Sale of Asset			9,845	
Net Loss	**(36,065)**	**(33,003)**	**(53,285)**	**(15,130)**
Shares Outstanding (millions)	**18.3**	**23.8**	**24.6**	**24.8**
Loss per Share ($/share)	**($2.13)**	**($1.63)**	**($2.19)**	**($0.61)**
Cash Flow Statement Data:				
Loss	(36,065)	(33,003)	(53,285)	(15,130)
Operating Adjustments	10,215	7,222	70	(1,532)
Cash Flow from Operations	(25,850)	(25,781)	(53,215)	(16,662)
Repayments from/(Advances to) Related Party	(134)	4,337		
(Purchases)/Sales of PP&E	1,207	(17,218)	(1,631)	(266)
(Purchases)/Sales of Assets	(58,517)	(68,107)	47,517	16,648
Net Cash Flow from Investing Activities	(57,444)	(80,988)	45,886	16,382
Sale of Stock and Warrants	82,458	84,237		
Dividend Payments[2]	0	0	0	0
Exercise of Stock Options and Warrants	1,541	14,387	8,516	1,736
Principal Payments on Long-term Debt	(12,319)	(17,426)	(3,919)	(4,111)
Proceeds from Long-term Debt (net)	29,228	21,073	1,838	
Net Cash Flow from Financing Activities	89,797	102,271	6,435	(2,375)
Net Decrease in Cash and Equivalents	**(503)**	**(4,498)**	**(894)**	**(2,655)**

Source: Cephalon financial statements.

[1] Debt consists of an unsecured bank loan, capital lease obligations, and mortgage loans, all unrated.
[2] Cephalon paid no dividends and had not announced any intention of doing so.

Exhibit 2 Analysts' projections of the value of Cephalon common stock, conditional on the FDA's decision about Myotrophin[1]

Analyst	Date of report	Approval Probability	Value if approved	Value if not approved	Discount rate[2]
Hambrecht & Quist[3]	3/20/97 5/9/97	not given	$30-35/share in twelve months - 3/20/97	"Our best sense is that the stock could find support in the $12 range" - 5/9/97	25-35%
Cowen[4]	2/20/97	not given	$40-45 per share at the end of fiscal year 1997	"Shares have a $20 present value ex-ALS"	25%
UBS Securities Equity Research[5]	5/7/97	70%	"A positive outcome should send Cephalon's stock into the thirties"	Likely in the "low teens"	25%

[1] Cephalon's share price on April 8, 1997 was $19.25.
[2] The discount rate assumed by the analyst in preparing valuations of Cephalon share prices.
[3] Meg Malloy, Hambrecht & Quist Biotechnology Company Reports, *Cephalon, Inc.*, March 20, 1997 and May 9, 1997.
[4] Joyce A Lonergan, David K. Stone, and Felicia L. Reed, Cowen & Co., *Cephalon, Inc.*, February 20, 1997.
[5] Timothy Wilson and Eric Schmidt, UBS Securities Equity Research, *Cephalon Inc.*, May 7, 1997.

Exhibit 3 Projected Myotrophin cash flows to Cephalon/CCP if approved by the FDA in 1997 — $millions

Cash Flow from Myotrophin:	Note	1997	1998	1999	2000	2001	2002	2003	2004	2005	2006	2007	2008	2009	2010	2011
ALS Revenues																
United States ALS Population	(1)	25000	25000	25000	25000	25000	25000	25000	25000	25000	25000	25000	25000	25000	25000	25000
Penetration Rate	(2)	0%	30%	50%	60%	70%	70%	70%	70%	70%	70%	70%	70%	70%	70%	70%
Revenue/patient	(3)	0.015	0.015	0.015	0.015	0.016	0.016	0.016	0.016	0.016	0.016	0.017	0.017	0.017	0.017	0.017
US Revenues		0	114	191	232	273	276	279	281	284	287	290	293	296	299	302
European ALS Population	(4)	35000	35000	35000	35000	35000	35000	35000	35000	35000	35000	35000	35000	35000	35000	35000
Penetration Rate	(5)	0%	10%	25%	30%	35%	40%	45%	50%	50%	50%	50%	50%	50%	50%	50%
Revenue/patient	(6)	0.015	0.015	0.015	0.015	0.016	0.016	0.016	0.016	0.016	0.016	0.017	0.017	0.017	0.017	0.017
European Revenue		0	53	134	162	191	221	251	281	284	287	290	293	296	299	302
Peripheral Neuropathies Revenues																
Potential Revenues	(7)	0	5	13	26	38	43	48	55	62	70	79	89	101	114	129
Total Revenues		0	172	338	420	502	540	577	618	630	644	659	675	693	711	732
Cost of Goods Sold	(8)	0	60	118	147	176	189	202	216	221	225	231	236	242	249	256
Taxes	(9)	0	38	75	93	111	119	128	137	139	142	146	149	153	157	162
EBIAT		0	74	145	180	216	231	248	265	270	276	283	289	297	305	314
Terminal Value Cash Flow	(10)															1322
Total Free Cash Flow	(11)	0	74	145	180	216	231	248	265	270	276	283	289	297	305	1637
Cash Flow to Chiron	(12)	0	37	73	90	108	116	124	133	135	138	141	145	149	153	818
Net Cash Flow to Cephalon/CCP		0	37	73	90	108	116	124	133	135	138	141	145	149	153	818

Cephalon Payment Options:	Note	1997	1998	1999	2000	2001	2002	2003	2004	2005	2006	2007	2008	2009	2010	2011
Make Tender Offer																
Total Tender Offer Cash Flow	(13)	125														
Exercise Purchase Option With Cash																
Milestone Payment	(14)	16														
Purchase Option Payment	(15)			40												
Royalties to CCP	(16)	0	17	34	42	50	54	58	62	63	32	33	34	35	36	
Total Cash Flow		16	17	74	42	50	54	58	62	63	32	33	34	35	36	
Don't Buy Myotrophin Rights																
Milestone Payment	(14)	16														
Royalties to CCP	(16, 17)	0	7	34												
Total Cash Flow		16	7	34												

Notes and references for this exhibit appear on the following page.

Exhibit 3 (con't) These pro forma projections draw upon a number of analyst reports and other public sources, but reflect the casewriters' interpretations of a composite of these professional analyses. Specific references are as follows:

(1) Based on estimates by Malloy (March 20, 1997, p. 9); Wilson and Schmidt (January 20, 1996, p. 4) Cephalon estimates 20K US patients in its December 1996 10-K, p. 4.

(2) Based on estimates from Malloy (p. 9) and Wilson & Schmidt (p. 8), and on private communications with Cephalon managers.

(3) Revenue per patient is $15K/yr, growing at a rate of 1% a year due to inflation (growth would probably occur at irregular intervals, but 1%/yr. is a reasonable simplification). Malloy estimates annual patient revenue of $15K/yr. Lonergan, Stone, and Reed (February 20, 1997) use 10K/yr. Malloy observes that Rilutek sells for approximately $9K/yr.

(4) Casewriters' estimate. Wilson & Schmidt (p. 8) claim the European patient population to be 40K. Malloy (p. 9) estimates 20K. Lonergan, Stone, and Reed (p. 4) estimate a combined US and European population of 60K.

(5) Based on Malloy (p. 9) and Wilson & Schmidt (p. 8).

(6) Same as US revenue per patient.

(7) Casewriters' estimates based on projections from Cephalon Clinical Partners Placement Memorandum, June 16, 1992, p. 8. Estimates for the years 1997-2011 are one-third of what Cephalon Clinical Partners project, based on more cautionary discussions in analyst reports.

(8) Malloy uses 45% (p. 22) and Wilson & Schmidt use approximately 20% (January 26, 1996, Table 2).

(9) 35% of revenues: As of the end of 1996, Cephalon had Net Operating Losses of $75 million, and based on these projections would create additional NOLS through the next few years. Rather than give Myotrophin the benefit of these NOLS, we assume that the NOLS are transferable and value the marginal revenues from Myotrophin at the statutory marginal rate.

(10) Terminal Value calculated using a 1% growth rate (as outlined in note (3) above) and a discount rate of 25% (this discount rate is used by Wilson & Schmidt, (p. 11), and Lonergan et al. (p. 3), in valuing Cephalon).

(11) From Cephalon's perspective, the capital expenditure and working capital requirements for commercializing Myotrophin are negligible.

(12) Cephalon and Chiron split after-tax profits on Myotrophin equally. This is indicated in Cephalon, Inc.'s 10-K, December 1996, p. 53.

(13) Cephalon estimates the tender offer at "possibly in the $125 million range" in Cephalon, Inc., 8-K, May 7, 1997, p. 3.

(14) The Milestone Payment will be made when the FDA approves Myotrophin, given here in the second half of 1997.

(15) The purchase option payment of $40.275 (if made in cash) occurs at the earlier of (a) the date which is the later of (i) the end of the first month in which the CCP partners have received payments equal to 15% of their capital contribution (approximately $6 million in total), and (ii) 24 months after the first commercial sale of Myotrophin, and (b) 48 months after the first commercial sale. Our estimates indicate that the option will be triggered 24 months after the first commercial sale of Myotrophin, so the advance payment of $40.275 occurs at the end of 1999, approximately two years after Myotrophin is approved by the FDA.

(16) The royalty arrangement is given in the Cephalon Clinical Partners Placement Memorandum, June 16, 1992, p. 6. The Memorandum indicates that the royalty payment is 10% of Myotrophin sales in the US and Europe until each partnership interest receives $400K, when the royalty rate switches to 5%. The Memorandum assumes 800 partnership interests, so this means the royalty rate switch occurs when total payments to CCP reach $320 million. This $320 million includes the "advance payment," including the Purchase Option payment of $40.275, but excluding the Milestone Payment. Royalties are paid for the 11 years following exercise of the purchase option.

(17) If Cephalon elects not to exercise its purchase option when it becomes available, the cash flows from Myotrophin and the royalty payments to CCP will be eliminated. This is assumed to happen at the end of 1999, and as a result, Cephalon will experience both cash flows in that year.

Cephalon, Inc. 298-116

Exhibit 4   Pro forma projections of Cephalon's internal cash flow[1]

Cephalon Cash Flow Projections (excluding the impact of Myotrophin)	Note	1997	1998	1999
EBIT	2	(84)	(66)	(71)
Net interest income/(expense)	3	1	(5)	(6)
Taxes	4	0	0	0
Net income/(loss)		(83)	(71)	(77)
Additions to net working capital	5	(7)	(7)	(7)
Total operating cash flow		(90)	(78)	(84)
Net investing cash flow	6	(6)	(6)	(6)
Net financing cash flow	7	25	(2)	(1)
Net cash flow		**(71)**	**(86)**	**(91)**

Incremental Cash Flow Impact of Myotrophin Approval, Purchase, and Commercialization				
Under Cash Exercise of Purchase Option:				
Free cash flow from Myotrophin	8	0	37	73
Cash flow required to purchase Myotrophin rights	8	(16)	(17)	(74)
Total Myotrophin Cash Flow impact		**(16)**	**20**	**(1)**
Under Stock Exercise of Purchase Option:				
Free cash flow from Myotrophin	8	0	37	73
Cash flow required to purchase Myotrophin rights	8	(16)	(17)	(34)
Total Myotrophin Cash Flow impact		**(16)**	**20**	**39**
Under Cash Tender Offer:				
Free cash flow from Myotrophin	8	0	37	73
Cash flow required to purchase Myotrophin rights	8	(125)	0	0
Total Myotrophin Cash Flow impact		**(125)**	**37**	**73**
Under Stock Tender Offer:				
Free cash flow from Myotrophin	8	0	37	73
Cash flow required to purchase Myotrophin rights	8	0	0	0
Total Myotrophin Cash Flow impact		**0**	**37**	**73**

Source: Casewriters' estimates.

(1) Cephalon's balance of Cash and Short-term Investments was approximately $119 million as of April 1, 1997.
(2) Estimates from Timothy Wilson & Eric Schmidt, UBS Securities Equity Research, *Cephalon Inc.*, January 26, 1996 and from Meg Malloy, Hambrecht & Quist Biotechnology Company Reports, *Cephalon, Inc.*, March 20, 1997, p. 22.
(3) Based on existing debt requirements and interest on cash balances.
(4) Cephalon had a net operating loss of $75 million as of the beginning of 1997, and would generate additional losses in the subsequent years so it would pay no taxes over the three-year horizon.
(5,6) Casewriters' estimates from historical data.
(7) Includes all Cephalon financing secured and planned as of the time of the case. Repayment schedule given in Cephalon Corporation 10-K, December 1996. Also included is a $30 million convertible Cephalon issued in early 1997.
(8) From **Exhibit 3**.

Exhibit 5 Cephalon external financing history

Year	Type of Financing	Announcement and Issue Date	Terms of Issue	Gross Proceeds	Fees as a % of Proceeds	Cumulative Abnormal Return[1] Benchmarks		Offering dilution[2] Benchmarks	
						S&P 500	Russell 2000	S&P 500	Russell 2000
1993	Public Stock Offering	Announcement: 2/8/93 Commenced: 4/7/93	2.3 million shares at $9.50/share	$20.539 million[3]	7.6%	-8.1%	-5.5%	-42.1%	-28.6%
1994	Public Stock Offering	Announcement: 1/10/94 Issue: 2/9/94	3.795 million shares at $15.00/share	$53.328 million	5.9%	-2.3%	0.0%	-8.8%	0.0%
1995	Public Stock Offering	Announcement: 6/27/95 Issue: 8/1/95	3.45 million shares at $22.50/share	$73.037 million[4]	5.9% (excludes expenses)	-7.3%	-6.8%	-31.2%	-29.1%
1997	Convertible Private Placement	Announcement: 1/16/97 Completed: 4/8/97	7% int. in year 1; 10.75% later if not converted. Convertible into stock at 6% discount to a market price at conversion.	$30 million	N/A	+8.5%	+9.4%	+162.4%	+179.6%

Source: Cephalon, Inc. SEC filings, casewriters' estimates.

[1] Reflects the abnormal return on Cephalon stock around the time of each equity issue. The abnormal return is calculated as the difference between the stock's actual return and the stock's expected return in absence of the equity issue. This expected return is estimated by calculating the stock's beta versus a benchmark portfolio (either the S&P 500 or the Russell 2000) and multiplying it by the return the benchmark delivered around the time of each equity issue.
[2] Offering dillution is calculated as the total abnormal return of the stock (CAR × # shares outstanding) as a percentage of the gross proceeds of the issue.
[3] Casewriters' estimate (Cephalon reported proceeds of $23.2 million from equity issues, including a July 1993 private placement of 285,714 shares at $10.50/share).
[4] Casewriters' estimate (Cephalon reported proceeds of $84.237 million from equity issues, including a private placement of 538,310 shares at $21.17/share).

Cephalon, Inc. 298-116

Exhibit 6 Funds raised by U.S. biotechnology industry participants, 1978-1995

Funds raised 1995 $ mil	Venture Capital	Initial Public Offering	Seasoned Equity Offerings	Private Placement	Debt & Convertibles	R&D financing organizations (1)
Average per year	7.08 $393	$378	$445	$51	$90	$90
Fraction of total raised	27%	26%	31%	4%	6%	6%
Mininum	$20	$0	$0	$0	$0	$0
Maximum	$770	$1,480	$2,730	$310	$440	$250
Number of years out of 17 in which:						
No funds raised	0	2	5	8	11	6
Less than $100 million raised	2	7	7	15	12	8

(1) Such as R&D Limited Partnerships

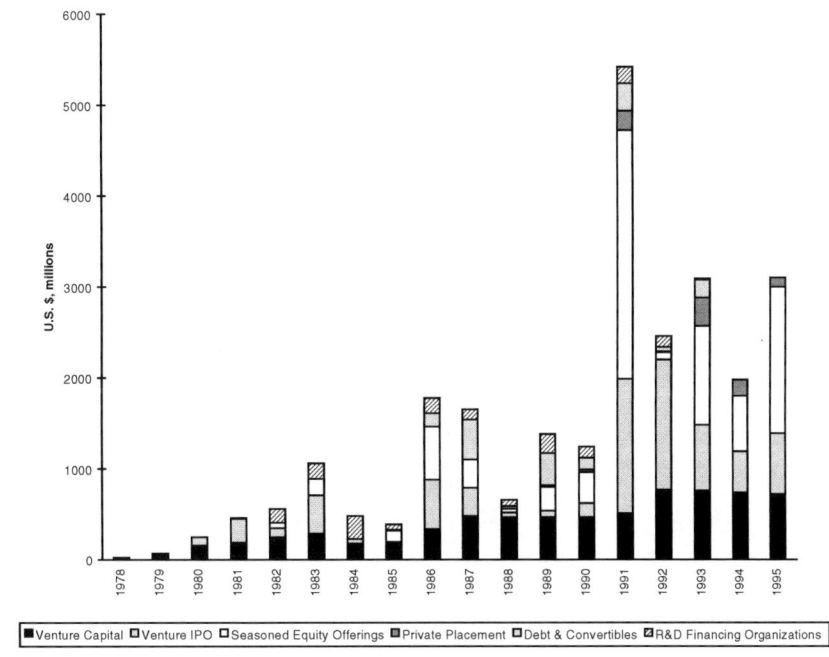

Source: Josh Lerner and Robert P. Merges, *The Control of Strategic Alliances: An Empirical Analysis of Biotechnology Collaborations*, NBER Working Paper 6014, 1997.

Exhibit 7 Terms of SBC's option proposal

Deal Terms (Italicized Terms are Defined Below):	
Deal:	• Cephalon Capped Call Options
Buyer:	• Cephalon, Inc.
Seller:	• SBC Warburg Dillon Reed (SBC)
Trade Date:	• May 7, 1997 • Premium to be delivered on May 8, 1997
Number of Options:	• 2,500,000
Total Premium:	• 490,000 shares of Cephalon, Inc. common stock
Share Equivalent:	• Each call option entitles the holder to purchase one share of common stock of Cephalon, Inc.
Exercise Date:	• 5:00 p.m. on October 31, 1997 (provided it is an *Exchange Business Day*) • If October 31, 1997 is not an *Exchange Business Day*, the options will expire on the following day • European-style
Strike Price:	• $21.50
Cap Price:	• $39.50
Settlement:	• The transaction will be cash settled upon expiration unless 30 *Exchange Business Day* notice is provided by Cephalon • Upon cash settlement, SBC will pay Cephalon the number of options outstanding multiplied by the greater of $0 and the difference between the strike price and a *Reference Price* (or the cap price if the Reference Price is greater than $39.50) • In lieu of cash, Cephalon can opt to have SBC settle the options by delivering shares of Cephalon common stock equal in value to the cash settlement value of the options. Deliveries of stock will be made according to the following schedule: |	1st Tranche	2nd Tranche	3rd Tranche
---	---	---	---
Delivery date	3rd day after the Exercise Date	4th day after the Exercise Date	5th day after the Exercise Date	
Automatic Settlement:	• The options will be exercised automatically if they are in-the-money on the expiration date unless: (1) Cephalon notifies SBC in advance; or (2) the closing price of Cephalon shares cannot be determined on the expiration date
Adjustments:	• The terms of the SBC options will be adjusted to reflect adjustments made to other Cephalon options (as a result of stock splits, etc.)
Transferability:	• The transaction is not transferable by either party without the prior written consent of the other party
Definitions:	
Exchange Business Day:	• A day that is a trading day on the NASDAQ National Market System and the American Stock Exchange • Neither exchange may close trading before their standard time for the day to qualify as an *Exchange Business Day*
Normal Price Point:	• Bid price points taken at 10am, 12noon, and 3pm from Bloomberg's QRM screen on any given *Exchange Business Day* for which no *Market Disruption* has occurred
Market Disruption:	• Any limitation imposed on trading in excess of the following time limits during a relevant time period prior to the calculation of a price point | Price Point time	10am	12noon	3pm
---	---	---	---
prior period	9:30am-10am	10am-12noon	12noon-3pm
max. trading limit	15 min.	1 hr.	1 hr.	
Reference Price:	• The arithmetic average of 60 *Normal Price Points* of Cephalon stock during the 20 *Exchange Business Days* prior to and including the Expiration Date of the options • If the 20 days do not contain 60 *Normal Price Points*, the two parties will jointly determine the missing price points and the *Reference Price* will again be the arithmetic average of the 60 price points

Source: May 7, 1997 Cephalon, Inc. SEC filing.

Exhibit 8 Cephalon historical stock price — October 10, 1991 - April 8, 1997[1]

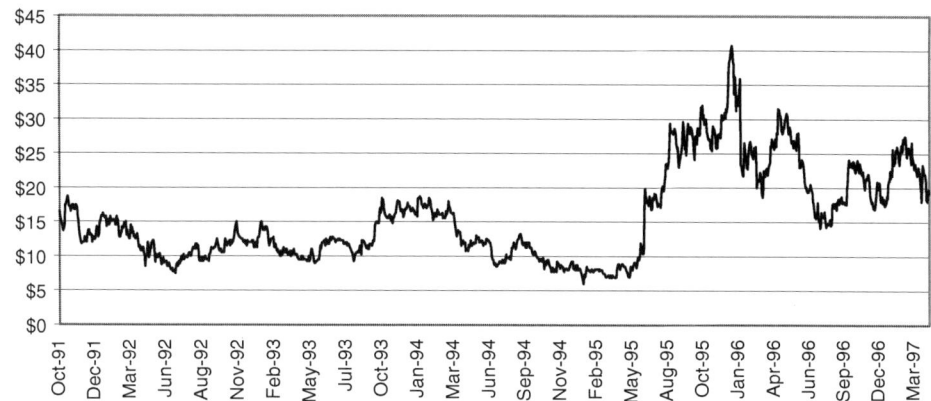

Source: Compiled from ReuterLink.

[1] On April 8, 1997, Cephalon stock closed at $19.25.

Historical volatility of Cephalon equity returns[1] — October 10, 1991 - April 8, 1997

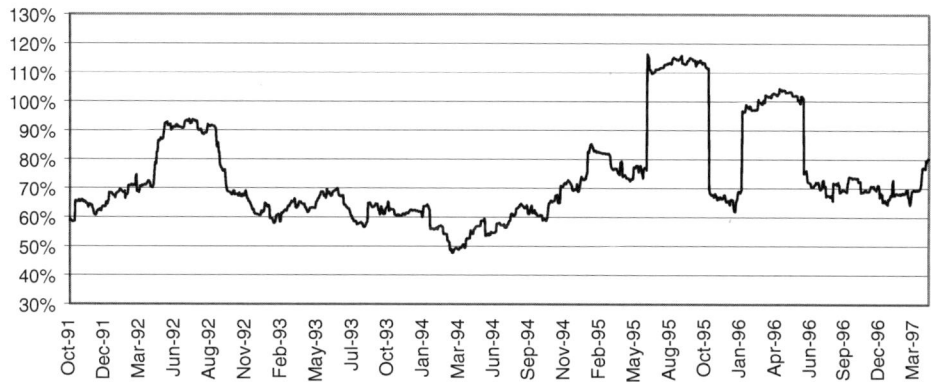

[1] Stock price volatility on any given day is calculated as the annualized standard deviation of the stock's daily returns over the 100 trading day period prior to and including that day. As of April 8, 1997, the volatility of Cephalon returns over the prior 100 trading days was 80.2%.

Implied volatility of outstanding Cephalon call options

Strike Prices	May Options	August Options	November Options
$15.00	145%		
$17.50	131%	93%	
$20.00	132%		76%
$22.50	128%	80%	74%
$25.00	123%	84%	69%

[1] Implied volatilities calculated from CBOE-traded options using the Black-Scholes option pricing formula and option and stock prices as of April 8, 1997. Calculated by casewriters from data compiled from Bloomberg.

Exhibit 9 Biotech company stock data[1]

Company	12/96 Market Capitalization ($ billions)	FY 1996 Total debt/equity (market value)	FY 1996 EPS	12/96 P/E Ratio	1996 Price-to-Book Ratio	Equity beta 10/1/96-3/31/97
Amgen	$14.4	0.01	$2.43	22.4	7.6	0.71
Biogen	$2.8	0.02	$0.54	72.4	5.8	0.84
Centocor	$2.5	0.02	($0.21)	Negative	9.7	1.39
Cephalon	$0.5	0.14	($2.20)	Negative	3.7	0.96
Chiron	$3.2	0.18	$0.32	58.2	4.2	0.57
Immunex	$0.8	0.02	($1.36)	Negative	5.6	1.39
Nexstar	$0.4	0.09	($0.88)	Negative	4.5	1.63
Sequus	$0.5	0.00	($0.60)	Negative	10.7	1.13
Vertex	$0.8	0.01	($2.22)	Negative	6.5	1.16

Source: Data compiled from Bloomberg.

[1] These companies were identified in analyst reports as being in the same industry as Cephalon.

Exhibit 10 Term structure of U.S. Treasury interest rates — April 8, 1997

	3-month	6-month	1-year	3-year	5-year	10-year
UST	5.23%	5.55%	5.95%	6.56%	6.75%	6.09%

Source: Compiled from Bloomberg. All rates quotes in bond-equivalent yield.

HARVARD | BUSINESS | SCHOOL

9-201-071
REV: FEBRUARY 28, 2002

GEORGE CHACKO

Pine Street Capital

Harold Yoon looked up from his workstation at the analysis that he had just printed out. Yoon had come in to work at 4am in the morning today, July 27, 2000, to look over this analysis one more time. As the managing partner for a $32 million equity hedge fund, Yoon was used to coming in early to the partnership's downtown San Francisco office, but this time he had more than the usual monitoring of pre-market news to take care of.

Immediately after the markets closed today, 1pm in San Francisco, he and the other partners of the hedge fund would meet to discuss a potential change of hedging strategy. The fund they managed tended to be a market-neutral fund, meaning that the fund hedged out all market risk. In the past, they had hedged this market risk by short-selling, or "shorting", shares of a market index. However, due to the unprecedented volatility (and valuation levels) seen in the markets over the past several months, the partners were now considering hedging this risk by purchasing put options on this market index rather than simply shorting.

Yoon picked up the analysis that an analyst employed by the fund had carried out. Prior to the partners' meeting this afternoon, he needed to have a recommendation ready as to which hedging strategy to pursue.

Hedge Funds

From 1988 to 1998, the number of hedge funds around the globe increased by almost 425%, reaching an estimated 5,830 funds with assets under management. Assets under management during this time period grew from $42 billion to $311 billion[1]. Hedge funds are private group investments that offer equity pooling advantages similar to mutual funds. However, because hedge funds are not publicly owned, they are less regulated than mutual funds and enjoy additional privileges. The lack of regulation gives hedge funds flexibility in investment strategies and risk management that mutual funds do not have. As **Exhibit 1a** shows, this flexibility seems to translate into higher expected

---

[1] "Size of Hedge Fund Universe." VAN Hedge Fund Advisors International, Inc. Nashville, TN. 1999.

Research Associate Eli Peter Strick prepared this case under the supervision of Professor George Chacko. HBS cases are developed solely as the basis for class discussion. Cases are not intended to serve as endorsements, sources of primary data, or illustrations of effective or ineffective management.

Copyright © 2000 President and Fellows of Harvard College. To order copies or request permission to reproduce materials, call 1-800-545-7685, write Harvard Business School Publishing, Boston, MA 02163, or go to http://www.hbsp.harvard.edu. No part of this publication may be reproduced, stored in a retrieval system, used in a spreadsheet, or transmitted in any form or by any means—electronic, mechanical, photocopying, recording, or otherwise—without the permission of Harvard Business School.

returns for hedge funds as compared to mutual funds.[2] Two important ways hedge funds differ from mutual funds are their ability to use leverage and their ability to hedge by shorting or using options.

Leverage

While hedge funds can use leverage, mutual funds, for the most part, cannot. By using debt to finance a portion of the assets in a portfolio, a higher return on the portfolio's equity is possible compared with an all-equity financed portfolio. See **Figure 1** for an example of the effect of leverage on a portfolio. The balance sheets of two portfolios, a portfolio that is leveraged and an all-equity portfolio, are shown when assets appreciate 100% (100% ROA). By keeping the initial equity amount ($50) the same in the two portfolios, the impact of leverage can be observed on the portfolio's Return on Equity (ROE).

Figure 1: Balance Sheet Effects of Leverage (ROA = 100%)

Leveraged Portfolio (Initial Debt/Equity=1)				Un-leveraged Portfolio			
Today		Tomorrow		Today		Tomorrow	
Assets 100	Debt 50	Assets 200	Debt 50	Assets 50	Equity 50	Assets 100	Equity 100
	Equity 50		Equity 150				
ROE = 200%				ROE = 100%			

Of course, if leverage is employed and the assets lose value, then leverage works against the investor, amplifying the loss on equity relative to an all-equity portfolio. Therefore, using leverage increases the risk of an investment. In response, many hedge funds seek arbitrage opportunities in different markets, searching for payoffs with little to no risk. While these opportunities may be overlooked for their marginal size by most investors, hedge funds are able to lever these payoffs to create higher returns.

Leverage doesn't come without a price. Prime brokers, who help finance and execute trades for hedge funds, offer loans to hedge funds and charge the interest. These loans are typically known as margin loans. Prime brokers minimize the credit risk associated with their loans to hedge funds. They do so by diligently monitoring their hedge funds' investments and risks. If the value of a fund's investments, or assets, drops to a level such that little equity remains, the broker can force the fund to put in more equity or the broker can liquidate part or all of the fund's portfolio, quite possibly putting the fund out of business.

Options & Derivatives

A hedge fund's ability to use options gives it another advantage over traditional mutual funds. While some funds use options and other derivative instruments to speculate on risky returns, most hedge funds use options as a hedging tool to limit the overall risk of their investments.

---

[2] This analysis is done with raw returns rather than risk-adjusted returns. However **Exhibit 1b** illustrates that the higher performance of hedge funds is not simply due to added risk-taking on the part of hedge funds. This exhibit shows that even in times when funds have negative performance, hedge funds continue to outperform mutual funds.

Pine Street Capital

Figure 2 gives an example of using put options to protect a portfolio's value. (Information given: S&P 500 is at 100, S&P volatility = 25%, the portfolio's beta = 1.5, Risk Free Rate = 5%, and the S&P options are two month, at the money puts.) This example shows the balance sheets of two portfolios, an "un-hedged portfolio," only invested in stock, and a "hedged portfolio" that uses put options to minimize changes in the value of the portfolio. At the beginning ("today") both portfolios have equal amounts of equity and assets. In either market outcome, up 5% or down 5%, the Return on Equity (ROE) for the hedged portfolio is more stable than the un-hedged portfolio.

Figure 2: Balance Sheet Effects of Hedging with Put Options

Un-Hedged Portfolio

Today		Tomorrow (S&P 500 +5%)		Tomorrow (S&P 500 -5%)	
ASSETS		ASSETS		ASSETS	
$100.00 stock		$107.50 stock		$92.50 stock	
	EQUITY		EQUITY		EQUITY
	$100.00		$107.50		$92.50
		ROE=	7.50%	ROE=	-7.50%

Hedged Portfolio

Today		Tomorrow (S&P 500 +5%)		Tomorrow (S&P 500 -5%)	
ASSETS		ASSETS		ASSETS	
$89.09 stock		$95.77 stock		$82.41 stock	
$10.91 S&P puts		$5.60 S&P puts		$19.07 S&P puts	
	EQUITY		EQUITY		EQUITY
	$100.00		$101.37		$101.48
		ROE=	1.37%	ROE=	1.48%

The value of the put options is negatively correlated with the value of the stock in the portfolio. In the example above, put options are held to insure the portfolio against market fluctuations. The ratio of put options to stock needed to perfectly hedge a portfolio is a function of the option and portfolio "deltas." While the hedge position protects the portfolio from the downside of risk, it also limits the potential gains.

Hedge Fund Strategies

One way of categorizing a hedge fund is by its investment strategy. Each fund's particular investment strategy is based on its fund manager's skills and where the fund manager feels he/she has a competitive advantage over other investors in assessing risks. Skilled managers will usually take and, in fact, leverage up those risks that they understand well, while they will hedge away risks where they feel they have no particular comparative advantage. For instance, a manager might feel confident about his ability to value individual companies but have no view on the performance of the entire market. This manager might then adopt what is called a "market-neutral" strategy, where market risk is hedged away while firm-specific risk is kept in the portfolio.

Pine Street Capital

Pine Street Capital (PSC) was a hedge fund that specialized in the technology sector. Holding undergraduate degrees in engineering/sciences as well as MBAs and/or PhDs specializing in finance, and having worked at an assortment of technology and financial services firms prior to forming PSC in January 1999, the partners of PSC felt their strength to be their ability to evaluate the technology sector and, specifically, to pick out-performing stocks in this sector. They felt less comfortable making bets on the direction of the entire market. PSC's portfolio reflected the partners' strengths, particularly Yoon's.[3]

Up to now, PSC had been using a short-sale strategy to eliminate general market risk from the fund. The short-sale was accomplished in the following way. Using the model:

$$\text{Expected PSC Portfolio Return} = \alpha + \beta * (\text{Market Return})$$

and data on PSC's portfolio holdings and market returns, PSC established a relationship between the performance of the market and PSC's portfolio. Beta (β) measured how PSC's portfolio responded to changes in the market, while alpha (α) was the amount of return in excess of that due to market risk. Thus, beta was a measure of the market risk of PSC's portfolio while alpha measured PSC's expected return if market risk were eliminated from the portfolio. **Exhibit 2 & 3** show PSC's current portfolio allocation and historical risk-return characteristics.

Since PSC's goal was to eliminate market risk, this risk was hedged from PSC's portfolio by shorting the market (PSC used the NASDAQ index as its proxy for the market) in proportion to the beta of the assets in the portfolio. **Exhibit 4** gives historical price data for the Nasdaq 100 index,[4] while **Exhibit 5** shows how PSC's portfolio would have performed on a monthly basis compared to the NASDAQ if the portfolio were completely unhedged.

An example of how short selling the market hedges market risk is given below in **Figure 3**. Eliminating market risk from the long portfolio leaves the portfolio with a guaranteed 1% return, which is precisely the alpha of the long positions in the portfolio. Thus, short-selling removes the market return component, and market risk correspondingly, leaving only an alpha return in the portfolio.

Figure 3: Example of Hedging by Short-Selling[5]

		Tomorrow's Value	
Today	Initial Value	NASDAQ +10%	NASDAQ –10%
Long Portfolio	$100.00	$116.00	$86.00
Short NASDAQ	$150.00	$135.00	$165.00
TOTAL	$250.00	$251.00	$251.00
	Return on Hedged Portfolio:	1.0%	1.0%

---

[3] Yoon held an engineering degree as well as an MBA from MIT. Yoon's work experiences included substantial time spent at a defense/communications firm, a pharmaceutical company, a consulting firm, and an investment bank.

[4] Selling the market portfolio did not require short selling every stock on the NASDAQ; this would be extremely expensive to finance and maintain. Instead, *Exchange Traded Funds* (ETFs) enable investors like PSC to trade single shares that mimic the performance of entire market indices. ETFs can be short sold and, unlike most common stocks, shorted on a downtick. The ticker for the ETF that follows the NASDAQ 100 composite is QQQ.

[5] Assuming an alpha of 1% and a beta of 1.5 for the long portfolio.

Of course, the alpha return that PSC was left with in their portfolio after hedging market risk could have been negative if they picked the wrong investments, but finding positive alpha stocks in the technology sector was exactly what PSC felt to be its comparative advantage. **Exhibit 6** shows historical performance of hedge funds in the technology sector, while comparing this performance with funds focusing on other sectors.

Immunizing the portfolio against market fluctuations left much less risk in the portfolio. This allowed PSC to increase the expected return, and corresponding risk, of the portfolio by levering. As a long-run goal, PSC generally maintained a debt ratio of 50% in the fund's capital structure.

Options-Based Hedging

Over the past year, and particularly over the past four months, the technology sector, as measured by the Nasdaq index, had been extremely volatile. The technology sector, especially any firms connected in any way to the Internet, delivered huge returns during 1999 and the first quarter of 2000. From January of 1999 to March 2000, the Nasdaq appreciated more than 115%. However, from early March 2000 to the end of June 2000, the Nasdaq declined nearly 40%. This enormous volatility exhibited by a fairly broad stock index was unprecedented in the recent history of the U.S. equity markets (**Exhibit 7** shows the implied volatility of Nasdaq puts options over the prior 1 ½ years).

While the fund was protected from market movements due to the short-sale hedging strategy it employed, this proved to be only partially effective during the previous few months. Consecutive, large dips in the Nasdaq had resulted in enormous losses for the fund on several days, particularly in March and April of the current year. PSC had been very careful to develop models that would allow it to accurately measure the beta of their portfolio in order to immunize the fund against market fluctuations. However, the volatility of the past few months had not been foreseen and the firm's models appeared to break down somehow, leaving the portfolio under-hedged.

To protect the fund from future periods of high volatility in the market, one of the partners suggested altering PSC's hedging program to use put options on the Nasdaq instead of shorting the Nasdaq. Because put options appeared to be more sensitive to market movements, this partner felt that using put options could better immunize PSC's portfolio to market movements.

To this end, Yoon had one of the analysts in the firm put together some analyses as to how PSC would have done over the previous 1 ½ years if the fund had used put options instead of short sales. **Exhibits 8** provides a graph comparing how the fund would have performed with an option-based hedging program vs. a short sale-based program vs. no hedging program at all. Additionally, **Exhibit 9** shows this comparative performance on the 20 worst-performing days of the Nasdaq over the previous 1 ½ years.

Conclusion

Yoon looked out the window of his office. The Internet was expanding at a breakneck pace, and he felt this was just the tip of a technological revolution. He could see it occurring all around him, and he wanted PSC to participate in it fully. One way to ensure this would be to use a more conservative investment style by utilizing less leverage, but he felt that this would not be in the best interest of the investors in the fund as it would not be maximizing their equity value.[6] However, given the nature of the technology sector he knew the market could see more volatile times ahead like the past few months, and he didn't want to see the fund liquidated, as it almost was back in April. Could an option-based hedging strategy allow the fund to keep utilizing the leverage it had in the past while also protecting against large, negative fluctuations in the market? Yoon picked up a printout of option prices from the previous day (see **Exhibit 10**) to recheck his calculations.

---

[6] PSC's compensation package dictated that 20% of any appreciation in the equity of the fund would be paid to PSC as management fees. So any reduction in returns was directly felt by the partners as well.

Exhibit 1a Hedge Fund VS Mutual Fund Performance

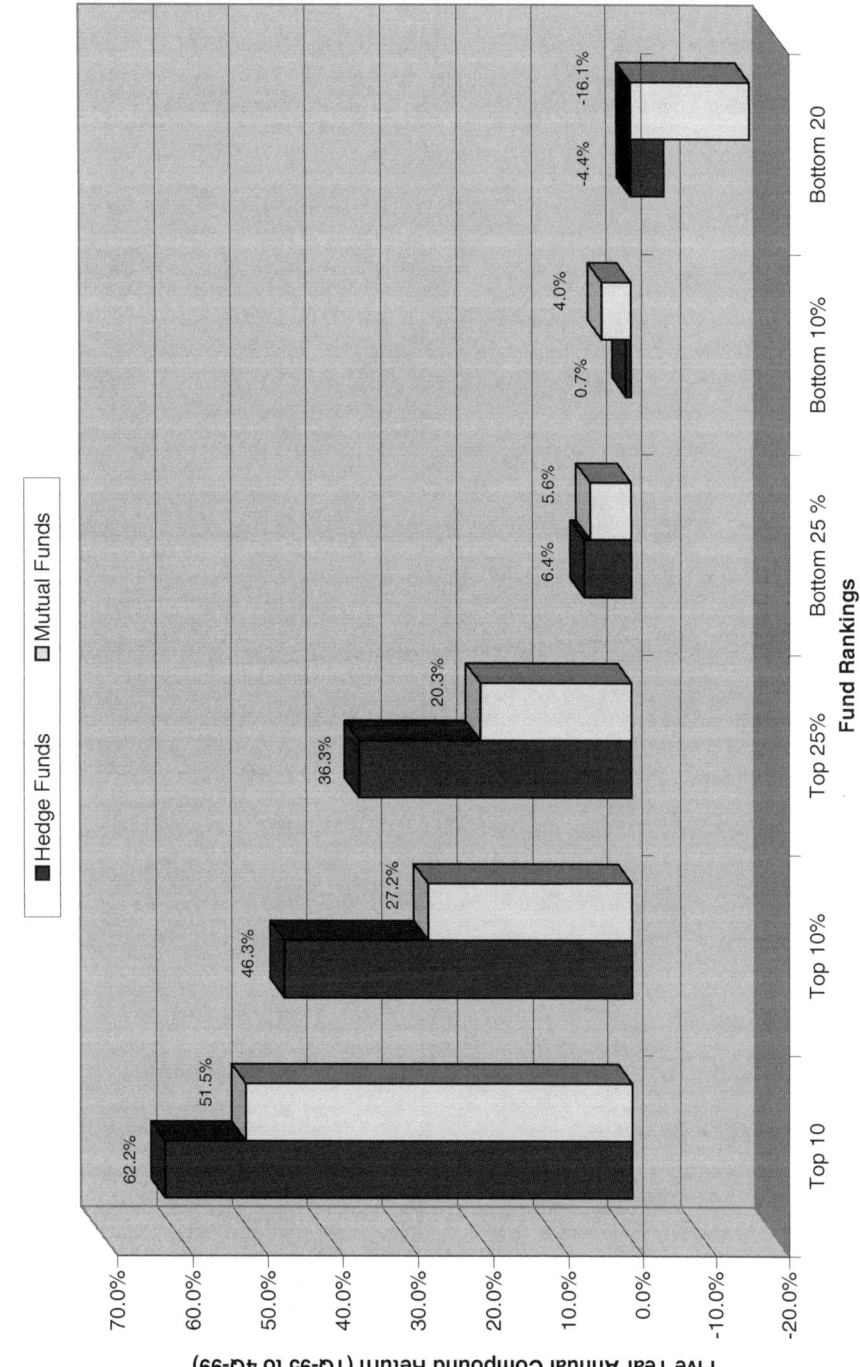

Source: Van Money Manager Research, Inc., Nashville, TN, USA

Exhibit 1b Hedge Fund and Mutual Fund Performance During Quarters with Negative Returns for the S&P 500 (1988-1999)

	1Q - 90	3Q - 90	2Q - 91	1Q - 92	1Q - 94	4Q - 94	3Q - 98	3Q - 99	Cumulative Return
S&P 500	-3.0%	-13.7%	-0.2%	-2.5%	-3.8%	-0.02%	-9.9%	-6.2%	-33.8%
VAN U.S. Hedge Fund Index	2.2%	-3.7%	2.3%	5.0%	-0.8%	-1.2%	-6.1%	2.1%	-0.7%
Morningstar Average Equity Mutual Fund	-2.8%	-15.4%	-0.9%	-0.7%	-3.2%	-2.6%	-15.0%	-3.2%	-37.2%
Morningstar Average Taxable Bond Fund	-0.9%	0.6%	1.5%	-1.1%	-2.4%	-0.2%	2.0%	0.3%	-0.3%

Source: Van Money Manager Research, Inc., Nashville, TN, USA

Exhibit 2 Pine Street Capital's Portfolio Allocation on July 26[h], 2000

Ticker	Company Name	Shares	Share Price[1]	Total $	Total Allocation	Beta[3]	NASDAQ[2] Alpha[4]	R-Squared[5]	Beta	S&P 500 Alpha	R-Squared
AMCC	Applied Micro Circuits	24000	162.875	$3,909,000	11.31%	2.15	6.42	0.58	3.06	6.91	0.29
AHAA	Alpha Industries, Inc.	45000	36.1875	$1,628,438	4.71%	1.63	2.14	0.39	2.39	2.16	0.20
ANAD	Anadigics, Inc.	70000	26.8125	$1,876,875	5.43%	1.65	1.22	0.45	2.36	1.24	0.22
CNXT	Conexant Systems Inc.	42500	35.75	$1,519,375	4.40%	1.42	-0.08	0.39	2.24	-0.08	0.24
CY	Cypress Semiconductor	15000	43	$645,000	1.87%	1.07	1.44	0.39	1.64	1.44	0.22
HLIT	Harmonic, Inc.	20000	28.0625	$561,250	1.62%	1.63	-0.81	0.36	2.29	-0.80	0.17
JDSU	JDS Uniphase Corporation	22000	135.9375	$2,990,625	8.65%	1.56	1.08	0.57	2.40	1.13	0.33
LSI	LSI Logic Corporation	12500	32.625	$407,813	1.18%	1.32	2.44	0.48	2.14	2.42	0.31
PWAV	Powerwave Technologies	40500	36.875	$1,493,438	4.32%	1.39	6.23	0.30	1.69	6.38	0.11
QLGC	QLogic Corporation	30000	77.9375	$2,338,125	6.77%	1.87	1.05	0.48	2.19	1.12	0.16
RFMD	RF Micro Devices, Inc.	21000	39.75	$834,750	2.42%	1.62	1.66	0.46	2.45	1.67	0.25
TQNT	TriQuint Semiconductor	25000	48.625	$1,215,625	3.52%	1.74	4.22	0.57	2.34	4.31	0.25
TXCC	TranSwitch Corporation	30000	41.6562	$1,249,686	3.62%	1.64	4.21	0.47	2.35	4.25	0.23
VTSS	Vitesse Semiconductor	20000	65.625	$1,312,500	3.80%	1.65	3.35	0.42	2.42	3.30	0.22
EMLX	Emulex Corporation	30000	55.81	$1,674,300	4.85%	1.86	-0.12	0.40	2.54	-0.10	0.18
PMCS	PMC-Sierra, Inc.	16000	197	$3,152,000	9.12%	1.79	9.99	0.54	2.60	10.07	0.28
SDLI	SDL, Inc.	20000	387.25	$7,745,000	22.41%	1.52	13.53	0.45	2.37	13.52	0.27
PSC PORTFOLIO				$34,553,799	100.00%	1.65	3.35	0.80	2.41	3.38	0.41

Source: Company

[1] Share prices are adjusted over time to include stock splits and dividends

[2] Assume there is minimal difference between NASDAQ Betas and QQQ Betas

[3] Alpha and Beta are calculated using the regression model and appropriate proxy for the market:

$$\text{Company Return (\%)} = \text{Alpha (\%)} + \text{Beta}[\text{Market Return (\%)}] + \text{Error}$$

[4] Alpha is given as an annualized number

[5] R-Squared measures how much of the underlying data is explained by the regression model

Exhibit 3 Portfolio Statistics for Days of Positive and Negative Market Returns

Half Year (1/3/2000 – 7/11/2000)[5]

	Nasdaq Up[1]			Nasdaq Down			S&P 500 Up			S&P 500 Down		
	Beta[2]	Alpha[3]	R-Squared[4]	Beta	Alpha	R-Squared	Beta	Alpha	R-Squared	Beta	Alpha	R-Squared
AMCC	2.53	-0.77	0.32	2.45	208.34	0.50	3.62	-0.55	0.15	3.44	67.61	0.23
AHAA	2.05	-0.60	0.20	0.92	-0.99	0.10	3.14	-0.74	0.12	1.74	-0.51	0.08
ANAD	1.81	-0.63	0.23	1.97	50.07	0.31	2.75	-0.77	0.14	2.86	25.64	0.15
CNXT	1.70	-0.83	0.22	1.08	-0.93	0.13	2.15	0.09	0.09	2.42	0.76	0.15
CY	1.50	-0.90	0.30	0.97	1.03	0.16	1.93	0.08	0.13	1.26	-0.30	0.07
HLIT	1.64	-0.72	0.20	1.37	-0.98	0.11	1.93	0.63	0.08	1.78	-0.98	0.04
JDSU	1.69	0.47	0.27	1.12	-0.95	0.30	3.52	-0.97	0.27	1.97	0.18	0.15
LSI	0.88	87.87	0.11	1.43	3.19	0.32	1.46	23.27	0.07	2.99	51.34	0.30
PWAV	1.81	-0.56	0.16	1.06	-0.16	0.11	1.31	46.17	0.02	1.49	1.15	0.05
QLGC	1.60	7.50	0.18	2.29	54.63	0.34	2.13	1.08	0.07	2.42	4.28	0.09
RFMD	1.78	-0.30	0.25	1.70	6.13	0.25	3.57	-0.95	0.22	1.75	-0.51	0.07
TQNT	2.09	-0.70	0.37	1.77	12.77	0.35	3.42	-0.95	0.21	2.42	21.71	0.15
TXCC	2.27	-0.97	0.30	1.80	62.88	0.36	3.14	-0.66	0.15	1.77	0.10	0.09
VTSS	1.69	1.65	0.15	1.76	11.60	0.34	2.34	3.38	0.08	2.67	10.21	0.15
EMLX	0.80	334.48	0.05	3.23	27706.21	0.43	2.23	-0.82	0.07	5.06	18466.43	0.27
PMCS	1.95	2.19	0.29	1.78	12.76	0.33	3.54	-0.74	0.19	2.36	10.37	0.16
SDLI	1.51	9.17	0.19	1.81	182.00	0.33	2.80	2.63	0.15	1.96	3.27	0.11
PORTFOLIO	1.71	0.89	0.57	1.86	31.15	0.66	2.89	-0.49	0.25	2.49	9.07	0.29

Source: Company

[1] Nasdaq and S&P 500 daily returns were separated into "up" days of positive performance and "down" days of negative performance

[2] Alpha and Beta are calculated using the regression model and appropriate proxy for the market:

$$\text{Company Return (\%)} = \text{Alpha (\%)} + \text{Beta}[\text{Market Return (\%)}] + \text{Error}$$

[3] Alpha is given as an annualized number

[4] R-Squared measures how much of the underlying data is explained by the regression model

[5] The standard deviations for the daily returns of the Nasdaq Composite and the S&P 500 during this half-year period were 3.07% and 1.54% respectively

Exhibit 4 Cumulative Returns [1] of QQQ (Nasdaq 100) Based on Historical Prices

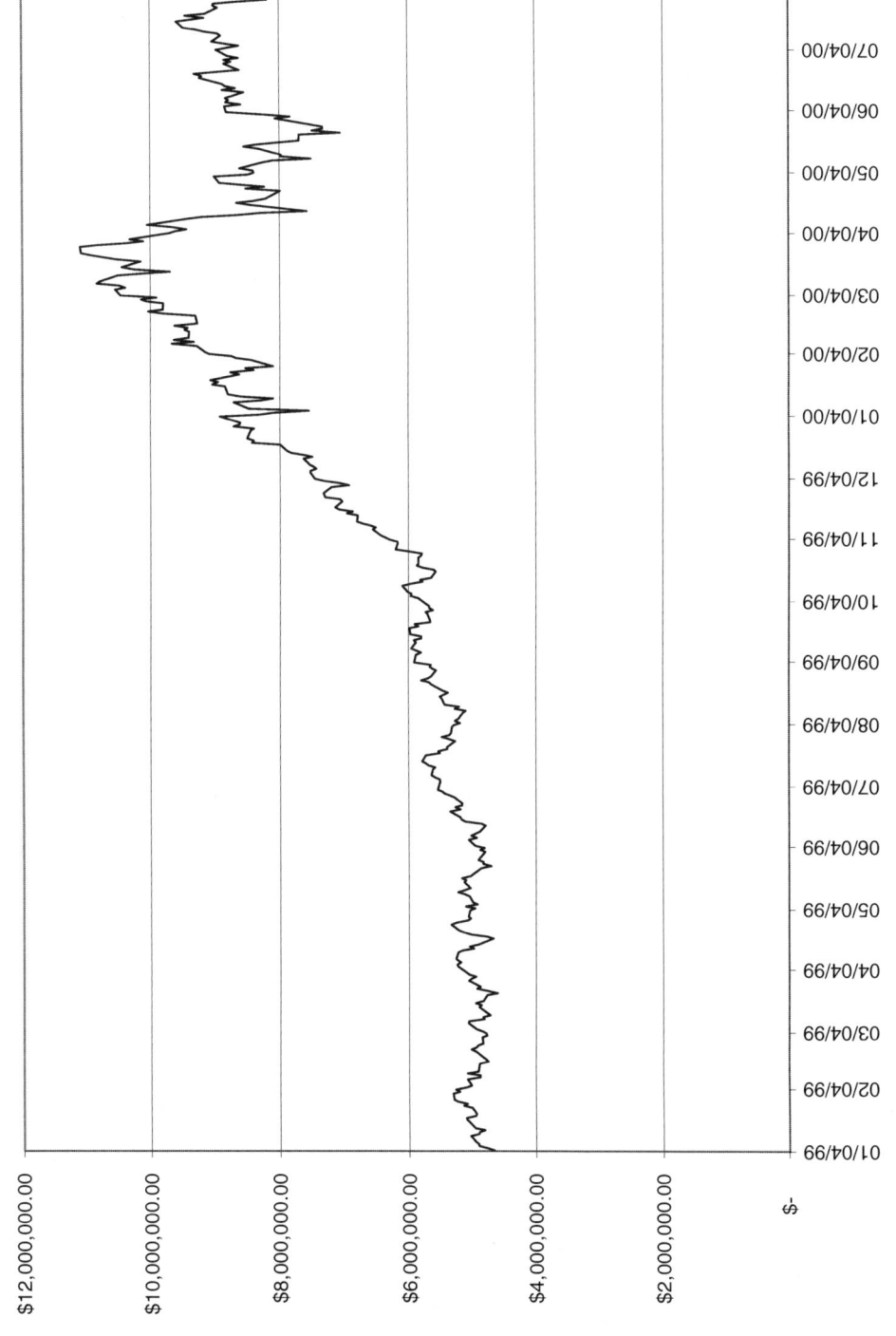

[1] This graph shows the value of equity over time if Pine Street Capital invested their initial equity, $4,663,656.85, in the Nasdaq 100 index.

Exhibit 5 Pine Street Capital's Portfolio Return Compared to the Market Return (Nasdaq Composite)

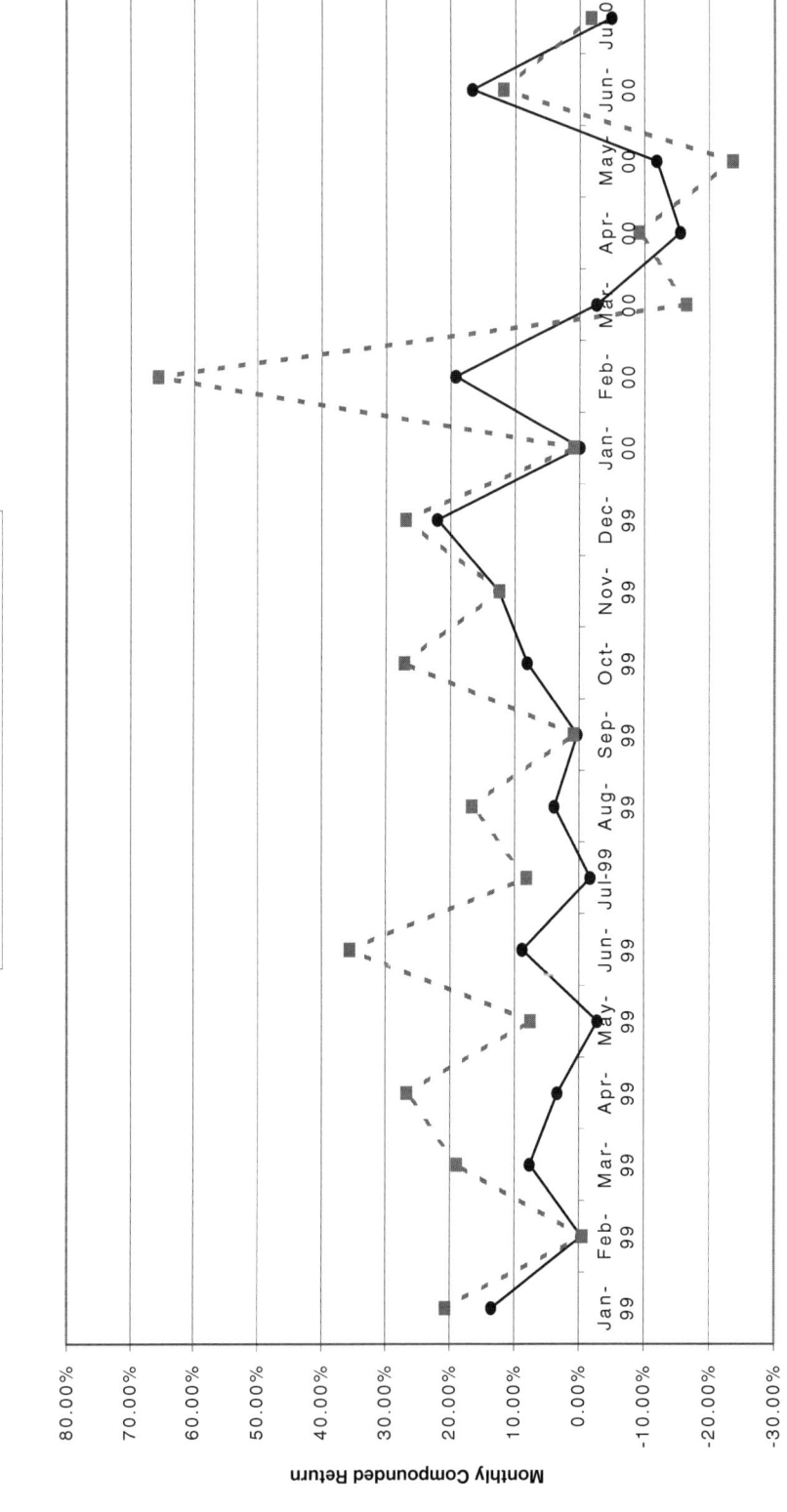

Source: Company

Exhibit 6 Hedge Fund Performance by Sector

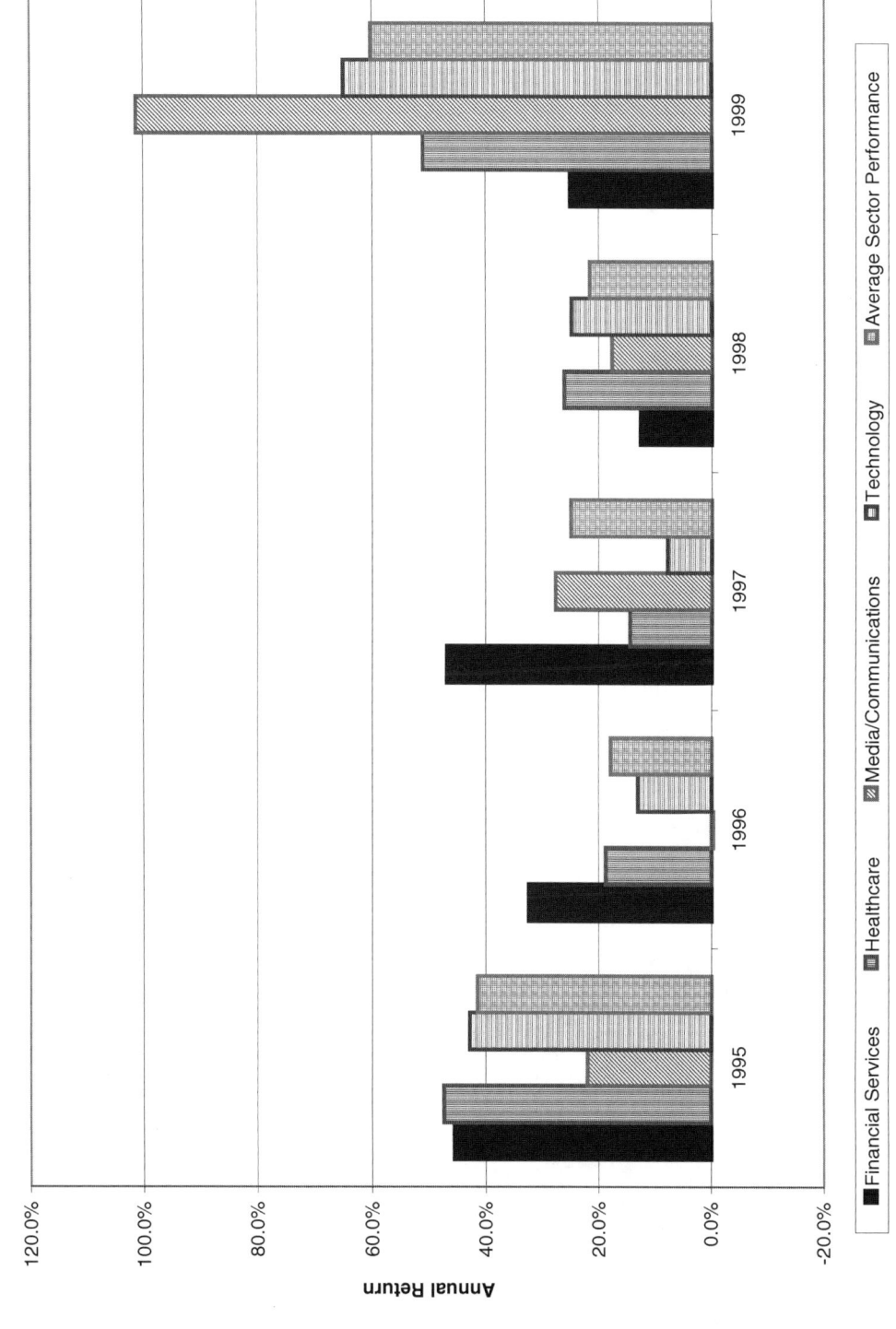

Source: Van Money Manager Research, Inc., Nashville, TN, USA

Exhibit 7 Implied Volatility of QQQ (Nasdaq) Two Month Put Options with Strike Prices 20% Out of the Money

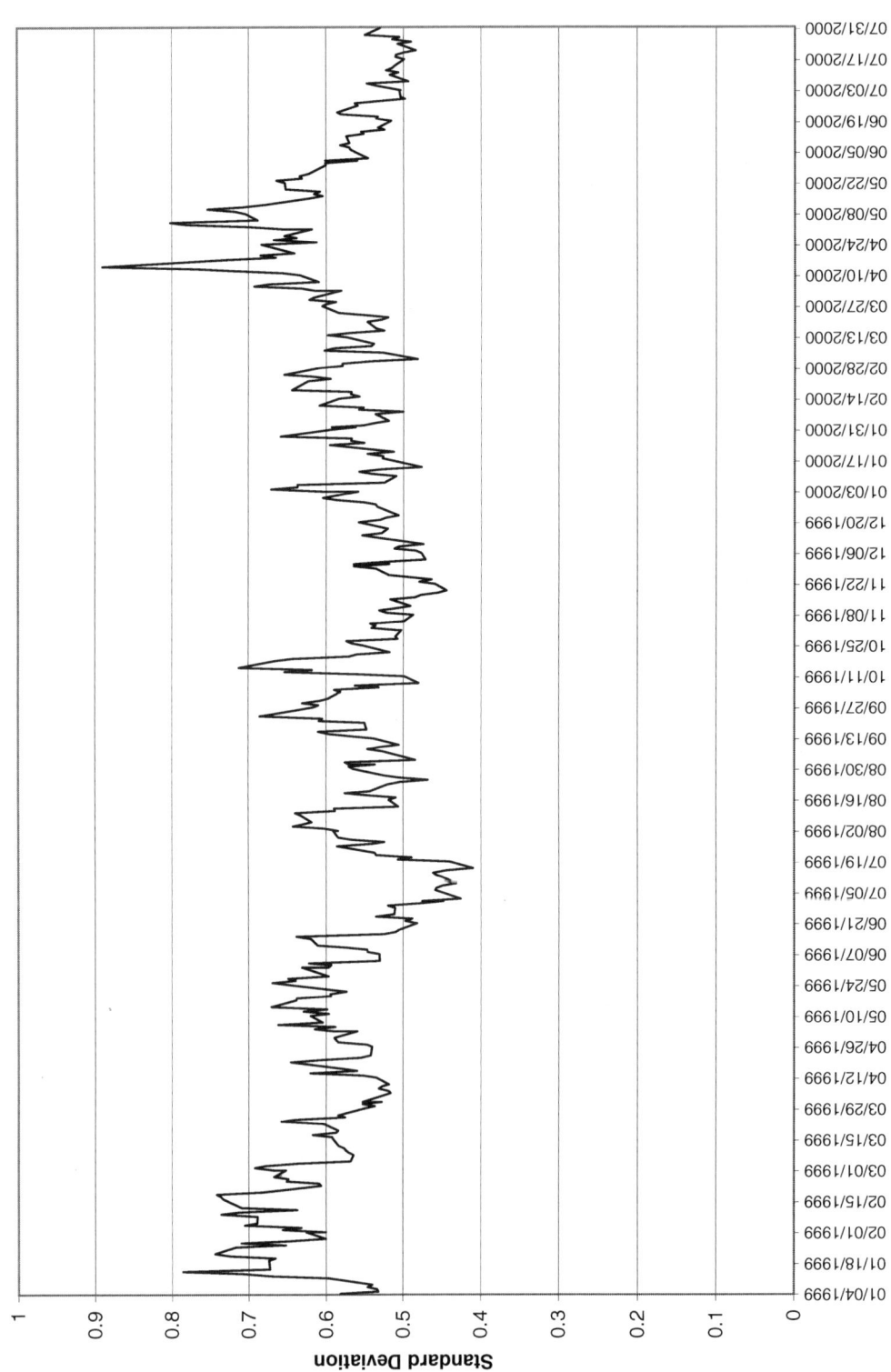

Source: Company

Exhibit 8 Changes in Equity Using Different Hedge Strategies (With No Transaction Costs Purchasing and Selling Options)

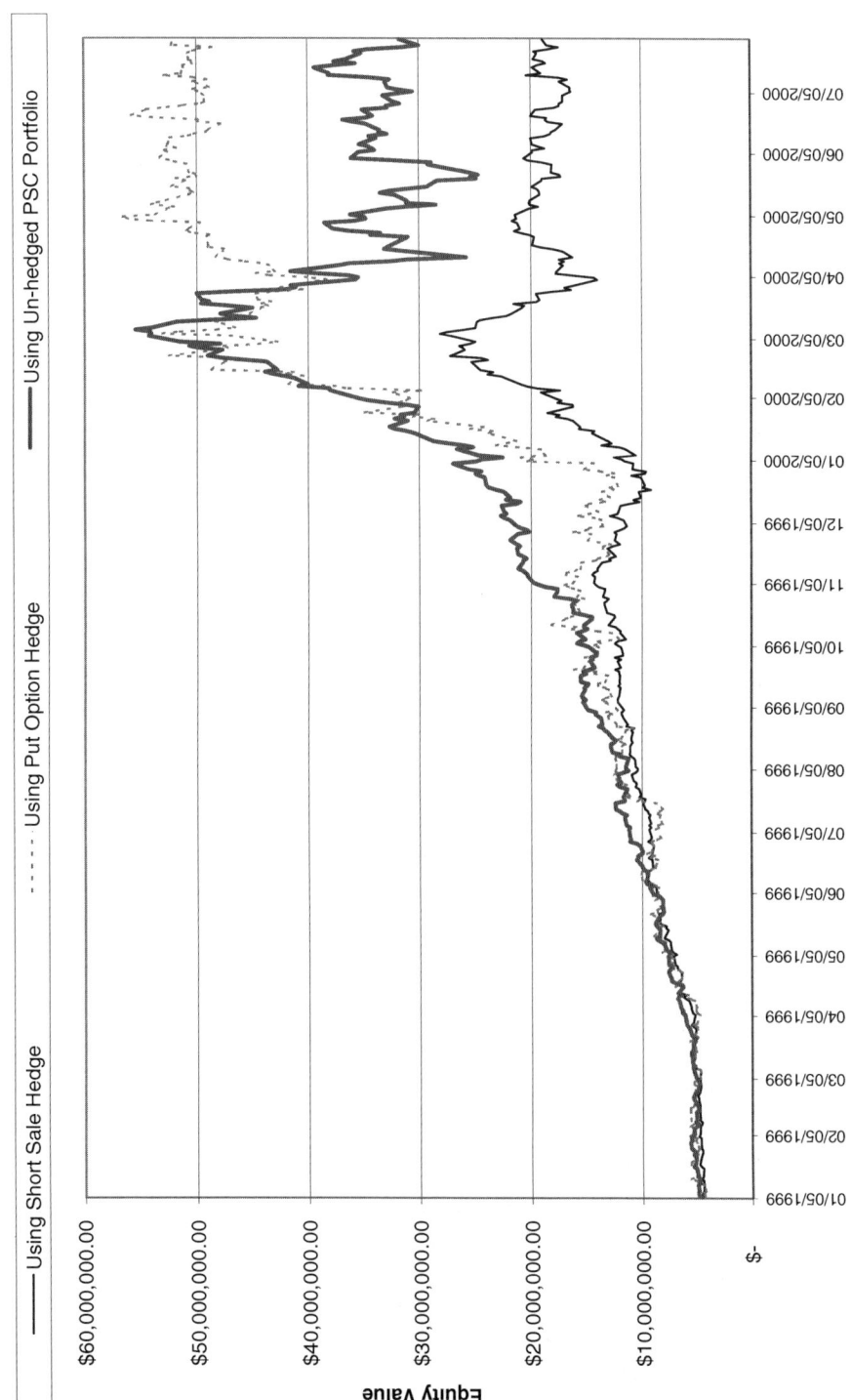

Source: Company

Exhibit 9 Performance of Pine Street Capital's Hedge Strategies During NASDAQ Worst 20 Days (Over the Period 1/04/99 to 7/26/00)

	NASDAQ	QQQ	Un-hedged PSC	Short Sale Hedge		Put Option Hedge [3]	
Date [1]	Return	Return	Portfolio Return	$ Profit/Loss	ROE [2]	$ Profit/Loss	ROE
14-Apr-00	-9.67%	-8.66%	-16.84%	(1,253,436.86)	-7.18%	935,932.36	1.98%
03-Apr-00	-7.64%	-5.99%	-14.20%	(2,182,183.49)	-13.50%	(3,004,361.57)	-7.27%
12-Apr-00	-7.06%	-5.88%	-9.93%	(437,810.11)	-2.51%	1,599,279.25	3.61%
23-May-00	-5.93%	-8.35%	-12.39%	(27,653.10)	-0.15%	838,441.15	1.64%
10-Apr-00	-5.81%	-6.10%	-10.53%	(615,272.36)	-3.48%	520,987.70	1.21%
10-May-00	-5.59%	-7.27%	-8.25%	751,321.71	3.89%	2,009,996.12	3.86%
19-Apr-99	-5.57%	-4.69%	-6.71%	8,681.20	0.13%	464,170.27	7.09%
04-Jan-00	-5.55%	-6.86%	-7.45%	746,550.20	6.94%	5,963,416.59	41.56%
28-Jul-00	-4.66%	-5.44%	-4.72%	1,082,841.42	6.22%	3,663,503.42	7.54%
24-Apr-00	-4.43%	-2.87%	-4.64%	(140,814.13)	-0.71%	91,294.87	0.19%
02-May-00	-4.36%	-5.75%	-7.21%	484,191.77	2.28%	4,483,090.41	9.01%
19-May-00	-4.19%	-4.74%	-5.53%	444,170.87	2.28%	1,602,169.02	3.16%
14-Mar-00	-4.09%	-3.70%	-6.05%	(287,101.52)	-1.15%	1,417,348.53	2.94%
30-Mar-00	-4.02%	-2.50%	-2.36%	572,243.01	3.49%	1,972,150.27	4.87%
20-Mar-00	-3.92%	-2.82%	-6.11%	(918,421.33)	-4.22%	(1,002,796.54)	-2.22%
29-Mar-00	-3.91%	-4.14%	-10.03%	(1,811,832.73)	-9.95%	(2,382,220.64)	-5.56%
09-Feb-99	-3.91%	-3.91%	-5.23%	26,606.64	0.55%	247,151.80	4.55%
06-Jan-00	-3.88%	-6.87%	-7.56%	646,208.46	5.46%	1,031,268.09	5.19%
08-May-00	-3.86%	-3.90%	-9.09%	(1,214,790.73)	-5.68%	(1,051,204.31)	-1.96%
23-Sep-99	-3.79%	-4.14%	-3.82%	347,743.29	2.88%	963,842.98	13.83%

Source: Company

[1] Days are listed by Nasdaq return (starting with the worst)

[2] ROE is Pine Street's Return on Equity

[3] Not including transaction costs

Pine Street Capital

Exhibit 10   QQQ Option Prices and Treasury Rates for July 26th, 2000

QQQ Share Price $95.63   **T-bill Rates** [a]   **1 Month:**   **5.97%**
                                                           2 Month: **6.13%**
                                                           3 Month: **6.14%**

Calls	Bid	Ask	Days to Maturity	Puts	Bid	Ask	Days to Maturity
00 Aug 70	25 1/2	26	23	00 Aug 70	1/16	3/16	23
00 Aug 75	20 5/8	21 1/8	23	00 Aug 75	3/16	5/16	23
00 Aug 80	16	16 3/8	23	00 Aug 80	1/2	11/16	23
00 Aug 85	11 3/4	12 1/8	23	00 Aug 85	1 1/16	1 1/4	23
00 Aug 90	7 7/8	8 1/4	23	00 Aug 90	2 1/8	2 3/8	23
00 Aug 95	4 3/4	5 1/8	23	00 Aug 95	4	4 1/4	23
00 Aug 100	2 1/2	2 3/4	23	00 Aug 100	6 3/4	7 1/8	23
00 Aug 105	1 1/16	1 1/4	23	00 Aug 105	10 1/4	10 5/8	23
00 Aug 110	3/8	1/2	23	00 Aug 110	14 1/2	14 7/8	23
00 Aug 115	1/8	1/4	23	00 Aug 115	19 3/8	19 3/4	23
00 Aug 120	0	1/8	23	00 Aug 120	24 3/8	24 7/8	23
00 Sep 70	26	26 3/4	58	00 Sep 70	1/2	11/16	58
00 Sep 75	21 1/2	22 1/4	58	00 Sep 75	7/8	1 1/16	58
00 Sep 80	17 3/8	17 7/8	58	00 Sep 80	1 9/16	1 3/4	58
00 Sep 85	13 1/2	14	58	00 Sep 85	2 9/16	2 13/16	58
00 Sep 90	10 1/8	10 5/8	58	00 Sep 90	4	4 3/8	58
00 Sep 95	7 1/4	7 5/8	58	00 Sep 95	6	6 3/8	58
00 Sep 100	4 7/8	5 1/4	58	00 Sep 100	8 5/8	9	58
00 Sep 105	3	3 1/4	58	00 Sep 105	11 3/4	12 1/4	58
00 Sep 110	1 11/16	1 7/8	58	00 Sep 110	15 1/2	16	58
00 Sep 115	7/8	1 1/16	58	00 Sep 115	19 3/4	20 1/4	58
00 Sep 120	7/16	9/16	58	00 Sep 120	24 1/4	25	58

Source: Chicago Board of Exchange

[a] Bond equivalent yields

9-204-024
REV: MARCH 11, 2004

MIHIR A. DESAI

Foreign Exchange Hedging Strategies at General Motors

In September of 2001, Eric Feldstein, Treasurer and Vice President, Finance for General Motors, Corp. paid little attention to his unobstructed view of Central Park from his office far above the Manhattan traffic. He had three risk management decisions to make: what to do about (i) GM's billion dollar exposure to the Canadian dollar, (ii) GM's exposure to the Argentinean peso in light of the expected devaluation in the months ahead, and (iii) the continuing strategic concern about fluctuations in the Japanese yen, which figured so heavily into the cost structures of some of GM's competitors.

Feldstein and his treasury team were responsible for all of GM's monetary transactions and for managing the myriad risks associated with the timing of those transactions. They handled everything from investing excess cash from vehicle sales receipts to hedging currency risks when a foreign subsidiary like Opel Austria announced it would remit a dividend to the worldwide parent company. The GM Treasury program invested heavily in its people, rotating them through functional positions and offices around the world, developing their skills and experience. The unit continued to produce individuals who went on to senior finance positions with GM subsidiaries or elsewhere within the GM organization or left for senior roles at other major U.S. companies.

As GM expanded around the world, the magnitude of its exposures to foreign currencies grew. Because exchange rate swings created gains and losses that flowed through GM's reported income statement, it was essential from a planning and management perspective to understand GM's foreign exchange flows and to manage the amount of earnings and cash flow volatility they imposed on GM. Feldstein constantly followed news on volatile political situations around the world and kept abreast of macroeconomic trends that might affect GM's finances.

GM senior executives had implemented a number of formal policies with respect to foreign exchange risk management and hedging procedures. These policies guided the vast majority of treasury operations, but on occasion situations arose that required special attention and possibly a deviation from the stated policy. Feldstein was reviewing proposals for the Canadian dollar (CAD), Argentinean peso (ARS), and Japanese yen (JPY). He had the authority to sign off on each deviation.

Professor Mihir A. Desai and Research Associate Mark F. Veblen prepared this case. HBS cases are developed solely as the basis for class discussion. Certain figures and details have been disguised and do not reflect the actual operations of General Motors, Corp. Cases are not intended to serve as endorsements, sources of primary data, or illustrations of effective or ineffective management.

Copyright © 2004 President and Fellows of Harvard College. To order copies or request permission to reproduce materials, call 1-800-545-7685, write Harvard Business School Publishing, Boston, MA 02163, or go to http://www.hbsp.harvard.edu. No part of this publication may be reproduced, stored in a retrieval system, used in a spreadsheet, or transmitted in any form or by any means—electronic, mechanical, photocopying, recording, or otherwise—without the permission of Harvard Business School.

Overview of General Motors and its Treasury Operations

General Motors[1]

General Motors was the world's largest automaker, with unit sales of 8.5 million vehicles in 2001—15.1% worldwide market share—and had been the world's sales leader since 1931. Founded in 1908, GM had manufacturing operations in more than 30 countries, and its vehicles were sold in approximately 200 countries. In 2000, it generated earnings of $4.4 billion on sales of $184.6 billion (see **Exhibit 1** for GM's consolidated income statement). The labor costs for its 365,000 employees in that year amounted to $19.8 billion, only $8.5 billion of which was for U.S.-based personnel. In addition to vehicles, other major product lines included (i) financial services for automotive, mortgage, and business financing, and insurance services through General Motors Acceptance Corporation (GMAC), (ii) satellite television and commercial satellite services through Hughes Electronics, and (iii) locomotives and heavy duty transmissions through GM Locomotive Group and Allison Transmission Division. GM traded on the New York Stock Exchange and was a component of the Dow Jones Industrial Average.

While North America still represented the majority of sales to end customers and the largest concentration of net property, plant, and equipment (see **Exhibit 2** and **Exhibit 3**), the importance of GM's international operations was growing as a percent of the overall business. With globalized production, these figures understated the degree to which intermediate goods in GM's supply chain moved around the world. Its market share in Latin America was 20% and in Europe had reached 10% (20% if Fiat's figures were included[2]). Increasing market share in Asia, which stood at 4%, was a major strategic objective for GM.

General Motors Treasurer's Office

GM's Treasurer's Office performed a full range of corporate treasury functions from its head office in New York and through additional locations in Brussels, Singapore and Detroit. The organizational structure shown in **Exhibit 4** demonstrates the nature and extent of those activities.

One of the key functions of the Treasurer's Office was financial risk management. This included management of not only market risk (foreign exchange, interest rate and commodities exposures) but also counterparty, corporate and operational risk. **Exhibit 5** outlines the components of this function and demonstrates the high degree of centralization in approach.

All of GM's financial risk management activities were subject to oversight by the Risk Management Committee, which was composed of six of GM's most senior executives including Feldstein.[3] The committee met quarterly to review the performance of GM's financial risk management strategies and to set treasury policy for GM and its subsidiaries. Treasury policy included evaluating the parameters and benchmarks for managing market risks, determining criteria for assessing counterparty credit risk, determining thresholds for property and liability insurance

---

[1] Statistics drawn from General Motors, 2001 Annual Report (Detroit: General Motors, 2002) and General Motors, December 31, 2001 10-K (Detroit: General Motors, 2002)..

[2] General Motors owned 20% of Fiat, and Fiat held an option to put the remaining 80% to GM.

[3] Other members of the Risk Management Committee were the Chief Financial Officer, the General Auditor, the Chief Accounting Officer, the Chief Economist, and a senior executive from General Motors Acceptance Corporation (GMAC), GM's financial services subsidiary.

coverage, as well as reviewing internal control aspects of operating policies and procedures. GM's formal, company-wide policies contained not only broad principles, but also detailed execution procedures such as, in the case of foreign exchange risk management, the types of instruments to be used and the appropriate time horizons.[4] At its meetings the committee also discussed any special topics that needed to be addressed. Such special topics often included precisely the deviations from usual policy Feldstein was currently considering.

Various groups within the Treasurer's Office were involved in the implementation of financial risk management policy. For foreign exchange, all of GM's hedging activities were concentrated in two centers:

- The Domestic Finance group in New York handled FX hedging for GM entities located in North America, Latin America, Africa and the Middle East

- The European Regional Treasury Center (ERTC) was GM's largest foreign exchange operation, covering European and Asia Pacific FX exposures

FX hedging activities were segregated in this way on the principle that there should be some geographic correspondence between where a business unit was actually managed and where treasury for that business was controlled. At the same time, though, it was considered desirable to reap the benefits of pooling exposures across groups. In a sense, the goal was to match treasury management to the footprint of the business. Having local market knowledge and a trading center in both the European and U.S. time zones was also very helpful, because GM was active in each of the major foreign exchange markets.

In managing the FX exposures, both the Domestic Finance group and the ERTC worked closely with other groups within Treasury that had the primary responsibility of providing strategic support to GM entities within that region. These groups were also the global coordinators for intercompany loans, moved cash around the world to finance overseas mergers and acquisitions activities, and managed dividend repatriations.

Review of Corporate Hedging Policy

General Motors's overall foreign exchange risk management policy was established to meet three primary objectives: (1) reduce cash flow and earnings volatility, (2) minimize the management time and costs dedicated to global FX management, and (3) align FX management in a manner consistent with how GM operates its automotive business. The first constituted a conscious decision to hedge cash flows (transaction exposures[5]) only and ignore balance sheet exposures (translation exposures[6]). The second objective was a consequence of an internal study that determined that investment of resources in active FX management had not resulted in significantly outperforming passive

---

[4] GM policy specified, for example, which risks were to be hedged using forward contracts rather than options contracts.

[5] Transaction exposures are the gains and losses that arise when transactions are settled in some currency other than a company's reporting currency. These exposures stem from buying and selling activities as well as financing decisions such as borrowing. For further detail see W. Carl Kester and Richard P. Melnick, "Note on Transaction and Translation Exposure," HBS Case No. 9-288-017 (Boston: Harvard Business School Publishing, 1987, rev. 1992).

[6] Translation exposures are the gains and losses that arise when the assets and liabilities of a multinational's foreign subsidiary are translated back into the multinational's reporting currency for the purposes of preparing consolidated financial statements. For further detail see W. Carl Kester and Richard P. Melnick, "Note on Transaction and Translation Exposure," HBS Case No. 9-288-017 (Boston: Harvard Business School Publishing, 1987, rev. 1992).

benchmarks. As a result, policy was changed and a passive approach replaced the active one. The third reflected a belief that financial management should somehow map to the geographic operational footprint of the underlying business.

Passive Policy: Hedge 50% of Commercial (Operating) Exposures

The policy adopted was generally to hedge 50% of all significant foreign exchange commercial (operating) exposures on a regional level.[7] GM policy differentiated between "commercial" exposures—cash flows associated with the ongoing business such as receivables and payables—and "financial" exposures such as debt repayments and dividends. GM policy also outlined what sorts of derivative instruments were to be used for hedging.

Commercial (operating) exposures With operations, sales units, and investments spanning the globe, GM had direct or indirect commercial exposures to virtually every meaningful currency. Each regional center collected monthly forecasts of accounts receivable and accounts payable, usually for the twelve coming months, from all of the GM entities within its region and totaled the net exposures (receivables minus payables) by currency pair.[8] This information was complied into a matrix presenting the exposure totals by currency pair for each regional unit (General Motors North America, General Motors Europe, General Motors Asian Pacific, and General Motors Latin America, Africa, Middle East) and then aggregating them up to a corporate grand total for General Motors as a whole. (See **Exhibit 6** for the summary of exposures by currency pair.) In practical use, this provided GM executives with granular information about the currency exposures created by ongoing business operations.

A determination of *"riskiness"* was then made on a regional basis, deciding which FX exposures were significant enough to warrant hedging. This determination was governed by the following formula:

Implied risk # Regional notional exposure $\forall$ Annual volatility of relevant currency pair

For example, if GM-North America's forecasted 12-month euro exposure was a $400 million net payable at December 31, 2000. This difference of euro receivables less euro payables would represent the notional euro exposure for GM's North America region. Give the Euro's annual volatility versus the U.S. dollar of 12%, this suggested an implied risk of $48 million. For all implied risks of $10 million or greater, the regional exposure was required to be hedged. In the case of particularly volatile currencies, exposures were only hedged for the coming six months rather than twelve, and the implied risk threshold was lowered to $5 million. In practice, GM's overseas operations were large enough that all major currencies exceeded this threshold in one or more regions.

Net exposures within a region were then hedged to a *benchmark hedge ratio* of 50%. For example, half, or $200 million, of notional euro exposure of GMNA's $400 million would be hedged.

---

[7] The fact that exposures were managed regionally meant that although there might be offsetting exposures in different regions, each region's exposure would still be separately hedged. For example, if with respect to the British Pound GM-Europe had a net receivables position $1 million and GM-Asia Pacific had a net payables position of $1 million, each region's GBP exposure would be hedged even though GM as a consolidated entity had no net exposure before or after this hedging activity took place.

[8] The business units were permitted some flexibility in netting across months so long as they established a currency hedge through their treasury center. For example, if $20 million net receivables exposure in one month was likely to be offset by a $15 million payables exposure in the next month in the ordinary course of business, the net exposure of $5 million could be hedged with a forward contract and a currency swap used to hedge the risk involved in the timing difference.

Having calculated the forecasted net exposure to a particular currency for each of the coming twelve months, the regional treasury center was then bound to use *particular derivative instruments* over *specified time horizons*: forward contracts to hedge 50% of the exposures for months one through six and options to hedge 50% of the exposures for months seven through twelve. Assuming that GMNA's $400 million euro exposure was distributed evenly over the twelve months of 2001, the $200 million exposure for months one through six would be hedged through forward contracts on $100 million, and the $200 million exposure for months seven through twelve would be hedged through options on $100 million. In general, at least 25% of the combined hedge on a particular currency was to be held in options in order to assure enough flexibility.

The evolution of the rolling forward twelve months naturally became more complicated when the exposures were not evenly spread across time (see **Exhibit 7**). First, as months rolled closer (cash flow G from month seven to six in **Exhibit 7**), the Treasury group replaced or supplemented options-based hedge positions with forward contracts, sometimes selling options previously purchased. This meant that the balance of forwards and options used to hedge the year ahead was constantly changing—and according to policy, options had to make up 25% of hedge positions. Second, the forecasts that the Treasury group received from managers in the operating subsidiaries frequently changed from month to month. This created situations where hedging actions from the previous month left the Treasury group either over- or under-hedged due to changing expectations.

Treasury centers were also expected to monitor the economic performance of their hedges and to readjust cover to levels which matched the levels achieved by a simulated benchmark hedge portfolio. This was done on a *delta basis*. The delta provided a measure of how effectively a particular instrument covered a risk, taking into account the probability that the instrument would be exercised. Forward contracts therefore had a delta of 100%. In purchasing currency options, GM sought to buy at-the-money-forward options that had an expected delta of 50% upon execution. Given the required mix of forwards and options in hedging an exposure, the hedge ratio of 50% initially corresponded, on a delta basis, to a hedge ratio of 37.5%. Taking again GMNA's euro exposure as an example, the first six months were hedged on a delta basis at the notional hedge ratio (50%) times the forward contract delta (100%) or a delta hedge ratio of 50%. Similarly the last six months were hedged notionally at 50% and using options with a 50% delta, which combined to a 25% delta hedge ratio. The average delta hedge ratio over the entire hedging horizon was therefore 37.5% at the outset.

Over time, the delta hedge ratios of both the actual and the benchmark hedge portfolios could be expected to depart from the initial 37.5%, primarily due to sensitivity of the value of options to movements in spot rates. Experience suggested that the delta hedge ratio of the benchmark portfolio would fluctuate somewhere between 30% and 45%. In addition, the delta hedge ratio of the actual portfolio would often vary from that of the benchmark portfolio because of the practical difficulties in executing exactly in line with benchmark. A tolerance of +/- 5% was therefore allowed in matching the delta cover of the actual portfolio to the cover of the benchmark portfolio. It was also possible, on an exception basis, to deviate from a passive hedging strategy and take a view on the future direction of a particular FX rate. Regional approvals were required in any such case. Even then, delta and notional cover levels had to be kept within certain prescribed ranges.

Commercial exposures (capital expenditures) Because capital expenditures did not exhibit the same month-to-month volatility or changing forecasts, GM adopted a different approach to hedging them. Unlike uncertain cash flows, planned investments (purchases of fixed assets or equipment) that met either of the following two tests were hedged with forward contracts using a 100% hedge ratio to the anticipated payment date: (i) amount in excess of $1 million, or (ii) implied risk equivalent to at least 10% of the unit's net worth. Such exposures were generally treated separately from ordinary commercial exposures.

Financial exposures Other certain cash flows, including loan repayment schedules and equity injections into affiliates were hedged on a case-by-case basis. Generally they were structured so as to create as little FX risk as possible, and as a rule of thumb they were also 100% hedged using forward contracts. Dividend payments, on the other hand, were only deemed hedgeable once declared, and even then were hedged in the same manner as ordinary commercial exposures, i.e. a 50% hedge ratio.

Translation (balance sheet) exposures Translation exposures were not included under GM's corporate hedging policy. At the same time, they could on occasion become large enough to warrant the attention of senior finance executives, and Feldstein therefore kept abreast of any such situations. Such exposures were closely related to management's determination of a subsidiary's functional currency, a topic discussed below. Insofar as these exposures became significant and were not covered by stated hedging policies, they took on increased importance.

Accounting treatment One of the goals of GM's hedging policy was to reduce earnings volatility. This goal was challenging given that, under the prevailing accounting standards (FAS 133), the forwards and options GM would use generally had to be marked-to-market and the gains and losses flowed through the income statement. At the same time, the underlying exposure being hedged was, in the case of commercial exposures (forecasts of receivables and payables up to 12 months in advance), often not on the books at all, and therefore changes in its market value did not hit the income statement. This mismatch was a potential source of earnings volatility.

FAS 133, however, provided the possibility of hedge accounting treatment for an exposure and associated hedge position. If the requirements for hedge accounting treatment were met, the above described earnings volatility was neutralized by taking gains and losses on the hedges to a shareholder's equity account in the balance sheet pending the realization of gains and losses on the underlying hedged exposures. Ultimately, gains and losses on the hedges would be released through the income statement contemporaneously with the recognition in the income statement of the gains and losses on the underlying exposures. Unfortunately, due to the complexity of compliance with hedge accounting regulations only a few of GM's more significant currency pairs were initially targeted for compliance.[9]

Reporting Hedging activities were closely tracked and regularly reviewed within the Treasury Group. The information was made available to senior management and to the Risk Management Committee to assist in policy review and creation. It was this internal monitoring that had led, just a few years earlier, to the decision to shift away from active FX risk management to passive management.

Understanding the Choice of a Subsidiary's Functional Currency

When U.S. multinationals established new overseas subsidiaries, management was required to determine whether the functional currency for each overseas subsidiary would be the local currency or the U.S. dollar. Under FASB #52, the functional currency had to be the primary operating currency of that subsidiary. (There was one exception: parent companies were required to use their own

---

[9] Compliance was voluntary: by providing extensive proof that derivative transactions were entered into for the purpose of hedging and by establishing the effectiveness of the hedge, companies could obtain hedge accounting treatment for the combined position and avoid asymmetric mark-to-market treatment of the underlying exposure and hedge position.

reporting currency in highly inflationary economies.) A self-contained unit with substantial local currency receipts and expenses had to select the local currency as its functional currency. However, a subsidiary that purchased much of its raw inputs from a U.S. parent or sold a substantial part of its production to its U.S. parent each year—in short, operations that were essentially an extension of the parent company's business—had to select the U.S. dollar as its functional currency. The choice of functional currency did not impact the consolidated entity's reporting currency, which was always the U.S. dollar in the case of U.S. multinationals.

While the choice of functional currency did not change the economic realities of the business and its operations, it did change how a company reported the changes in value resulting from fluctuating exchange rates. The following example illustrates the consequences of the choice of functional currencies (see **Exhibit 8** for an illustration of these issues).

Imagine that GM-Strasbourg (GMS) has nothing but cash held in a U.S. dollar-denominated checking account and a euro-denominated checking account. The respective balances are $100 and €50. The subsidiary is financed entirely with equity. Furthermore, assume for simplicity that the U.S. dollar and the euro are trading at parity. Suppose GMS has a choice whether to use the U.S. dollar or the euro as its functional currency.[10] The difference between these alternatives is examined by tracing the consequences of a 10% devaluation of the euro against the U.S. dollar.

When GMS's functional currency is the same as GM's reporting currency (U.S. dollars), GM's consolidated income statement will include a gain or loss on the changes in value, as measured in U.S. dollars, of GMS's foreign currency denominated monetary asset/liability.[11] (GMS's income statement will show the same.) When GMS instead uses its local currency (euros) as its functional currency,

1. GM's consolidated income statement will include a gain or loss on the changes in value, as measured in GMS's local currency of GMS's non-local currency denominated asset/liability (GMS's income statement will show the same)

2. GM's balance sheet will show an adjustment to shareholders' equity for the translation to U.S. dollars of GMS's assets/liabilities.

The critical insight is that, while the overall impact of the devaluation of the euro will be the same regardless of the functional currency chosen, there is a difference in what impact is recognized in the income statement and what impact is recognized directly in the shareholders' equity of GM.

In the case where the dollar is chosen as the functional currency, the euro exposure is considered the foreign currency. The illustrative 10% depreciation of the euro against the U.S. dollar reduces the value of GMS's euro holdings: the €50 that used to be worth $50 are now only worth $45. This $5 loss is the economic impact on GM Worldwide (see **Panel A** in **Exhibit 8** for an illustration). At the subsidiary level, that $5 loss is similarly recorded as a decrease in value of the €50 that are held in the euro-denominated account. Both the subsidiary and GM as a consolidated entity report on their income statements a foreign exchange loss of $5. This

---

[10] As described above, the functional currency was determined by objective standards rather than a choice. This example contemplates a choice of functional currencies for illustrative purposes.

[11] For completeness, it should be noted that there would be an income statement impact resulting from any GMS foreign currency denominated non-monetary assets such as inventory and fixed assets if the historical exchange rate at which these assets were carried on the books needed to be adjusted retrospectively.

reduction in net income flows through to the balance sheet reducing equity (retained earnings) by $5.

In the next case, where the euro is the functional currency, GMS reports a $100 foreign exchange exposure. When the euro depreciates, the value of GMS's foreign exchange exposure ($100) changes. GMS's foreign currency-denominated asset (the $100 checking account balance) must be remeasured into the functional currency and the gain of €11.1 (or $10.0) is credited to the income statement. Upon consolidation, GMS's entire assets and liabilities of €161.1, including the $100 checking account after remeasurement into euros, are translated into U.S. dollars. (See **Panel B** in **Exhibit 8** for an illustration).

Feldstein realized that volatility in GM's earnings would to some degree depend on how GM accounted for the operations of its many subsidiaries. In particular, when considering policy deviations, it was important to understand which currency constituted a "foreign exchange" exposure from the perspective of the subsidiary—because it would be fluctuations in the value of that currency (as measured in dollars) that would affect GM's net income and retained earnings. Feldstein was less concerned with the foreign exchange adjustments to equity that did not flow through the income statement.

Monthly Review—the Canadian Dollar

GM-Canada was an integral part of GM's worldwide production process. In addition to serving the Canadian domestic market, it served as a core supplier to other GM operations in North America, especially those in the United States, and it also relied on many U.S. based suppliers. At GM-Canada the U.S. dollar-denominated flows were so large that the U.S. dollar was effectively the primary operating currency of the company. As a result, accounting standards required that the U.S. dollar be selected as the functional currency (despite GM-Canada's very large Canadian dollar assets and liabilities).

GM-Canada therefore recognized its foreign currency exposure as a Canadian dollar exposure. The income statement impact arose from gains and losses on both the CAD-denominated cash flows (see **Exhibit 9**) and on the balance sheet CAD net monetary liability position (see **Exhibit 10**). Both exposures were equivalent to short positions in the Canadian dollar. The net payable cash flow exposure resulted largely from payments due to Canadian suppliers, and the size of the net monetary liability stemmed mainly from future pension and postretirement benefit obligations to employees in Canada.

Feldstein was aware of the fact that GM's passive hedging policy called for hedging 50% of the CAD 1.7 billion cash flow exposure projected over the subsequent twelve months. Nonetheless Feldstein acknowledged that GM's policy of not hedging the translation exposure stemming from the CAD 2.1 billion net monetary liability left a large CAD exposure that could impact GM's year-end financial results significantly.

Feldstein met with his FX and Commodities Manager, Doug Ostermann. Ostermann was proposing to increase the hedge ratio for the CAD to the maximum allowed under GM policy—75%. The internal memorandum requesting permission to deviate so far from the standard 50% policy read as follows:

> Historically, GMNA has a short CAD commercial exposure of approximately CAD 1.6 – 1.8 billion, primarily due to CAD denominated supplier payments being larger than CAD denominated sales.... In order to reduce global earnings volatility at year-end, we recommend

to hedge up to 75% of GMNA's commercial exposure (approximately 30% hedging ratio for the balance sheet exposure). According to the FX policy, any deviation from the passive hedging strategy (50% of notional hedging ratio), requires the approval...

Feldstein felt he needed a comparison of the income statement impact of a 75% versus a 50% hedge ratio. The proposal suggested that the expected volatility of the CAD/USD exchange rate was plus-or-minus 3.1% around the 1.5780 exchange rate on the date of the memo. Using this volatility, Ostermann could do a sensitivity calculation with a favorable scenario (gain due to FX movements) and an unfavorable scenario (loss due to FX movements) based on the after-tax gain/loss impact from the projected CAD cash flow as well as from the CAD net monetary liability. Dividing this amount by the 550 million shares GM had outstanding, Ostermann could determine how much the proposed deviation would reduce EPS volatility. To simplify the calculation, Ostermann ignored the costs of hedging (such as option premiums).

As Feldstein prepared to make a decision about the CAD deviation, he had to keep in mind both what economic risks he wanted to hedge and what was called for under GM's corporate hedging policy.

Implementing a Foreign Exchange Hedge

If Feldstein signed off on this deviation, Mercedes Michel and the team in Domestic Finance would oversee putting on the hedge position. Michel was in regular communication with several of the largest currency-dealing banks and maintained up-to-date price quotations. On any day when GM was active in the market to adjust its hedge positions, she was on the phone with the banks virtually all day getting quotations and executing trades. On an ordinary day, she could get most of the information she needed from electronic data sources. When a hedge position was being created or modified, she handled transactions in both forward and options contracts.

Suppose on September 15, 2001 Michel needed to hedge a CAD 10 million cash outflow three months in the future (in other words, 50% of a CAD 20 million notional exposure). First, she checks the market price levels using a Bloomberg terminal. The spot price on the CAD/USD exchange rate is bid-ask of 1.5621-1.5624. (Spreads were very small when transacting in significant amounts in the currency markets; players typically only referred to the last two digits of the spread because it was assumed that buyers and sellers knew the levels to the $1/100^{th}$ of a point.) With that information she dials one of her regular bankers:

Michel: Can you give me a two-way price on 10 Canada?

Trader: CAD spot is 21 to 24.

Michel: I'll do it at 21.

Trader: So, you are buying 10 million Canadian dollars against U.S. dollars at 1.5621.

Michel: Actually, I want to roll it 3 months out. Can you tell me the forward points?

Trader: That's 45 points.

Michel: Can you improve it a pip?

Trader: Humm...OK...You get it at 46.

Michel: Done. Thanks.

Trader: Good. Then GM buys 10 million Canadian dollars at 1.5667 and sells USD 6,382,842.92 with value December 17, 2001.

Michel: Agreed. Bye.

Now assume that instead of hedging the exposure with a forward contract, Michel needed to use a currency option to hedge the CAD 10 million exposure. Michel will buy a CAD call / USD put with a notional amount of CAD 10 million. Assume the spot price is 1.5621. Again, before calling the trader, Michel checks Bloomberg to find the forward rate—1.5667 in this example. Michel will use this as the strike price for a 3-month at-the-money-forward (ATMF[12]) CAD call / USD put.

Michel: Can you give me a price for a CAD call / USD put with delta exchange?[13]

Trader: Sure. Give me the details.

Michel: I need a 10 Canada call, maturing on December 17th, with a strike price of 1.5667 and delta exchange at 1.5621. Can you give me the premium price as a percentage of USD?

Trader: Yes. Hold on a moment...So, the strike is at 50% delta[14]...the premium price is 1.45% of USD offered.

Michel: Let's see. The U.S. dollar put amount is 10 million divided by 1.5667, that's USD 6,382,842.92; that times 1.45% makes the premium amount 92,551.22 U.S. dollars. Let's do it.

Trader: Done. GM buys a 10 million Canadian dollar call / U.S. dollar put with maturity on December 17, value December 18, at a strike of 1.5667. On the delta exchange GM sells CAD 5 at 1.5621.

Michel: Agreed. Bye.[15]

Comparing Forward Contracts with Options

Because GM's hedging operations constituted a substantial volume of currency trading, GM was concerned with executing its hedging policies in a cost efficient manner. Forward contracts and options, however, were not easily comparable on straight cost basis. A forward contract was always a zero cost contract on the trade date, whereas buying an option involved paying a premium. Thus, the treasury group needed a different way of analyzing the two strategies with respect to one another. The framework devised by the Treasury group involved comparing how one strategy or the other would have fared at the different possible exchange rates that might prevail at the future date (the date of the exposure to hedge).

Specifically, it compared: (1) the combination of the outright exposure plus a 50% hedge using forward contracts, with (2) the combination of the outright exposure plus a 50% hedge using options. On a graph of future spot prices (x-axis) against cash flow payoff (y-axis), these two produced lines that intersected. That point of intersection represented a sort of break-even point—if GM Treasury's expected future spot exchange rate was different from that point, GM could choose the strategy that was more profitable.

---

[12] Rather than being at-the-money with respect to the spot price, such an option is at-the-money with respect to the forward price.

[13] The delta exchange effectively allowed the bank to offer a price quotation based on a fixed spot rate (of 1.5621 in this case). As a result, GM was able to contact multiple banks and obtain competitive price quotations and select the best one for executing the options trade. **Appendix A** discusses the mechanics of a delta exchange in detail.

[14] An at-the-money-forward option was characterized by a delta (sensitivity to changes in the underlying exchange rate) of 50%.

[15] Michel might have asked the trader to hold the price quotation while she contacted other banks in search of a better price. The fact that she immediately executed the trade with this trader suggests that she had already called two other banks and that their price quotations were not as competitive.

Foreign Exchange Hedging Strategies at General Motors 204-024

Forward contracts   Continuing the example from Michel's conversations with traders above, Michel constructed a spreadsheet that considered a range of future spot rates of 1.4000 to 1.8000 CAD per USD. The outright exposure measured the foreign exchange gain or loss GM would recognize on the CAD 20 million position. At a 50% hedge, Michel knew she had to layer on a CAD 10 million hedge at a forward price of 1.5667. This would produce a partially offsetting cash flow in the future. The sum of the outright gain/loss and the cash settlement of the forward contract amounted to the net consequence of a forwards strategy.

Options contracts   Instead, Michel could layer on top of the outright exposure just calculated an option contract purchase. The sum of the outright exposure and the option payoff amounted to the net consequence of an options strategy. The option characteristics were as described above: a strike price equal to the forward price of 1.5667 and a premium cost of 1.45% of the notional hedge amount. When the option was in the money, the contract returned a profit (less the premium), whereas when it expired out of the money, the gain (loss) on the outright exposure was reduced (increased) by the premium amount.

Special Situations—the Argentinean Peso

Argentina presented GM Treasury with a real headache for GM's extensive operations there. In order to cure rampant inflation, the government exercised control over foreign currency exchange and maintained a peg to the U.S. dollar at USD 1 : ARS 1. With a debt-to-GDP ratio of 45% and $16.5 billion coming due in 2002, the "zero-deficit" law passed by the Senate in 2001 put Argentina at serious risk of defaulting on its debt. Credit analysts at Standard & Poor's and Moody's had downgraded Argentina to six and seven grades below investment grade, respectively. GM Treasury's Latin America experts believed the short-term probability of default had reached 40%. In the medium term, the probability rose to 50% because Argentina had not addressed key issues such as trade liberalization, state reform, and pension and healthcare reform. A default would undoubtedly be accompanied by a massive devaluation.

The Argentina situation appeared grim. Feldstein reviewed the figures before him. The treasury analysts had provided the ARS and USD denominated components of the balance sheet (see **Exhibit 11**)—and described a potential devaluation of the peso against the dollar from 1 : 1 to 2 : 1. Feldstein saw two immediate impacts. First, local currency equivalent of USD borrowings by GM Argentina (a local currency functional subsidiary) would grow, putting financial pressure on the subsidiary. In fact, the $300 million USD net liability position would double in peso terms to an ARS 600 million liability. There would be a consequent ARS 300 million adverse income statement impact for the subsidiary. Second, there would be a substantial translation loss on GM Argentina's ARS denominated net assets when these net assets were consolidated in USD with all other assets of GM Worldwide. This loss would negatively impact consolidated shareholders' equity. With a few calculations, Feldstein figured the value at risk to GM—an amount that included the maximum EPS hit GM might be forced to take into net income in 2002 together with the shareholders' equity impact.[16]

---

[16] In fact, the accounting consequences were more complex.   As a local currency functional entity, GM Argentina would first convert all non-ARS denominated asset and liabilities to ARS. The gain or loss would be reflected in GM Argentina's income statement and ultimately impact the consolidated net income of GM Worldwide. On consolidation, the entire GM Argentina balance sheet, now denominated exclusively in ARS, would be translated into USD, and any gain or loss would be reflected as an accumulated translation adjustment (ATA) flowing directly to shareholders' equity.

Hedging the Peso Exposure

This time, Michel had sent some materials along with the policy deviation proposal. She reviewed the market for forwards and options on the ARS and suggested a method for thinking about how costly it would be to hedge the ARS exposure in the financial markets. Michel had compiled historical prices on one-, six-, and twelve-month forward rates of the peso vs. the dollar (see **Exhibit 12**). Feldstein's first observation was the rapid rise in forward rates over the recent months. With the peso pegged at 1 : 1 to the dollar, the forward premium, approximately 4.56% on a one-month contract, would be lost if the peso peg was maintained (since pesos could instead still have been purchased at 1 : 1). Michel extrapolated from the historical prices the costs of hedging a $300 million exposure based on rolling over shorter term contracts or purchasing year-long contracts (see **Exhibit 13**).

These figures led Feldstein to consider what alternative hedging opportunities might be available to mitigate the impact of a likely devaluation. He hoped to find some natural business hedges or creative ways to reduce peso-denominated assets and substitute peso-denominated liabilities for hard currency-denominated ones. Similarly, creating exports—even if to other GM affiliates—from Argentina could bring in revenues in more stable foreign currencies. GM Argentina had already eliminated peso cash balances and transferred them in USD to the European Regional Treasury Center. It was also considering the purchase of some materials locally in ARS for export to other entities in the region that would pay for them in hard currency. GM-Argentina's USD borrowings would certainly have to be addressed. The Argentina situation was more complex than most currency deviation requests—although Feldstein had to consider all of the same issues as with the CAD deviation, it was less clear how to accomplish an ARS deviation effectively.

Feldstein and Ostermann needed to decide how to proceed: was it worth the costs to increase the size of GM's hedge position beyond what was required by usual policy?

Understanding Competitive Exposures

Source of Competitive Exposure

All this thought devoted to changing a fundamental business process to minimize exposures readied Feldstein for tackling the final proposal—the Japanese yen. This exposure was not created by GM's inflows or outflows or how it chose to run its business. Rather, it was a result of competing against companies with different home currencies. The major Japanese automakers had large portions of their cost structure denominated in yen. As a result, any depreciation in the yen lowered their relative cost structure as compared to the U.S. and European auto manufacturers. If some of GM's competitors achieved significantly reduced costs through currency depreciations, this meant that the performance of GM's business faced currency risk: lower costs for Japanese firms would lead to lower required prices to achieve the normal profitability levels, thus eroding GM's market share—and market value.

The dollar/yen exchange rate had fluctuated widely over the past two decades and was again depreciating (see **Exhibit 14**). Japanese automakers derived 56% and 43% of their revenues from the U.S. market in 1999 and 2000, respectively. In the most recent year, they sold 4.1 million units in the United States. Equity analysts had estimated that the yen appreciation from 117 to 107 during the first half of 2000 had reduced Japanese automakers' combined global operating profits by $4 billion. Feldstein reversed that statistic in his mind: for every 1 yen depreciation against the dollar, Japanese competitors' collective operating profit grew by more than $400 million. Rough estimates from research reports suggested that the Japanese firms were unprofitable when the yen was stronger than 110 to the dollar and profitable at 120 or more yen to the dollar.

Measuring Competitive Exposures

Feldstein thought of this exposure as a competitive one rather than a financial one. There was no projected receivable or payable and no capital investment or loan to be repaid, yet there was still a bottom-line impact that stemmed from fluctuations in exchange rates. Because of the lack of an explicit transaction, Feldstein realized he was outside the usual territory of GM's hedging policy. Any action with respect to the yen based on this perceived competitive exposure would be setting a new precedent—something Feldstein felt he had to consider very carefully. At the very least, he needed an airtight story justifying the magnitude of the exposure and how it could be effectively hedged.

Feldstein felt that a compelling case could be made for the following chain of events. (1) A depreciation in the yen lead to (2) additional gross margin for Japanese automakers, who (3) passed along some of this benefit to consumers in the form of lower prices, and (4) as a result of lower prices the Japanese automakers gained market share in the U.S., which (5) ate into unit sales at GM, which (6) lowered GM's profits, which (7) reduced GM's market value. The key was numerically estimating these variables and effects.

Of course, he would also need to place his estimated competitive exposure in the context of GM's overall yen exposure. This included a commercial exposure based on forecasted receivables and payables of $900 million, an investment exposure resulting from equity stakes in several Japanese companies (see **Exhibit 15**), and a financing exposure through a yen-denominated loan. GM had recently completed a yen bond issue, one of the objectives of which had been to partially offset the yen competitive exposure. Approximately $500 million worth of bonds were outstanding.

Feldstein realized that estimating the magnitude of the competitive exposure depended on a number of assumptions and involved a fair amount of guesswork. In any event, he could calculate sensitivities for each input variable later. After consultations with the business development team, he figured that the average Japanese car had between 20% and 40% Japanese content. This included parts sourced from suppliers in Japan as well as labor and plant expense incurred in Japan. A yen depreciation, therefore, had the potential to reduce cost of goods sold substantially. Hoping for insights into what portion of cost savings might ultimately be passed on to end buyers, Feldstein conferred with colleagues of his in GM's sales and marketing organizations. The feedback he received suggested that a reasonable estimate of what the Japanese automakers might give away in terms of added incentives or lower sticker prices would be between 15% and 45% of the cost savings. In 2000, Japanese automakers had given away relatively little in incentives in comparison to the rest of the industry (see **Exhibit 16**). GM, on the other hand, had given away more than the industry average—and almost one third of per vehicle profits.

The two most difficult factors to estimate were the consumer sales elasticity and the cross elasticity to GM sales. Feldstein consulted with one of sales managers for dealer networks and was told that a 5% price increase could be expected to lower unit sales by around 10%. In an effort to isolate the impact on GM, Feldstein assumed that any market share losses to Japanese automakers would be shared equally among and entirely by the Big Three in Detroit.

Feldstein figured that a rough calculation around a 20% yen devaluation would capture an upper bound of the likely exposure. The consequent annual impact on GM's income statement could then be valued as a perpetuity at a 20% discount rate—clearly a simplification, but if he needed more detailed figures he could ask his team to delve deeper into the numbers.

A Place for Competitive Exposures in GM's Corporate Hedging Policy?

Unlike the CAD and ARS deviations, the yen exposure was simply more difficult to measure. Feldstein was going to have to make a case for considering nominal exposures of a type not usually contemplated by the FX hedging policy. In the context of a passive policy, implementing too many deviations might create a *de facto* active policy. Feldstein was hesitant to broaden the scope of hedgeable exposures without carefully assessing the consequences. What about the German car makers? Should euro exposures be measured too? Either way, the first step was getting a handle on the magnitude of the yen exposure.

Conclusion

Feldstein had a great deal of thinking to do. None of the three cases—the CAD deviation, the ARS deviation, or the JPY deviation—was a simple one. He was being asked to sign off on some very significant exposures, some in ways not necessarily contemplated by GM's hedging policy. It was important for him to understand not just what the policy permitted, but what the economics of each exposure were, and what was best for GM as a consolidated global entity in each case.

Appendix A Mechanics of a Currency Option Purchase with a Delta Exchange

Key variables for a currency option (1) Spot exchange rate, 1.5621; (2) forward rate (sometimes stated in forward points or forward premium), 1.5667; (3) strike price (an exchange rate), 1.5667; (4) risk free interest rate in both currencies, available instantly from Bloomberg; (5) time to expiration, three months; and (6) volatility of the currency pair, the price quoted by the bank.

What happens when GM buys and option from a bank? After Michel and the trader agree on a price and the bank has written an option, the bank has taken on a naked option position. However, the bank usually does not take currency positions for the purpose of gain, but instead acts as an intermediary and earns a commission on each trade. As a result, it wishes to eliminate the exposure created by having written the option to GM. Typically the bank does so by immediately creating an offsetting position. It might be that the bank has another client who wants to take the exact opposite side of the option GM bought. This is rare, however, and the bank normally resorts to "delta hedging." At any given point in time, an option has some price sensitivity to the underlying asset price. For example, if an exchange rate appreciates one percent, this would increase the value of a call on that currency. The amount by which the call value increases is called the delta. If a bank is short an option on CAD 10 million but has bought CAD 5 million and the option has a delta of 50%, then the bank is perfectly hedged: if the CAD exchange rate appreciates one percent, the short option will lose one percent on CAD 10 million times 50%, but the long currency position will gain one percent on CAD 5 million times 100% in value. (The delta of a long position in the underlying asset is necessarily one.) As the spot rate changes, the bank will have to increase and decrease the size of its delta hedge position so that changes in the exchange rate will always create offset gains and losses on the option and delta hedge positions.

What if GM wants to get competitive price quotations? In order to get multiple price quotations, it is necessary to call several banks. This requires that the first bank called agrees to leave their quoted price open for some time while GM accumulates other price quotations. Spot rates, however, change constantly, so no bank will leave a price quotation open for long. GM must, therefore, find a device that protects the bank against changes in the spot rate between getting the price quotation and calling back to execute the trade. In effect, GM must promise to help the bank retroactively create the delta hedge that the bank would have created on its own, had the order been placed during the same phone call that the price quotations was given.

What is a "delta exchange" Mechanically, by agreeing to the delta exchange, GM is agreeing to act as the counterparty for the bank's delta hedging transaction at the spot rate prevailing when the option price quotation was given. This protects the bank's ability to hedge the option exposure. It also requires that GM purchase CAD 5 million on the spot market before placing the option trade so that when it purchases the option from the bank it has CAD 5 million on hand to sell to the bank when it is called upon to complete the delta exchange.

Exhibit 1 GM Consolidated Income Statement

December 31, ($ millions)	2000	1999	1998
Total net sales and revenues	184,632	176,558	155,445
Cost of sales and other expenses	145,664	140,708	127,957
Selling, general, and administrative	22,252	19,053	15,915
Interest expense	9,552	7,750	6,629
Earnings before taxes and minority interests	**7,164**	**9,047**	**4,944**
Income tax expense	2,393	3,118	1,636
Equity income (loss) and minority interests	(319)	(353)	(259)
Income from discontinued operations	-	426	(93)
Net income	**4,452**	**6,002**	**2,956**
Dividends on preference stocks	(110)	(80)	(63)
Earnings attributable to common stocks	**4,342**	**5,922**	**2,893**

Source: General Motors, December 31, 2000 10-K (Detroit: General Motors, 2001).

Exhibit 2 GM Segment Breakdown of Sales to End Customers, 2000

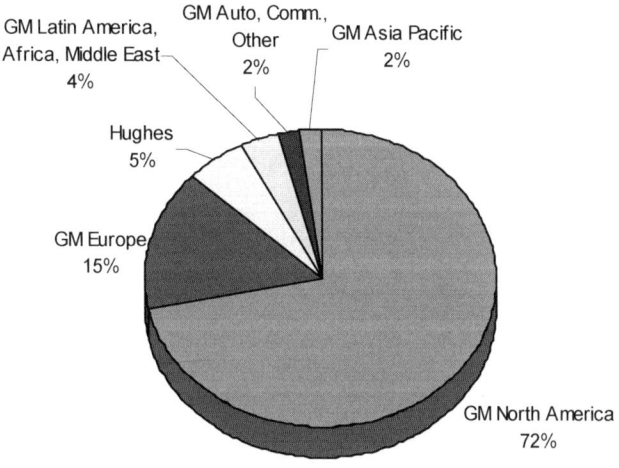

Source: General Motors, 2001 Annual Report (Detroit: General Motors, 2002).

Exhibit 3 GM Geographic Breakdown of Net Property, 2000

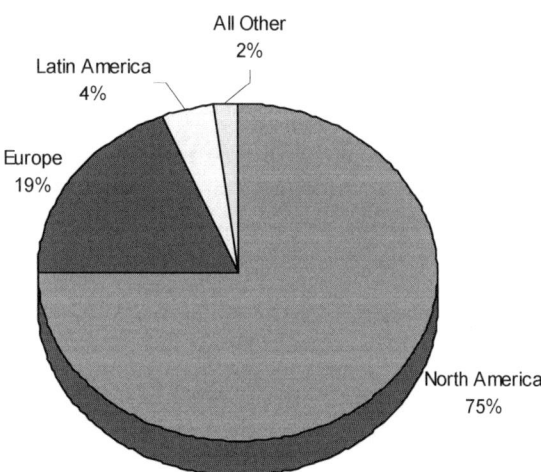

Source: General Motors, 2001 Annual Report (Detroit: General Motors, 2002).

Exhibit 4 GM Treasury Group – Organizational Structure

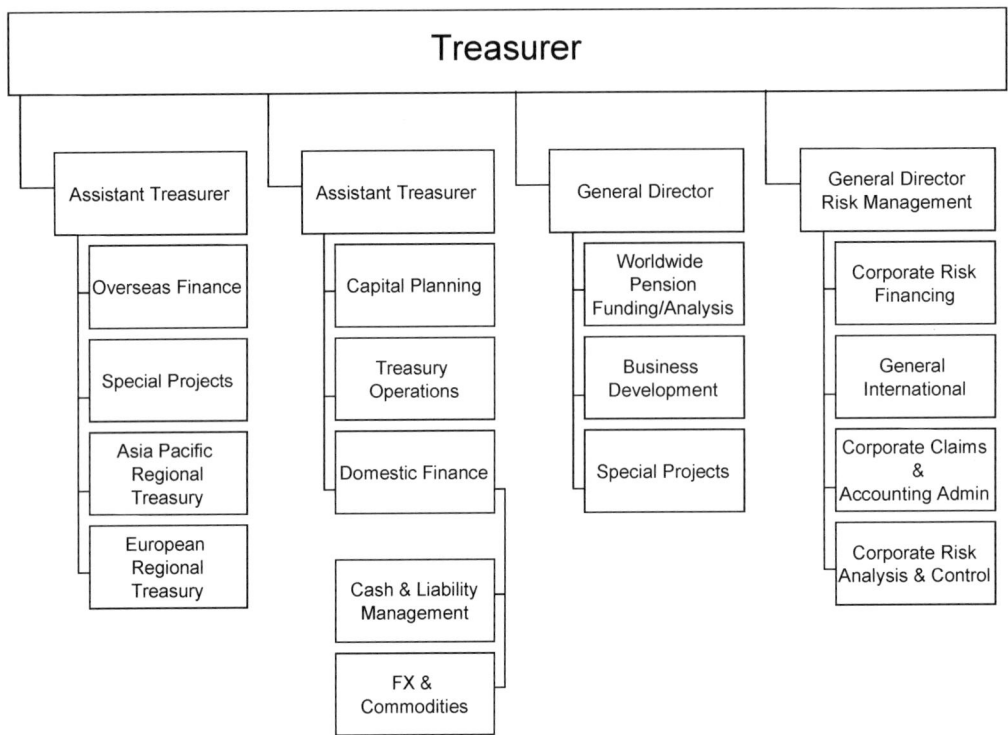

Source: Company documents.

Exhibit 5 GM Treasury Group – Functional Structure

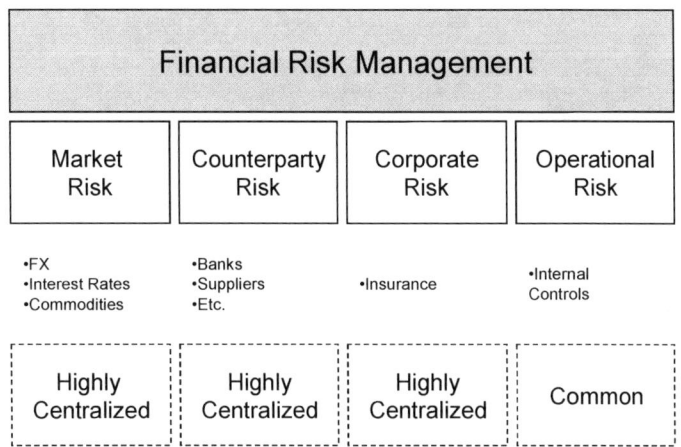

Source: Company documents.

Exhibit 6   GM's Largest Currency Exposures (Forecasted Receivables Less Payables)

As of 12/31/00 ($000)	USD	EUR	JPY	GBP	SEK	AUD	CAD	CHF	PLN	MXP	OTHER
GMNA	800	(400)	-	-	(200)	-	(1,400)	-	-	1,200	-
GME	400	(2,400)	(200)	1,400	(800)	400	(200)	400	200	-	800
GMAP	200	(200)	(200)	200	-	200	-	-	-	-	200
GMLAAM	600	(400)	(400)	-	-	-	-	-	-	-	-
GM Total	**2,000**	**(3,400)**	**(800)**	**1,600**	**(1,000)**	**600**	**(1,600)**	**400**	**200**	**1,200**	**1,000**

Source: General Motors
Figures have been disguised and do not reflect the actual operations of General Motors, Corp.

NOTES:
    GMNA: General Motors North America
    GME: General Motors Europe
    GMAP: General Motors Asian Pacific
    GMLAAM: General Motors Latin America, Africa, Middle East

Foreign Exchange Hedging Strategies at General Motors

Exhibit 7 Evolution of Net Receivables / Payables Exposure, Rolling Forward Twelve Months

Month	1	2	3	4	5	6	7	8	9	10	11	12
			FORWARDS						OPTIONS			
t=0 CFs	A	B	C	D	E	F	G	H	L	I	K	L
t=1 CFs	B*	C*	D*	E*	F*	G*	H*	I*	J*	K*	L*	M

Source: Casewriter analysis

(*) Forecasts received from operations managers for future months may change from month to month.

Exhibit 8 Illustrative Example of the Effect of a EUR Depreciation / USD Appreciation Depending on the Choice of Functional Currency

	Exchange Rate (EUR / USD)	Impact on **GMWorldwide's Financial Statements**
	1.0 0.9	

USD Functional

GMS Net Assets

In functional currency	USD	100.0	100.0
In foreign currency	EUR	50.0	50.0
GMS - Reported	USD	150.0	145.0

(A)

Income Statement:	USD	-5.0
Translation Adjustment:	USD	0.0
Shareholders' Equity:	USD	-5.0

EUR Functional

GMS Net Assets

In functional currency	EUR	50.0	50.0
In foreign currency	USD	100.0	100.0
GMS - Reported	EUR	150.0	161.1

(B)

Income Statement:	USD	10.0
Translation Adjustment:	USD	-5.0
Shareholders' Equity:	USD	5.0

A A depreciation of the EUR against the USD causes a decline in the dollar value of GMS's foreign currency (EUR) net asset, generating a loss for GM Worldwide's income statement

B The increase in the euro value of GMS's foreign currency net asset generates a gain for GM Worldwide's income statement. Given that the GMS functional currency is not GM's reporting currency, there is a translation adjustment of -$5.0.

Source: Casewriter analysis

Foreign Exchange Hedging Strategies at General Motors

Exhibit 9 GM Canada – Projected Cash Flow Exposure

Cash Flows	Amount as of September 30, 2001
INFLOWS	
Canadian sales	10,564
Tax refunds (GST)	1,049
OUTFLOWS	
Material purchases	(10,180)
Capital expenditures	(113)
Other structural costs	(1,737)
Tax expenditures	(1,258)
Other expenditures	(6)
12 month C$ cash flow forecast	**(1,682)**

Source: Company documents.
Figures have been disguised and do not reflect the actual operations of General Motors, Corp.

Exhibit 10 GM Canada – Net Monetary Asset/Liability Exposure

Balance Sheet Account	Amount as of September 30, 2001
ASSETS	
Cash & cash equivalents	683
Accounts & notes receivable	271
Deferred income taxes	118
Pension asset	1,525
LIABILITIES	
Outside – all other	(93)
Other postretirement benefits	(1,949)
Warranty	(132)
Accounts payable and other	(2,565)
C$ Monetary asset / (liability) position	**(2,143)**

Source: Company documents.
Figures have been disguised and do not reflect the actual operations of General Motors, Corp.

Exhibit 11 GM Argentina Balance Sheet, Monetary Assets and Liabilities by Currency, as of September 30, 2001

ARS Monetary Assets		ARS Monetary Liabilities	
Scrap incentive owed by govt.	45.8	Payables to local suppliers	24.1
Interest subsidy owed by govt.	3.2	Provisions to local suppliers	11.3
VAT credit and other tax owed by govt.	130.6	ARS loan (VAT financing)	13.7
Receivable (tax credit reimbursement)	2.7	Other provisions	9.8
Other	7.8	Tax payable	2.0
Total	**190.0**	**Total**	**60.9**

USD Monetary Assets		USD Monetary Liabilities	
Cash	2.5	Accounts payable	224.5
Receivables	20.5	Loans	101.3
Total	**23.0**	**Total**	**325.7**

Source: Company documents.

Figures have been disguised and do not reflect the actual operations of General Motors, Corp.

Foreign Exchange Hedging Strategies at General Motors

Exhibit 12 Argentinean Peso/U.S. Dollar Forward Rates by Contract Maturity

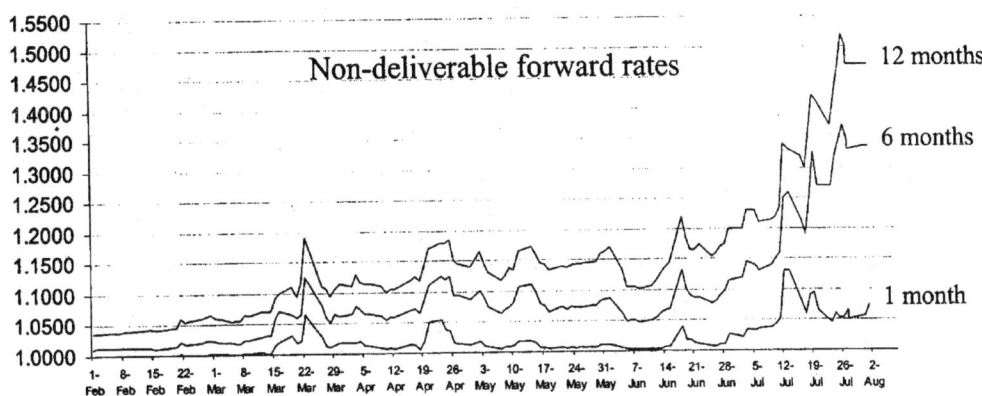

Source: Company documents.

Exhibit 13 Cost of Hedging the ARS Exposure in Argentina

Time Horizon / Hedging Period	Cost ($ millions)
One-month Forward	$6.4
Three-month Forward	18.2
Six-month Forward	28.7
Twelve-month Forward	40.3

Source: Company documents.

Exhibit 14 Historical Japanese Yen/U.S. Dollar Exchange Rate (Yen per Dollar)

Source: Thomson Financial Datastream.

Exhibit 15 General Motors Investments in Japanese Automakers

Affiliate	Affiliate Exposure Long/(Short) ($ billions)	GM Ownership Stake
Fuji	(1.50)	20%
Isuzu	(1.02)	49%
Suzuki	(0.09)	20%

Source: General Motors
Figures have been disguised and do not reflect the actual operations of General Motors, Corp.

Note: Exposures are net yen exposures (measured in dollars) and are presented for each affiliate entity. For example, Fuji's yen-denominated liabilities exceed its yen-denominated assets by $1.2 billion. GM's exposure is limited by the relevant ownership share in the affiliate.

Exhibit 16 2000 Average Incentive per Unit in the United States

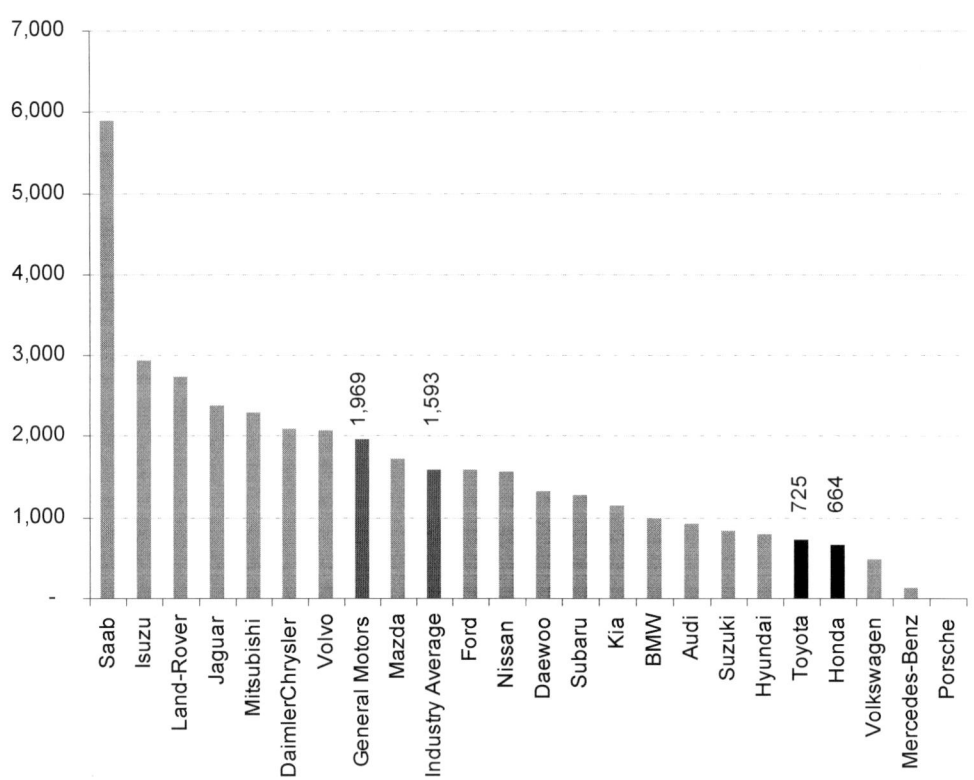

Source: Company Documents

HARVARD | BUSINESS | SCHOOL

9-203-001
REV: AUGUST 11, 2004

GEORGE CHACKO
RANDOLPH B. COHEN
MARC CHENNAULT

Note on Risk Arbitrage

Give a man a fish and you feed him for a day. Teach him how to arbitrage and you feed him forever.[1]
—Warren Buffet

Risk arbitrage is an event-driven investment process involving the purchase and/or sale of securities affected by announced transactions including mergers, tender offers, recapitalizations, spin-offs, and corporate reorganizations. The arbitrageur invests with the intention of profiting from changes in the value of the securities once the transaction is consummated.

Although a small community of professionals had practiced risk arbitrage in the United States for several decades, the strategy was popularized during the corporate takeover frenzy of the early 1980s.[2] Today, risk-arbitrage strategies are employed by investment mangers at a wide range of firms who recognize its potential to generate significant returns with low correlation to systematic stock market risk. These characteristics have made risk arbitrage an attractive investment management diversification tool.

The main purpose of this note is to provide an introduction to risk arbitrage. A discussion on the origins and development of modern-day risk arbitrage, an overview of the risk-arbitrage community, and a description of the basic mechanics of the investment process are included.

Background[3,a]

The origins of modern-day risk arbitrage can be traced to commercial practices dating back centuries. *Arbitrage*, in its classic form, involves the identification and capture of value resulting from price differences between two or more identical or related assets. Venetian merchants practiced this basic form of arbitrage during the Medieval period. At the crossroads of Western commerce and information flow, these merchants traded in various interchangeable securities in order to profit from differences in price.

Later, with the development of international securities markets, speculators began to participate in a particular form of classic arbitrage known as *tendency arbitrage*. Several modern dictionary definitions of "arbitrage" actually describe this variant of the investment strategy: "The purchase of

---

[a] Much of the material in this section is taken directly from Guy P. Wyser-Pratte's 1971 monograph, "Risk-arbitrage," originally the subject of the author's MBA thesis at the Graduate School of Business Administration, New York University.

Professors George Chacko and Randolph B. Cohen and Marc Chennault (MBA '01) prepared this note as the basis for class discussion.

Copyright © 2003 President and Fellows of Harvard College. To order copies or request permission to reproduce materials, call 1-800-545-7685, write Harvard Business School Publishing, Boston, MA 02163, or go to http://www.hbsp.harvard.edu. No part of this publication may be reproduced, stored in a retrieval system, used in a spreadsheet, or transmitted in any form or by any means—electronic, mechanical, photocopying, recording, or otherwise—without the permission of Harvard Business School.

securities on one market for immediate resale on another in order to profit from a price discrepancy."[4,b] As identical securities began trading on different European exchanges, speculators participated in tendency arbitrage by taking advantage of price differences occurring on various exchanges resulting, largely, from unique local supply and demand characteristics.[5]

These early strategies evolved into *riskless arbitrage*, practiced in U.S. securities markets. This form involved traders' simultaneously buying and selling convertible securities and the underlying equivalents in order to profit from value discrepancies. Since the convertible and underlying security were practically equivalent in certain circumstances, simultaneously buying and selling these securities when they traded out of line could lock in profit with very little risk.

Eventually, investors began to participate in modern *risk arbitrage*. This strategy began to appear in American securities markets in the early 20th century. According to research by Guy Wyser-Pratte, risk-arbitrage trading initially occurred in response to two important events in the history of American capitalism. The first event was the era of railroad reorganization beginning in the 1930s. During this period, several large insolvent railroad lines underwent bankruptcy reorganizations involving the issuance of new securities in exchange for existing ones in order to ease the companies' debt-service burdens. The new securities began trading on a "when-issued" basis (that is, they could be traded before the restructuring plan was actually confirmed), creating opportunities to take advantage of differences between prices prevailing in the market for when-issued securities and those of existing securities. The arbitrageur, recognizing that the when-issued security was trading higher than the existing security, would purchase the existing security and simultaneously sell the when-issued security. The profit (price difference, or "spread") could be locked in as long as the reorganization plan was confirmed and new securities were actually issued in exchange for the existing securities. The arbitrageur would simply transfer the new security to the purchaser of the when-issued security and walk away with the original spread. With this development, arbitrageurs were now specifically taking on and being compensated for the risk of the restructuring exchange transaction occurring.

The 1935 Public Utility Company Act signaled the second major event in the development of risk arbitrage in the United States. The act mandated that several public utilities divest themselves of subsidiaries. When-issued securities began trading prior to many of the divestitures, and profit could be made by buying and selling between the parent company's existing securities and the when-issued securities of the subsidiaries.

Modern risk-arbitrage opportunities expanded with the waves of corporate mergers and acquisitions in the 1970s and 1980s.[6] These situations, involving the exchange of an acquirer's stock for that of a target company, allowed the arbitrageur to capture a spread, as long as the deal was consummated.

Risk-Arbitrage Community

U.S. merger volume during the first nine months of 2000 was approximately $1.4 trillion, up from $1.2 trillion the previous year.[7] Opportunities to arbitrage mergers and acquisitions have increased with the rise in deal volume and, as a result, have attracted new groups of investors. Originally confined to a small and close-knit community of specialists, risk arbitrage is practiced today by a wider variety of investment professionals.[8] According to one recent estimate, more than 200 firms controlling over $30 billion in investment capital participated in the arbitrage business in late 1998.[9]

---

[b] Note that in tendency-arbitrage transactions, the resale of securities need not be immediate.

Note on Risk Arbitrage

These practitioners recognize the potential for risk arbitrage to generate positive returns with low correlation to overall returns in the equity markets.[10,11,c]

The practitioner community has long included dedicated risk-arbitrage partnerships and individuals acting as arbitrageurs. Ivan Boesky, one of the most infamous figures of the 1980s Wall Street, headed a well-known dedicated risk-arbitrage partnership. Today, several hedge funds operate focused risk-arbitrage groups or opportunistically pursue risk-arbitrage strategies—examples include Farrallon Capital, Och-Ziff Capital, and M.H. Davison. Many major brokerage firms, including Bear Stearns, Morgan Stanley Dean Witter, and Goldman Sachs & Co., have also established dedicated risk-arbitrage desks; former U.S. Secretary of the Treasury Robert Rubin rose through the ranks as a trader on Goldman Sachs's risk-arbitrage desk prior to leaving for government service. Finally, several institutional shareholders, such as pension funds, have begun to engage in risk-arbitrage investing.

The Risk-Arbitrage Investment Process

The risk-arbitrage position is essentially a "bet" on whether the proposed transaction event or deal is consummated. The bet's "payoff" is reflected in the spread between the market values of consideration to be received in the deal (i.e., acquirer's stock, cash, etc.) minus the market values of securities to be given up (i.e., target's stock). Between the time the deal is announced and its close, the magnitude of the spread is dictated primarily by two factors: the time value of money and the risk premium.[d]

As an example, on October 5, 1999, Worldcom, Inc. (WCOM) and Sprint, Inc. (FON) formally announced their plans to merge in a stock-for-stock exchange that would have given approximately $76.00 in WCOM stock for each share of FON held.[e] Shares of FON, however, never reached $76.00 during the entire deal period—FON peaked to a high of only $75.3225 briefly on November 19, 1999 (see **Exhibit 1** and **Exhibit 2** for FON and WCOM historical price charts). Why did the spread persist? First, since any potential gain from the spread would not be fully realized until months later when shares were to be exchanged at closing, investors demanded a time value of money premium as compensation for committing capital to the arbitrage investment for the deal period. Second, investors were concerned about whether the merger, which faced serious antitrust regulatory hurdles, would actually close. This element of completion risk discouraged investors from bidding

---

[c] Baker and Savasoglu (August 2000) find that risk-arbitrage positions held in a diversified portfolio between 1981 and 1996 produced an abnormal return of 0.8% per month and reflected betas of 0.3 to 0.5 and zero in all cash and all stock deals, respectively. After accounting for transaction costs, Mitchell and Pulvino (May 2000) find that risk arbitrage generates excess returns of 4% per year. They also find that risk-arbitrage returns are uncorrelated with those of the market in flat and appreciating markets but positively correlated in depreciating markets.

[d] In certain circumstances, the appropriate total spread would be measured using prices prior to deal announcement. This could be the case where rumors of the anticipated deal leak into and affect the public markets before the official "announcement."

[e] Note that the WCOM/FON deal was actually slightly more complicated. The terms of the merger included a "collar" where the exchange ratio (and, therefore, value of stock exchanged in the transaction) would have changed if FON traded at predefined extreme price levels at the merger date.

FON up to the $76.00 level, establishing a risk premium in the spread.[f] In retrospect, investors were correct; the merger eventually failed due to government antitrust challenges.

In general, the risk-arbitrage investment process involves three analyses:

- Estimating the potential return on the arbitrage investment
- Determining the securities and amounts in which to establish a position
- Continuously assessing the deal risks in order to refine and update return expectations and rebalance positions as necessary

Estimating Potential Returns

The first step in calculating the potential return on a risk-arbitrage investment is to estimate the gross spread. The formula for determining the gross spread is the value of cash and securities to be received upon completion of the transaction less the initial cost of establishing the arbitrage position. In stock-for-stock mergers, this can be given as:

$$\text{Gross Spread} = \text{Value to be Received in the Transaction} - \text{Stock Price of Target}$$

Once the gross spread is estimated, the net spread is calculated as:

$$\text{Net Spread} = \text{Gross Spread} \, \forall \, \text{All Other Cash Flows from the Investment}$$

or

$$\text{Net Spread} = \text{Gross Spread} - \text{Interest Cost of Carry} + \text{Short-Sale Rebate} \, \forall \, \text{Dividends}$$

Finally, the net spread is used to calculate the potential return on investment (ROI), as follows:

$$\text{Potential ROI} = \text{Net Spread} / \text{Total Capital Employed}^{g}$$

Arbitrageurs will typically annualize the potential ROI calculated above in order to compare deals with different time horizons as well as to evaluate target annual rates of return.

$$\text{Annualized Potential ROI} = \text{Potential ROI} \times (365 / \text{Number of Days Until Completion})^{h}$$

When annualizing returns, the arbitrageur must understand how long the transaction will likely take to complete. Note that from the beginning of the deal process until completion, a series of legal and regulatory steps must be performed, and one of the most critical aspects of the arbitrageur's timing analysis is to understand where the deal is in relation to these milestones. (**Exhibit 3** presents a general legal and regulatory timeline for most corporate mergers in the United States.)

---

[f] Baker and Savasoglu (August 2000) report that the risk premium portion of the spread is actually made up of two components: completion risk and selling pressure. In other words, part of the arbitrageur's return is compensation for providing scarce liquidity to a large number of selling shareholders.

[g] Some arbitrageurs prefer to use unlevered gross return (gross spread/investment in target stock) to measure the relative profitability of arbitrage investments. This method reflects the idea that, depending on the deal, an arbitrageur may employ different amounts and forms of leverage and that the attractiveness of individual arbitrage opportunities should be compared ignoring financing choices.

[h] Similarly, some arbitrageurs may prefer to use unlevered annualized rates of return instead.

Note on Risk Arbitrage

Consider the following example to illustrate the risk-arbitrage investment process. Assume ABC Corporation and XYZ Corporation are competitors in a highly fragmented and largely unregulated industry. Neither company controls more than 10% of any market into which it sells. ABC has made a tender offer for all of the outstanding shares of XYZ. ABC is offering $63.00 in cash and one ABC stock warrant for each share of XYZ, currently trading at $62.00. Using option-pricing models, each ABC warrant is valued at $2.50. Neither company is expected to pay dividends prior to the merger. The Securities and Exchange Commission has declared the registration documents effective, and the merger is expected to close within 90 days. Margin requirements restrict this particular arbitrageur to 50% borrowing at an interest rate of 7% per annum.

The arbitrageur decides on the following investment strategy: borrow on margin (restricted to 50% of the total investment) to acquire shares of XYZ and hold through merger date.

$$
\begin{aligned}
\text{Gross Spread} &= \text{Value to be Received in the Transaction} - \text{Stock Price of Target} \\
&= 63.00 + 2.50) - 62.00 \\
&= 3.50
\end{aligned}
$$

$$
\begin{aligned}
\text{Net Spread} &= \text{Gross Spread } \forall \text{ All Other Cash Flows from the Investment} \\
&= \text{Gross Spread} - \text{Margin Interest} \\
&= 3.50 - ((7\% \times 50\% \times 62.00) \times (90/365)) \\
&= 3.50 - 0.54 \\
&= 2.96
\end{aligned}
$$

$$
\begin{aligned}
\text{Potential ROI} &= \text{Net Spread} / \text{Total Capital Employed} \\
&= 2.96 / (62.00 \times 50\%) \\
&= 9.6\%
\end{aligned}
$$

$$
\begin{aligned}
\text{Annualized Potential ROI} &= \text{Potential ROI} \times (365 / \text{Number of Days Until Completion}) \\
&= 9.6\% \times (365/90) \\
&= 38.9\%
\end{aligned}
$$

Establishing a Position

The arbitrageur's objective in establishing a position is to maximize return on the investment while exposing herself only to the risk of the deal's not closing (completion risk). In the effort to maximize return, the arbitrageur may look for positions that utilize leverage and minimize the amount of net cash committed. Note that, in the previous example, the use of leverage allowed for a net cash investment of only $31. Had no leverage been used, annualized returns would have been only (3.50/62.00) x (365/90) = 22.9%.[i]

Ensuring that the arbitrageur is exposed only to deal risk involves establishing a position designed to hedge out all other risks. Deal terms can often be more complicated than cash tender offers. They often involve the exchange of one or more securities for another, and often in exchange ratios other than one-for-one. In these situations, the arbitrageur must be creative in order to maximize return through leverage and isolate deal risk.

---

[i] Leverage choices vary from investor to investor and, often, from deal to deal. In making decisions about leverage, the arbitrageur must consider, among other things, additional risks borrowing may inject into the investment, costs of financing and deal time horizons, and the various methods available to obtain leverage. For example, one large hedge fund is able to achieve leverage ratios of 10-to-1 by employing swaps.

Consider the following example in **Figure A**. ABC is acquiring XYZ in a tax-free stock-for-stock merger. As above, the SEC has declared the registration documents effective, and the deal is expected to close within 90 days. ABC is offering to issue 1.3 shares of its common stock (each share currently trading in the market at 50 ½) for each share of XYZ stock outstanding (currently trading at 62).

Figure A

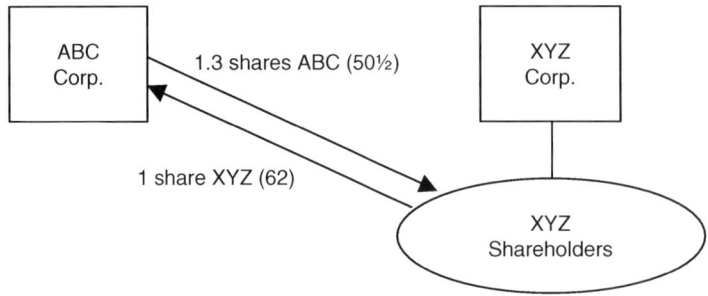

Source: Author.

Furthermore, assume that our arbitrageur can earn a rebate of 6% per annum on short-sale proceeds but is required to put up 50% collateral on short-sale borrowings. She, therefore, decides to establish the following position: Short 1.3 shares of ABC stock to purchase one share of XYZ, using margin and the short sale to increase returns and isolate deal risk.

$$
\begin{aligned}
\text{Gross Spread} &= \text{Value to be Received in the Transaction} - \text{Stock Price of Target} \\
&= \text{Value of ABC Shares to be Received} - \text{Price of XYZ} \\
&= (50.50 \times 1.3) - 62.00 \\
&= 3.65
\end{aligned}
$$

$$
\begin{aligned}
\text{Net Spread} &= \text{Gross Spread } \forall \text{ All Other Cash Flows from the Investment} \\
&= \text{Gross Spread} - \text{Margin Interest} + \text{Short-Sale Rebate} \\
&= 3.65 - ((7\% \times 50\% \times 62.00 \times (90/365)) + (6\% \times (50.50 \times 1.3) \times (90/365)) \\
&= 3.65 - 0.54 + 0.97 \\
&= 4.08
\end{aligned}
$$

$$
\begin{aligned}
\text{Potential ROI} &= \text{Net Spread}/\text{Total Capital Employed} \\
&= 4.08/((50\% \times 62.00) + (50\% \times 1.3 \times 50.50)) \\
&= 4.08/63.83 \\
&= 6.4\%
\end{aligned}
$$

$$
\begin{aligned}
\text{Annualized Potential ROI} &= \text{Potential ROI} \times (365/\text{Number of Days Until Completion}) \\
&= 6.4\% \times (365/90) \\
&= 25.9\%
\end{aligned}
$$

The arbitrageur in this example has used leverage by means of the margin on the long position to maximize return. Furthermore, by entering into the short sale, she has eliminated the risk of receiving less than the anticipated gross spread due to a dramatic price move in ABC's stock between now and completion of the merger. She has exposed herself only to completion risk.

Note on Risk Arbitrage

To see this, observe the outcome assuming the merger is completed on schedule and, at close, the shares of ABC stock transferred to the arbitrageur are trading either at 60, 50½, or 45.

Figure B

Per Share Market Value of ABC at Merger Completion	60	50½	45
Gain/(Loss) on Long Position:			
Value of each ABC share received	60.00	50.50	45.00
X Number of ABC shares received	1.3	1.3	1.3
Value of consideration received	78.00	65.65	58.50
− Basis in XYZ stock	(62.00)	(62.00)	(62.00)
Gain/(Loss) on Long Position	**16.00**	**3.65**	**(3.50)**
Gain/(Loss) on Short Position:			
Price of ABC at time of short sale	50.50	50.50	50.50
− Market value at merger completion	60.00	50.50	45.00
	(9.50)	0.00	5.50
X Number of ABC shares shorted	1.3	1.3	1.3
Gain/(Loss) on Short Position	**(12.35)**	**0.00**	**7.15**
Total Gross Spread at Merger Completion	**3.65**	**3.65**	**3.65**

Source: Author.

Assessing Risk

A critical part of the work performed by the arbitrageur is continuously monitoring the deal as it progresses through the various approval processes and assessing, at each stage, the probability of the deal's actually being completed at the spreads anticipated. In other words, the arbitrageur must monitor the *risk* initially taken on in the arbitrage. As the deal develops, events may occur that could have the effect of either lengthening or shortening the time until completion. Other events may have the effect of either improving or reducing the likelihood of the deal's being completed at all. Further, announced deal terms may change altogether. It is the arbitrageur's job to be aware of these events as they occur, assess how these developments will likely affect his position, and make the appropriate adjustments to the position.

Some common deal risks include the following:[12]

Double price risk   If the transaction is called off, the arbitrageur faces price risk on both long and short positions. The acquirer's stock price (which has been shorted) could rise, and the target's stock price (which is held long) can fall to predeal trading levels. Note that predeal trading levels are not necessarily limited to the prices at which investment is made. Prices immediately preceding the announcement may reflect a premium as a result of rumors in anticipation of a deal. A "busted" transaction might result in prices settling to levels far worse than those at which the arbitrageur establishes his position, exposing him to more substantial losses. Note that the existence of leverage in the investment may amplify losses if the deal fails.

Change in the terms If the exchange ratio is altered or a change is made in the nature of securities offered, original arbitrage positions may have to be unwound or rebalanced at a high transaction cost.

Dramatic increase in acquirer's price A sharp rise in the price of the acquirer will deteriorate profit in the short position and may threaten the deal if the acquirer tries to renegotiate for better terms.

Dramatic decrease in acquirer's price A sharp fall in the acquirer's price may cause the target's shareholders to reevaluate the value they are receiving, thus threatening the deal.

Competing bids A competitive bidding situation may result in a liquidity problem as investors rush to cover short positions in the event that the original acquirer is not successful. This could make exiting the initial position very costly. Note, however, that competitive bidding situations are often positive for the arbitrageur since they increase the chances of a higher price on the long position.

Shareholder dissent Shareholders who disagree with merger plans could pursue various legal measures to block the deal.

Material adverse change clause Most definitive merger agreements include clauses that allow the acquirer to walk away if a material adverse change arises in the target's business prior to merger completion.

Tax approval IRS approval for attempted tax-free reorganizations is not guaranteed. An adverse ruling by the IRS could dramatically change the economics of the contemplated transaction and force it to be called off.

Regulatory agency interference The federal government must approve business combinations in order to ensure that antitrust rules are not violated. In the United States, the Department of Justice (DOJ) and the Federal Trade Commission (FTC) have responsibility for reviewing and approving or challenging mergers and acquisitions on general antitrust grounds. A challenge from one of these agencies will, more often than not, cause the deal to be called off or altered dramatically. At the very least, it will lengthen the time to completion, which may reduce the arbitrageur's return by increasing her costs of carry. Note that multinational corporations may also be required to seek approval from regulatory bodies in countries where both the acquirer and target have operations. In addition to the DOJ/FTC approval, companies in regulated industries seeking combination must often get approval from other federal or state industry regulatory bodies. For instance, merging telecommunications companies may be required to seek clearance from the Federal Communications Commission.

Management personalities Personalities may impact deals. In some instances, management teams leading the target and acquirer corporations find themselves clashing throughout the process. This may threaten successful deal completion.

Other Strategies—Derivatives

Arbitrageurs often engage in strategies that employ securities other than stock or cash, such as derivatives. The use of options, for instance, can expand the possibilities for leverage and provide tools for hedging away certain risks.

Note on Risk Arbitrage

Reconsider the first example above in which ABC offers $63.00 in cash and $2.50 worth of stock warrants for each share of XYZ, currently trading at 62. Assume now, however, that an American call option on XYZ stock with a strike price of 60 and expiration in exactly 90 days is available. Following the merger announcement, each call option is trading at a price of 4 ½.

The arbitrageur decides on the following investment strategy: Buy one XYZ 60 call for each share of XYZ stock that she wishes to own.

$$
\begin{aligned}
\text{Gross Spread} &= \text{Value to be Received in the Transaction} - \text{Cost of Establishing the Position} \\
&= \text{Intrinsic Value of Call Options at Merger Date}[j] - \text{Initial Cost of Option} \\
&= ((63.00 + 2.50) - 60.00) - 4.50 \\
&= (5.50 - 60.00) - 4.50 \\
&= 1.00
\end{aligned}
$$

$$
\begin{aligned}
\text{Net Spread} &= \text{Gross Spread} \, \forall \, \text{All Other Cash Flows from the Investment} \\
&= \text{Gross Spread} - \text{None} \\
&= 1.00
\end{aligned}
$$

$$
\begin{aligned}
\text{Potential ROI} &= \text{Net Spread}/\text{Total Capital Employed} \\
&= \text{Net Spread}/\text{Initial Cost of Option} \\
&= 1.00/4.50 \\
&= 22.2\%
\end{aligned}
$$

$$
\begin{aligned}
\text{Annualized Potential ROI} &= \text{Potential ROI} \times (365/\text{Number of Days Until Completion}) \\
&= 22.2\% \times (365/90) \\
&= 90.1\%
\end{aligned}
$$

Note that in addition to intensifying leverage and boosting potential return, the use of the call option also reduces the potential impact of deal risk in a way not possible earlier when we simply bought XYZ on margin. Assume that after the arbitrageur has established a position, the deal is cancelled. In the call option scenario, if the price of XYZ declines, the position loss is limited to the amount originally invested in the call option, $4.50. In the stock purchase on margin scenario, however, the arbitrageur could potentially lose up to $62.00 plus any costs of carry. On the other hand, using options in this manner introduces term risk in that the expiration dates of available options and the merger closing date may not coincide.

Options can also be helpful in hedging risks introduced by collars, where the deal terms (such as the exchange ratio or other considerations) change if the market price of the target company stock reaches extreme levels. Options, in addition, can be employed to protect against losses in stock positions in the case of deal failures (for instance, purchasing put options on the target's stock as insurance against an anticipated price decline following a cancelled deal).

---

[j] Assuming the merger is completed as anticipated, the intrinsic value of the option immediately prior to the merger should represent floor or minimum value. The value of a call option approaching maturity can be described as the sum of its intrinsic value, insurance value (the value of downside protection), and savings in carrying costs (the value of risk-free borrowing).

Exhibit 1 Historical Price Chart for FON

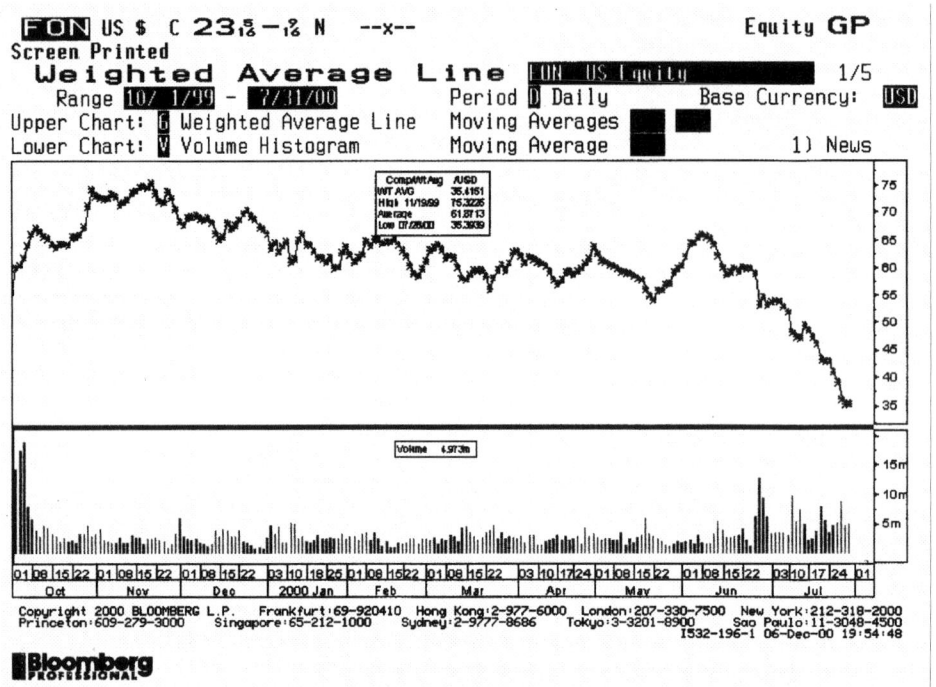

Exhibit 2 WCOM and FON Historical Price Spread

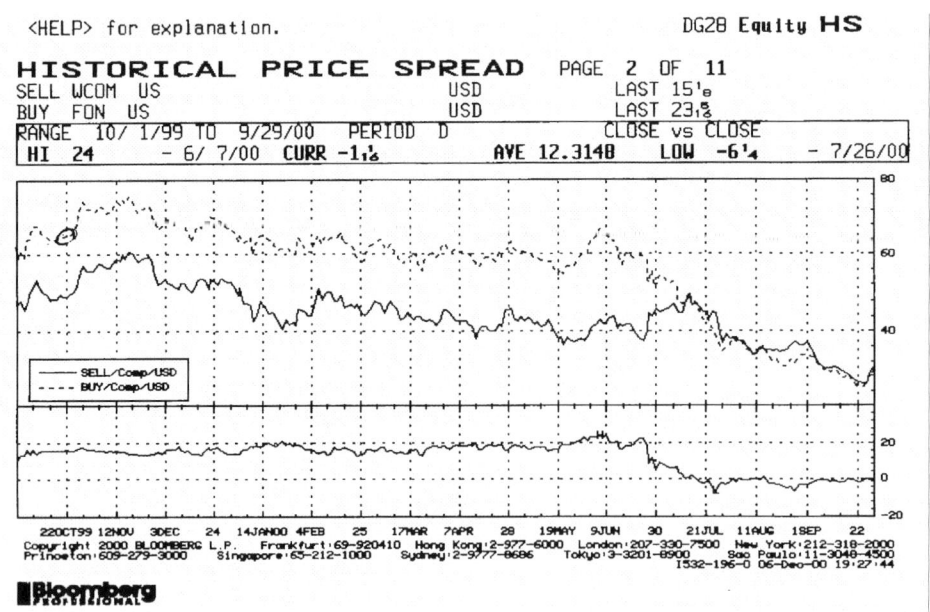

Exhibit 3 General Legal and Regulatory Timeline for Corporate Merger in the United States

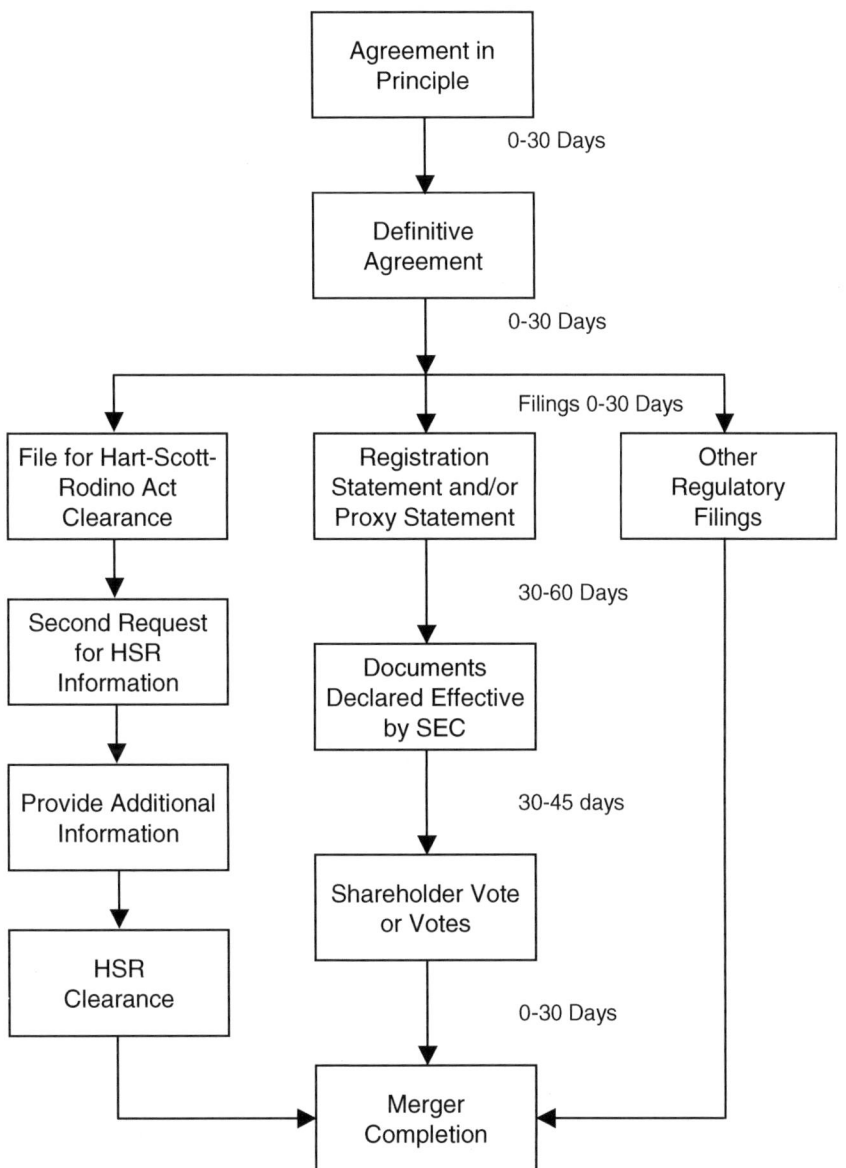

Source: Reproduced from Keith M. Moore, *Risk-arbitrage—An Investor's Guide* (New York: John Wiley & Sons, Inc., 2000), p. 49.

Endnotes

¹ Berkshire Hathaway, Inc., 1988 Annual Report, <http://www.berkshirehathaway.com/letters/1988.html>, November 28, 2000.

² "Risk and Reward—The Arbitrage Game Provides Plenty of Both," *Barron's*, November 30, 1981.

³ Guy P. Wyser-Pratte, "Risk-arbitrage," *The Bulletin,* New York University Graduate School of Business Administration Monograph No. 74-75, May 1971, pp. 1–3.

⁴ *The American Heritage Dictionary,* 2nd College Edition (Boston: Houghton Mifflin Company, 1985).

⁵ Ivan F. Boesky, *Merger Mania* (New York: Holt, Rinehart & Winston, 1985), p. 17.

⁶ Regina M. Pitaro, *Deals, Deals, and More Deals* (New York: Gabelli University Press, 2000), pp. 19–29.

⁷ Nikhil Deogun and Kara Scannell, "Quarterly Stock Market Review—Old Economy Finds New Life in Mergers," *The Wall Street Journal*, October 2, 2000.

⁸ Keith M. Moore, *Risk-arbitrage—An Investor's Guide* (New York: John Wiley & Sons, Inc., 1999), pp. 21-26.

⁹ Katrina Brooker, "Why Companies Hate Risk-arbitrageurs—They Call Them 'The Swarm,'" *Fortune* Magazine, August 3, 1998, pp. 270–272.

¹⁰ Malcolm Baker and Serkan Savasoglu, "Limited Arbitrage in Mergers and Acquisitions," HBS Working Paper, August 2000.

¹¹ Mark Mitchell and Todd Pulvino, "Characteristics of Risk and Return in Risk Arbitrage," HBS Working Paper, May 2000.

¹² Wyser-Pratte, pp. 14–16; Berkshire Hathaway, Inc., 1988 Annual Report, <http://www.berkshirehathaway.com/letters/1988.html>, November 28, 2000; "Risk and Reward—The Arbitrage Game Provides Plenty of Both," *Barron's*, November 30, 1981; Wyser-Pratte, pp. 1–3; *The American Heritage Dictionary,* 2nd College Edition (Boston: Houghton Mifflin Company, 1985); Boesky, p. 17; Pitaro, pp. 19–29; Deogun and Scannell; Moore, pp. 21–26; Brooker, pp. 270–272; Baker and Savasoglu; Mitchell and Pulvino.

 **Harvard Business School**

9-297-086
Rev. March 12, 1999

An Overview of Credit Derivatives

Introduction

Conventional market theory describes two main risk categories: market or price risk and credit risk. Market risk refers to general risks and instabilities inherent in the market, such as inflation, interest rates, and production of goods. To protect themselves against changes in these areas, many investors purchase futures or options on exchange rates or prices of assets. Some simple types of this protection against market risk include: buying a put option to protect against a decline in stock values or purchasing a bond which has a coupon tied to some variable rate, such as the London Interbank Offer Rate (LIBOR) to protect against inflation. But while a variable rate protects the investor against inflation, he or she still may not receive the entire return on the bond, as the bond issuer may not be able to make all its coupon payments, and thereby default. This is but the simplest manifestation of credit risk. The credit derivative market is a lucrative one which aims to structure and price this risk and other types of credit risk, thereby protecting investors.

Credit Risk: A History

Credit risk is pervasive in market relationships; it affects bond issuers, bond holders, and commercial banks. As the credit rating of a bond issuer worsens, its cost of issuing debt increases because it is forced to pay a higher interest rate due to its higher risk of default. Bondholders face the risk of a downgrade in the firm's credit rating. If this occurs, the value of the bond will decrease, as there must be a greater risk premium in holding the bond. Commercial banks sustain large amounts of credit risk. Most of the risk a bank takes on when making a loan is credit risk – default on the loan. This risk is often compounded by the fact that banks tend to concentrate their loans in a specific region or industry, which affords them less opportunity to diversify their portfolio to protect against shocks in the economy.

To protect against credit risk, firms traditionally have looked at the standards of their loans – to acquire debt with low likelihood of default – and then diversified those loans across geography and industry to try to protect against serious market shocks. Diversification is tough for some firms to accomplish as it is not always possible to balance a portfolio as well as one would like. Beyond diversification, some investors choose to securitize some of their loans and sell off pieces to other investors. Investors purchasing these packages find them attractive in their own diversification and securitization also allows the original writers of the loans to move the credit risk off their books. However, this approach only works well for loans with standardized payment schedules and similar

---

Research Associate Stephen Lynagh prepared this case under the supervision of Professor Sanjiv R. Das as the basis for class discussion rather than to illustrate either effective or ineffective handling of an administrative situation.

Copyright © 1997 by the President and Fellows of Harvard College. To order copies or request permission to reproduce materials, call 1-800-545-7685 or write Harvard Business School Publishing, Boston, MA 02163. No part of this publication may be reproduced, stored in a retrieval system, used in a spreadsheet, or transmitted in any form or by any means—electronic, mechanical, photocopying, recording, or otherwise—without the permission of Harvard Business School.

credit risk characteristics, such as home mortgages and automobile loans. Other commercial or industrial loans have widely different purposes and credit risks and are therefore more difficult to securitize. Additionally, in the early 1990s the volume of trading in risky products increased very rapidly, making it extremely difficult for portfolio managers to protect their portfolios against all the different credit risks they faced. This environment created the credit derivative market, a more specialized way to provide insurance against credit-related losses.

What is a credit derivative?

Credit derivatives are simply a means of protecting against credit risk. They come in many shapes and sizes to protect against the different kinds of credit risk, but all serve the same general purpose. Simply put, a credit derivative is a security with a payoff linked to a credit related event, such as default, credit rating downgrade, or structural change in a security containing credit risk.

CIBC Wood Gundy estimated the size of the credit derivatives market in June 1996 at about $39.2 billion, a monumental increase over its virtual nonexistence two years earlier.[1] Still, many analysts anticipated much further growth in the credit derivatives market as they took aim at a new risk category.

Why investors use credit derivatives

Banks and corporations use credit derivatives in a variety of ways. The most basic use is to separate credit risk from market risk. The ability to separate credit risk from market risk is a crucial one, since it then allows the two risks in the same instrument to be decoupled and traded separately by traders more well-versed in handling the risks of each component. Some more specific reasons why banks and corporations use credit derivatives are:

- **Constructing efficient portfolios:** Credit derivatives allow investors to hedge their portfolios very easily. To achieve the same benefits without using derivatives could require extensive purchases of bonds and many other securities. By purchasing a credit derivative instead, an investor can easily reduce overall transactions costs. Additionally, having the ability to make these hedging moves might allow investors to deal with assets that were previously not available. It also provides portfolio managers the ability to leverage bond or loan positions.

- **Increased flexibility in portfolio:** Part of the reason credit derivatives allow efficient portfolios is because they are extremely flexible. They can incorporate whatever part of the credit risk of an asset an investor chooses. For example, an investor may own a five-year corporate bond, but only be concerned about the credit risk over the next two years. Credit derivatives will allow that investor to pass that risk to someone else. Furthermore, by designing this type of security, an investor effectively creates a two-year security with many of the pricing characteristics of the five-year bond. The creative possibilities for other securities are endless.

- **Increase portfolio value by taking risk on highly unlikely scenarios:** Some investors feel selling credit derivatives is a good way to add value to their portfolio; the cost of a credit derivative far exceeds the probable payout. This is a

---

[1] Allen, James C. "Credit Derivatives Getting Off Ground." *The American Banker*, June 14, 1996.

An Overview of Credit Derivatives

possible means of generating additional revenue, but as the market efficiency of pricing credit derivatives improves, this use may drop off.

- **Low cost interest rate exposure hedge:** Investors who decide that changes in interest rates will affect the value of their fixed income assets can use credit derivatives as a low-cost means of hedging against large shifts in rates.

When dealing with credit derivatives, it is also important to consider the credit rating of all participants. It makes little sense for an investor to purchase a credit derivative on a AA-rated institution from an institution with a lower credit rating. Imagine a mom-and-pop convenience store offering credit protection to Wal-Mart. By the time Wal-Mart needs credit protection, the likelihood of the mom-and-pop store remaining in business is low, so its protection is meaningless.

Types of credit derivatives

There are many different kinds of credit derivatives. To write an exhaustive description is impossible. Here is a brief description of some popular types of credit derivatives.

- **Total Return Swaps:** Far and away, the most popular credit derivative instrument is the total return swap. As in a conventional swap, there is a payer and a receiver. In a total return swap, the payer gives the receiver the total return of an asset such as a corporate bond (including interest payments and price appreciation or depreciation). In exchange, the receiver gives the payer regular contracted payments, for example, the 3-month LIBOR plus a spread. The receiver gets the return of an asset without the need to hold the asset on its balance sheet. From the other side, i.e. that of the payer, this transaction is also preferred as a means of negotiating credit protection without liquidating the underlying asset. Total return swaps usually have far lower administrative costs than liquidation, and they allow banks to diversify credit risk without revealing confidential client financial records, since the asset is never transferred.

  Here is an example of a total return swap. Suppose Textron issues a bond at LIBOR + 5/8 maturing in 10 years. The price of the bond is 99 ½. An investor enters into a three-year swap paying LIBOR + 100bp, and receiving the Textron quarterly return. The investor pays more than the Textron coupon because the market believes there will be an increase in the price of the bond as well. If the terms of the swap were to pay LIBOR + 25bp, then the market opinion would be for price depreciation of the bond. The swap considers the return on capital as well as the coupon.

  The mechanism of the total return swap is as follows. The total return on the Textron bond consists of two components: interest rate risk related and credit risk related. If interest rates rise, the price of the Textron bond does not change much since it pays a floating rate. But, if Textron's credit quality changes, it does affect the price of the bond substantially. Now, the Textron bond is swapped with a floating rate LIBOR instrument which has no interest rate risk, and very little credit risk. Hence, the predominant component of the value of the total return swap derives purely from credit risk. Thus, it is an ideal credit derivative, allowing the buyer and seller to make a pure trade on credit risk.

- **Credit Default Swaps:** A credit default swap provides a hedge against *default* on some payment, such as a bond. The investor buying credit protection pays a provider to guarantee payment in case the investment defaults. This payment could be a lump sum at the beginning of the contract or periodic payments over the life of the contract. The credit guarantor only pays the investor if the original investment defaults in some way – by missing a coupon payment or total default. While the terminology of a swap may be inappropriate here, the credit default swap is an instrument where payout only occurs on default.

- **Credit Risk Options:** A default option protects an investor only against defaults on an investment; a credit risk option provides broader protection – against changes in payments as well as defaults. Suppose a Baa-rated company plans to issue a series of bonds in two months. When it makes this plan, it calculates the cost of the issue, assuming its interest payments are going to be a certain amount above an index rate, such as LIBOR. However, if in the time before the bonds are issued, the credit risk premium for Baa-rated companies increases, then the coupon payments over the life of the bond will also increase. As a result, the issuance will be worth much less to the company. To hedge this increase, the company can buy credit protection for increases in coupon payments. To do so, the company buys a credit risk option from a bank willing to make a market in the issuer's credit risk. The writer of the credit risk option provides a simple European option to the issuer with a fixed maturity, agreeing to compensate the issuer if the issue brings in less than the expected value due to a credit rating decline.

Bond investors can also protect themselves against declines in a bond issuer's credit rating. If a company's credit rating declines, the price of a bond falls, as the market requires a greater risk premium for holding the bond. Owning this type of credit protection helps an investor protect against that kind of loss.

- **Credit Intermediation Swaps:** In a credit intermediation swap, one entity serves as an intermediary between other entities to alleviate credit concerns in swaps. For example, suppose there are two small businesses, one in Seattle and the other in Miami. They want to enter into a swap contract with each other, but because they are both small businesses, still searching for their market identity, neither one is convinced of the other's ability to live up to their end of the swap. To facilitate the deal, they call up a big firm in New York with a AAA-credit rating. They use this firm as a vehicle to guarantee the swap. The Seattle business pays a fixed rate of 5.0% to the New York firm and receives a floating rate of LIBOR in return. The Miami business pays LIBOR plus 10bp to the New York firm, while receiving the same fixed rate of 5.0%. Each small business is convinced of the New York firm's credit worthiness, and the New York firm takes 10bp as payment for accepting the credit risk of the two small businesses

- **Credit Spread Derivatives:** Credit spread measures the difference between the interest rate on a risky bond and a government security. Assuming that interest rates move consistently with respect to market events – a 1% increase in government interest rates leads to a 1% increase in corporate bond rates, then any changes in the difference between the two rates can be attributed to changes in credit risk for the corporate bond. Derivatives written on this difference, or credit spread, are credit spread options, forwards, and swaps. For example, a credit spread call is a call option written on the level of credit spreads. If spreads rise, the call increases in value, and pays off if the credit spread at maturity of the option is greater than the strike spread. (Some participants define a spread call in the opposite way, i.e. it pays off if the spread is below the strike spread at maturity, as in the example below.)

An Overview of Credit Derivatives

example,

This type of credit derivative allows a financial manager to replicate a security with the return of one asset and the credit risk of a second asset. Consider a note issued by a AAA-rated firm that pays a coupon of three-month LIBOR plus 1.25%.[2] This note is linked to the credit spread of five-year bonds issued by a fictitious company, ABC Inc. These bonds currently trade at a spread of 250 basis points over Treasuries. This issued note also contains a two-year zero-coupon spread collar (a collar is the simultaneous purchase of a call and sale of a put at different strike prices). This collar effectively gives the investor a spread call struck at the current level of 250bp. The call is financed by effectively selling a spread put struck at 280bp. Adding the spread collar increases the sensitivity of the bond to changes in total interest rates (risk free rates plus spreads), thereby increasing its duration. As a result, the investment has five-year credit spread duration but minimal interest rate duration. **Exhibit 1** shows a graph of total return after two years in relation to the credit spread of ABC Inc. for the structured collar note and an outright purchase of ABC bonds. Notice that after the addition of the collar, the slope of the line for the bond increases, i.e. duration or risk has been enhanced. Investors looking for more bang per buck often adopt such strategies when they believe they understand the credit markets better than the average market participant.

- **Default Substitution Swaps and other Credit Derivatives:** Many credit derivatives are simply standard credit derivatives with a slight wrinkle thrown into the pricing or payment structure. For example, two investors could agree on a contract requiring them to trade assets if a credit spread moved past a certain level (a default substitution swap). A derivative could have a singular payoff, regardless of the size of credit change. For example, suppose a credit spread call is struck at 75bp over LIBOR, so the owner of the call will win if the credit spread narrow to less than 75bp over LIBOR. In a standard credit spread call, the size of the payment would depend on the magnitude of the change in credit standing. In this binary case, only one payment will occur no matter how large the change in credit risk.

Recent market features

The credit derivative market has grown considerably since 1994. This increase in credit derivatives has led to greater market liquidity. More and more firms use credit derivatives for a variety of purposes, and as a result, it has become much easier to create and trade these securities. With increased liquidity, pricing credit derivatives becomes much more efficient.

The legal status of credit derivatives is still unclear. Some people believe credit derivatives act less as a financial instrument and more as insurance against loss. If credit derivatives are classified as insurance, they face an entirely different set of legal restrictions. This issue has not yet been tested in court.

---

[2] This example was created by Bjorn Flesaker, Lane Hughston, Laurence Schreiber, and Lloyd Sprung in "Taking All The Credit." *Risk*, Vol. 7, No. 9, September 1994

A simple pricing model[3]

A simple way to price a defaultable bond is to use a binomial pricing model. Binomial pricing models used to price bonds are similar to ones used to price stocks and options, except that bond pricing models measure interest rate changes. The price of the bond at maturity is always known – the model accounts for possible fluctuations in interest rates along the way.

Suppose we are modeling a *zero-coupon* bond over two periods. It will mature with a face value of 100, and it currently has an interest rate of 10%. In the next period, the interest rate will either rise to 12% or fall to 8%. There is a 5% chance the bond will default in either period. If the bond defaults, it will pay 30% of its value. Before pricing the risky bond, we may want to check what a riskless bond would cost – a bond with all the same attributes but without the possibility of default. Chart 1 summarizes the pricing method for the riskless bond.

Chart 1

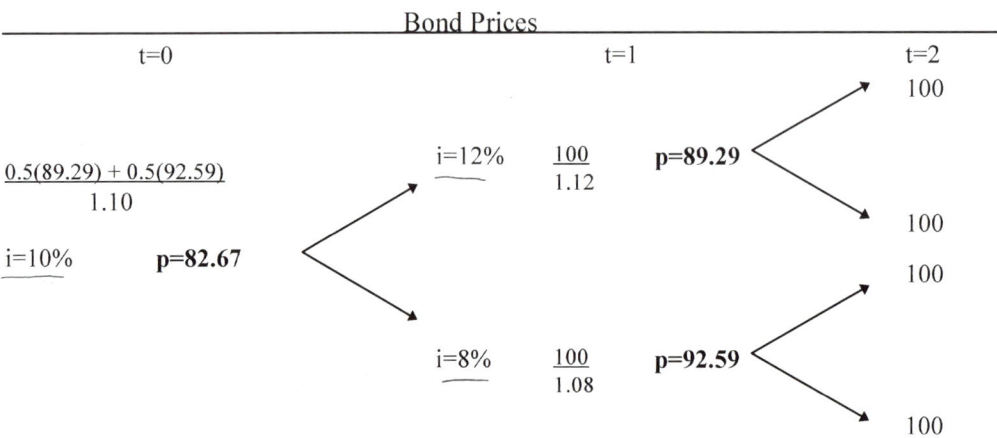

The riskless bond guarantees a payment of $100 at t=2. The price of the bond at t=1 will vary with the interest rate at t=1. Regardless of the rate, the price will equal the expected value of the bond ($100) discounted by the interest rate (either 8% or 12=%). The two possible prices at t=1 are in bold. To determine the price of the bond at t=0, we use the same methodology – discount the expected price by the interest rate. The interest rate is known – 10%. The expected price of the bond is simple to calculate: the probability of an outcome (each outcome has equal probability) multiplied by the price at that outcome (the prices at t=1). These calculations find the price of the bond at t=0 to be $82.67.

There are two ways to price a risky bond: by discounting the risky (or default-adjusted) cashflows with the riskless rates, or by discounting the riskless cashflows with the risk-adjusted (i.e. default-spreaded) rates. Because we do not know the risky rates yet, it will be much easier initially to price the bond by discounting the risky cashflows with riskless rates. Calculating the risky cashflows is simple: find the expected cashflow based on the probability of default. In this case, there is a 5% chance of receiving $30 and a 95% chance of receiving $100, for an expected final cashflow value of $96.50. Chart 2 calculates the price of the bond given these cashflow patterns.

---

[3] For a more detailed explanation of the model see "Modeling Term Structures of Defaultable Bonds." Working Paper, June 1996, by Darrell Duffie and Ken Singleton.

An Overview of Credit Derivatives

The information in Chart 2 is similar to the information in Chart 1. Instead of having an expected payoff of $100, the bond has an expected payoff of $96.50. This expected value is discounted by the same interest rates at t=1, resulting in two possible prices for the bond at t=1. These prices are in bold in the chart. To find the price of the bond at t=0, again we have to calculate the expected payoff (95% chance of the full payoff at t=1, and 5% chance of only 30% of the payoff at t=1), and discount that expected payoff by the interest rate at t=0. Again the interest rate is 10%, so calculating the price of the bond at t=0 is very straightforward. The price, $76.99, is in bold in the chart.

Chart 2

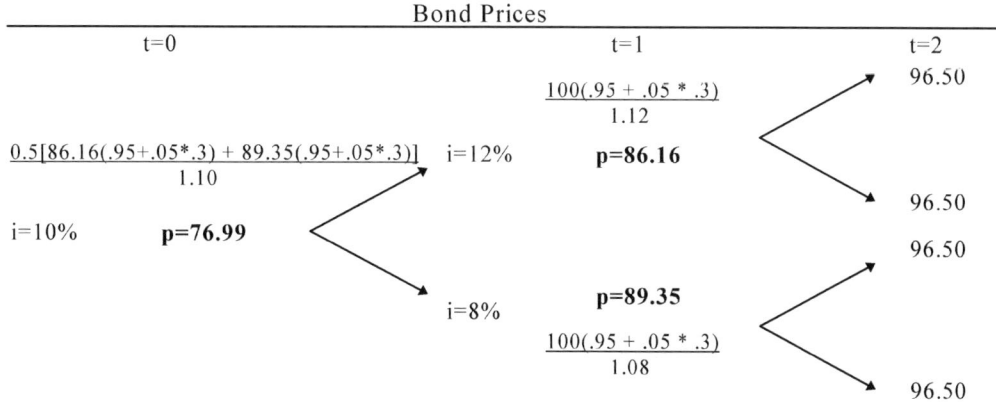

Calculating the rate of return on the risky bond is easy once the price of the risky bond is known. The expected prices of the bond in time 0 and time 1 are known from Chart 2. The risky rates of return assume the bond will pay the promised value of $100 in time 2 instead of the expected value of $96.50. Since the earlier prices for the bond are known, calculating the rates required to achieve those values is simple. In this example, we must find what rate of return is required to have $100 in the next period, given $86.16 or $89.25 in the first period. These rates are in bold in Chart 3. To find the rate at t=0 requires the same method: finding what interest rate will allow $76.99 to increase to the expected value at t=1 (with equal probability of each outcome). In this case, the rate is 14%.

Chart 3

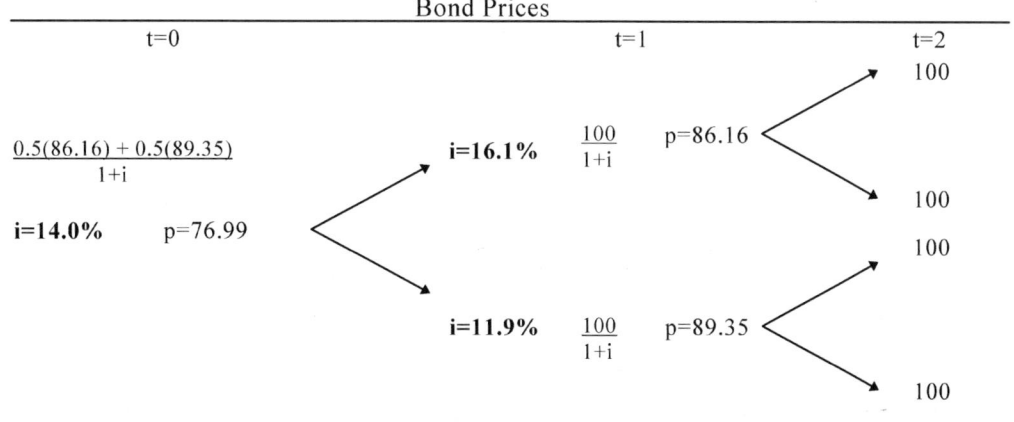

Once risky rates are known, it is easy to use those rates as a check to make sure the risky bond was properly valued. Follow the steps from Chart 1, except substitute the risky rates of return (14%, 16.1%, 11.9%) for the risk free rates of return (10%, 12%, 8%). The new prices calculated should equal the prices from Chart 2, give or take a little for rounding error. These rates can then be used to value any bond with similar credit characteristics. Hence, it is often easier to value a slew of bonds with the same risk level once the risky rates are known.

An example

Strategic Management of Asset Return Trends is a rapidly growing financial firm. It prides itself on being at the cutting edge of the capital markets. To stay on the cutting edge, it constantly searches for hot new talent in the field, and tries to hire those people from their current employment. Presently, the Strategic Management executives are developing their credit risk analysis department. Their star recruit so far is Elizabeth Brown, who they hired as a specialist in this field. They felt bringing Brown in from Massive Equity Transaction Services was a real coup, as Brown had shown a spectacular ability to anticipate market movement.

Over the weekend, Brown played racquetball with an acquaintance of hers from Classic Widget Production, a major industrial firm. She started formulating her opinions about the two-year credit risky bond recently issued by CWP, and she hoped she could make a move on this bond. When she got to the office at 4:30 am Monday morning, she checked out market opinion on these bonds.

Brown discovered the current price of the bond is 84.1979 for a face value of 100. The spot rate for one year is 7% and the forward rate between 1 and 2 years is 8%. The credit spread for one year is 1% and forward, between 1 and 2 years is 1.2%. Brown realized the price of the bond made sense because it followed the pricing formula: $100*\exp[-(0.07+0.01)-(0.08+0.012)] = 84.1979$. (The market uses continuous compounding, hence the 'exp' or exponentiation formula).

Next, Brown checked what the market anticipates will occur in the future. She found the market has assumed no correlation between interest rates and spreads in their pricing. Also, there are only two possible interest rates in the future and two possible spreads, which she summarized in the following table (with four possible outcomes):

Interest Rate	Spread	Probability
9%	1.5109%	0.25
9%	0.9%	0.25
7%	1.5109%	0.25
7%	0.9%	0.25

Brown checked to make sure the market priced this bond accurately, and she found the price consistent with the market again:

$100*¼*[\exp(-0.09-0.015109)+\exp(-0.09-0.009)+\exp(-0.07-0.015109)+\exp(-0.07-0.009)]*\exp(-0.07-0.01)$

$=84.1979$

By 7am, Brown was convinced the bond was priced fairly given market expectations. But her expectations differed from the market. Specifically, she thought there was a negative correlation between interest rates and spreads – if interest rates rose, spreads would fall. She had every

An Overview of Credit Derivatives

confidence the market would see things her way in a short time, and she intended on showing them the way to act. Now she just had to figure out specifically what to do.

Should Brown go long or short on this bond?

How else can she profit from this correlation view?

Exhibit 1

The investor receives LIBOR + 125bp on a two-year 250 spread call / 280 spread put leveraged collar note. The purchase of a collar note allows the investor to benefit more from spread tightening than an equivalent purchase of the underlying five-year ABC bond, while maintaining 30bp spread-widening protection. If interest rates rise by 200bp the spread can widen up to 330bp (spot + 80bp) before the collar note underperforms an outright purchase of the ABC bond.

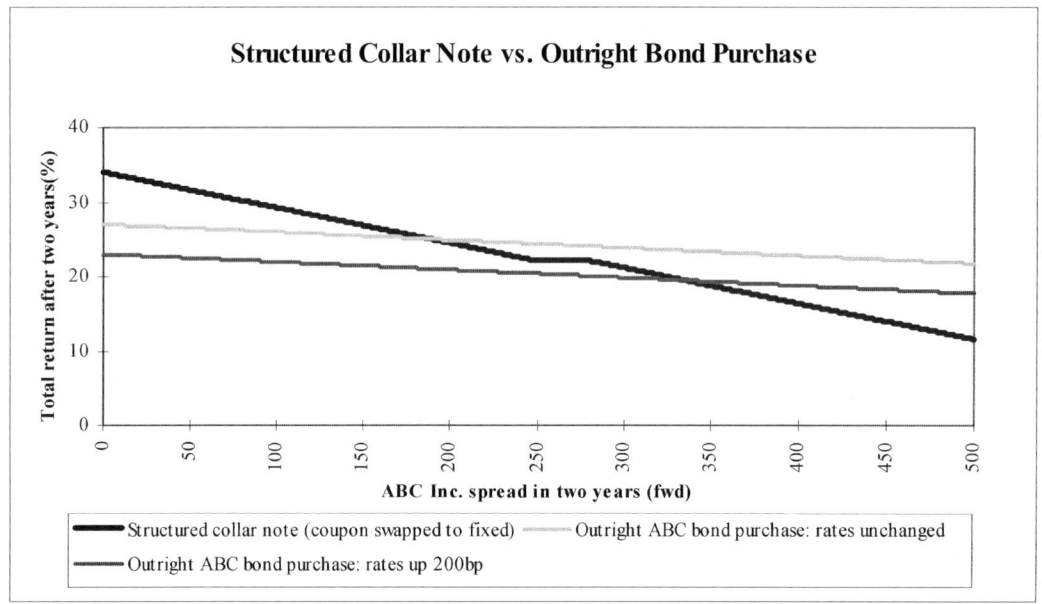

 **Harvard Business School**

9-299-020
Rev. November 17, 1999

Farallon Capital Management: Risk Arbitrage (A)

On August 1, 1997, Tom Steyer, David Cohen and Bill Duhamel stared pensively out of Farallon Capital's conference room admiring the morning lights of the San Francisco Bay Bridge. The sun was starting to rise as they discussed the news that British Telecom was conducting an in-depth review of its bid for MCI Communications. Nine months had passed since Farallon had taken its initial investment in the $25 billion acquisition by purchasing MCI shares and selling short BT shares. While the transaction had proceeded smoothly up to now, MCI sent tremors through the risk arbitrage industry in early July when it announced that its attempts to enter the local telephony market were proving more difficult than anticipated, resulting in an expected $800 million of losses during 1997, and even worse in 1998. This announcement threatened to jeopardize the groundbreaking transaction between BT and MCI and to cause severe trading losses to many merger arbitrage investors.

The BT/MCI investment represented Farallon's largest risk-arbitrage exposure, and Steyer, Cohen and Duhamel were trying to decide whether to stay in the position, or unwind it and cut their losses. While the United Kingdom press had been calling for BT to amend its bid for MCI, two of the leading Wall Street equity analysts in the telecommunications sector had taken opposing views on the prospects of the merger; and other risk arbitrageurs in the hedge fund community still appeared supportive of the deal. Farallon would have to draw its own conclusions, and did not have much time.

Farallon Capital Management, L.L.C.

Farallon Capital managed a hedge fund founded in 1986 by Tom Steyer and Fleur Fairman. Prior to forming Farallon Capital, Steyer had gained experience in private equity and distressed security investing at Goldman, Sachs & Co. Fairman, on the other hand, had developed expertise in the public markets working at some of the major New York hedge funds. Steyer's and Fairman's strengths complemented each other well when they formed Farallon Capital to take advantage of public market investment opportunities in risk arbitrage and distressed securities.

David Cohen joined Farallon in 1993 from the Equities Arbitrage Group at Goldman, Sachs. At Goldman, Cohen had developed an extensive understanding of the risk arbitrage business, with three years in international risk arbitrage in London, and one year in domestic risk arbitrage in New York City. In 1995, Bill Duhamel joined the company after several years in Mexico, where he had

---

Robert Howard (MBA '98) and Professor André F. Perold prepared this case as the basis for class discussion rather than to illustrate either effective or ineffective handling of an administrative situation.

Copyright © 1998 by the President and Fellows of Harvard College. To order copies or request permission to reproduce materials, call 1-800-545-7685 or write Harvard Business School Publishing, Boston, MA 02163. No part of this publication may be reproduced, stored in a retrieval system, used in a spreadsheet, or transmitted in any form or by any means—electronic, mechanical, photocopying, recording, or otherwise—without the permission of Harvard Business School.

managed a group of cable systems for the private equity firm, Hellman and Friedman. Steyer was responsible for Farallon's overall portfolio, and Cohen and Duhamel presently shared responsibility for the BT/MCI position.

In 1998, Farallon Capital had several billion dollars in assets under management across more than eight funds and its clients were primarily major university endowments and wealthy individuals. As manager of the funds, Farallon charged investors traditional hedge fund fees with a percentage of its revenues based on performance. The firm now had thirty-five employees, including fifteen investment professionals. The hedge fund segmented its operations into four major investment strategies: (i) Public Equity or Arbitrage; (ii) Distressed Securities, including bank debt and high-yield securities of companies in financial distress; (iii) Distressed Real Estate; and (iv) Private Investments, including equity and subordinated debt in leveraged buy-outs and the factoring of receivables. Farallon had performed well within each of these asset classes, but also derived extra returns from strategic allocations of capital among these four businesses.

Risk Arbitrage

As a general investment strategy, arbitrage refers to the buying of one security and the selling of another security to lock-in a risk-free profit. Risk arbitrage, or merger arbitrage, refers to an investment strategy that attempts to capitalize on the outcome of a merger situation after it has been disclosed to the public. The business became popular during the merger frenzy of the 1980s, but suffered from the insider trading indictments and convictions of traders like Ivan Boesky, Dennis Levine, and Martin Siegel.

In many announced mergers, there exists a discount between the price of the target company's stock and the consideration proposed in the merger. Merger arbitrageurs attempt to gain from the elimination of this discount when the merger is consummated. In a cash deal, arbitrageurs will tend just to purchase the equity of the target company. In a stock-for-stock deal, they typically purchase the target company's stock and sell short the stock of the acquiring company. Often, this apparently simple trading strategy can become complicated by the presence of multiple bidders for the target, defensive strategies in hostile takeovers, or the use of collars that alter the terms of the deal based on the performance of the acquirer's stock.

The outcome following the announcement of a proposed merger can be quite uncertain, hence the name "risk" arbitrage for this method of investing. One possibility is that the proposed acquisition falls due to resistance by the target company. Resistance can be effected through various anti-takeover provisions such as "poison pills" and staggered boards which make a potential merger more costly, if not impossible. In addition, the management of the target company may appeal to its shareholders to vote against a proposed acquisition on the basis that the terms do not adequately reflect the full value of the company's assets. Alternatively, the target may decide to sell the company to another bidder. Even if the target company agrees to a merger, a deal still can face complications from regulatory agencies, such as the Federal Trade Commission, the Department of Justice, or the Board of Governors of the Federal Reserve System. Merger agreements are typically subject to a variety of conditions, any one of which can lead to termination of the transaction if unfulfilled. For example, changes in business conditions or the general economic environment can alter the attractiveness of the deal and cause it to be revised or to fall apart. Lastly, even if a deal will eventually be consummated, the closing date remains uncertain and the final terms may be revised.

Arbitrageurs demand compensation for the risks associated with proposed mergers. Farallon believed that a typical rule of thumb in the arbitrage community was a required return of 3 x LIBOR. In addition, arbitrageurs calculate the potential upside in a deal as weighed against the downside if the deal were to fall apart. For example, consider Company A which has public common stock currently trading at $70. Suppose Company B announces an acquisition of Company A for $100 a share in cash and Company A's shares rise in value to $95. Arbitrageurs would see $5 of upside if the deal were to close but a likely downside exposure of $25 if the deal were to fall apart and Company A's shares fell back to $70. The $5 of upside versus the $25 of downside would have to be weighed in conjunction with the probabilities of these outcomes.

In some deals, shareholders have a choice of consideration, such as cash, stock or securities. Such choice can be via an election or via a tender for less than 100% of the target. In such situations, the arbitrageur must value the various alternatives, decide how much to tender or what to elect, and hedge the expected outcomes and pro rations.

In hostile deals, arbitrageurs can end up owning a significant percentage of the target company. As such, they can influence the success or failure of the hostile bid. In situations with competing bidders, arbitrageurs also can determine which bidder is eventually successful.

There are a variety of explanations usually given for the discounts in the prices of the target firm's shares. One is that investors require compensation for the risks to the proposed merger. A second argument is that natural selling occurs in the shares of the target company due to a change in investor clientele. A merger is a complicated corporate event and very news intensive. Many fund managers do not have the expertise nor the time to follow the company once it has been bid for by an acquirer. In the above example, many of Company A's investors might be happy to lock-in the $25 gain in Company A's stock price and may not want to wait around for only $5 more of upside. Additionally, forced selling may occur by investors who are restricted from owning companies involved in takeovers or from receiving the specific form of consideration being paid by the acquirer. For example, in a share-for-share deal, if the charter of a mutual fund allows it to own only dividend-paying stocks, and the acquirer's stock pays no dividends, then the mutual fund might be forced to sell its shares in the target prior to its receipt of the acquirer's shares at closing.

Farallon Capital's Equity Arbitrage Group

Farallon Capital's Equity Arbitrage Group consisted of five research professionals and two traders. Over the past few years, the group had been invested in 80 to 120 merger arbitrage positions at any one time, with an additional 165 to 200 deals being followed closely.

The amount of money allocated to risk arbitrage depended on the level of merger activity and alternative uses of funds. In the late 1980s, Farallon was primarily involved in merger arbitrage with about 80% of its funds invested in this area. In the early 1990s, when the merger market was relatively inactive, Farallon's risk arbitrage business declined significantly to less than 10% of the total fund. In 1997, with merger activity at record levels and the equity markets hitting all-time highs, Farallon's risk arbitrage business again represented a significant part of the total fund. As shown in **Exhibit 1**, Farallon's returns ranked highly when compared with those of the premier hedge funds specializing in this area.

As one measure of historical returns within the industry, there existed a retail mutual fund, The Merger Fund, with $446 million in assets under management that invested in merger arbitrage situations. The fund had become so successful that it closed itself to new investors on June 1, 1996. In addition, the mutual fund rating company Morningstar had assigned it four out of five stars for its historical performance. As **Exhibit 2** illustrates, the returns of The Merger Fund were in the range 4.45% to 18.15% over the period from 1988 to 1997, averaging 11.16%. In addition, the fund had a beta of less than 0.2 over the previous three years.

In managing its portfolios, Farallon placed a very high emphasis on capital preservation. Farallon had managed to achieve high returns while experiencing very little volatility (see **Exhibit 1**).

In fact, Farallon had not had a down month since 1989. Also, given the historically low volatility of risk-arbitrage investments, clients had come to view merger arbitrage as a low-risk investment strategy that yielded equity-type returns thus reinforcing the need to maintain market neutrality and manage the overall volatility of the portfolios' returns. Where appropriate, Farallon used stock index futures to reduce the market risk of its positions.

Use of Leverage

Farallon consistently tried to get high returns on assets but resisted opportunities to leverage low returns on assets into high returns on equity. The risk arbitrage market had seen periods of significant dislocation such as the period following the guilty plea of Ivan Boesky on illegal stock parking charges in October 1986 and the collapse of the United Airlines leveraged buyout in October 1989. Arbitrageurs who were highly levered going into these periods of dislocations were put out of business. Farallon therefore tried to maintain conservative levels of leverage that were well below the 50% margin restriction in the Federal Reserve Board's Regulation T.[1] Furthermore, a number of institutional investors, such as tax-exempt endowments, could not use any leverage as it would generate unrelated business taxable income, or UBTI.

Initiating a Risk Arbitrage Position

With its dependence on the public equity markets, Farallon Capital found itself a West Coast firm operating on East Coast time. Since the equity markets opened at 6:30 a.m. in San Francisco, the investment professionals usually arrived at the office between 5:00 a.m. and 5:30 a.m. On Monday mornings, however, two analysts usually would arrive at 4:30 a.m. to scour the press releases for merger announcements. Within a half hour, decisions would be made about which deals to investigate further. According to Farallon, about 50% of mergers were announced on Monday morning so that final discussions between companies could be completed over the weekend when markets were closed and the risks of leaks were mitigated. Thus, Mondays tended to offer a particularly rich supply of investment opportunities.

Given the highly competitive nature of the merger arbitrage market, Farallon tried to establish a position as soon as possible. A decision whether or not to commit capital would often be made within a period of two to three hours after a deal had been announced. During this period, Farallon's analysts focused on understanding the potential risks of the deal as well as the proper valuation for the target company. For the latter, Farallon's analysts used break-up valuations, relative valuation tables, and discounted cash flow models incorporating estimates of potential synergies from the merger. In addition, the analysts would calculate the potential accretion or dilution to earnings per share for the combined companies, as well as any other ratios that might shed light on the attractiveness of the deal.

In order to perform this due diligence, Farallon's analysts would draw upon numerous sources. To start, they would call Wall Street equity analysts to get their perspectives on the company, its industry, appropriate valuation metrics, the outlook for the deal, and potential synergies. Wall Street firms were usually very responsive to arbitrage funds, given their high turnover. (For example, a risk arbitrage fund with $100 million in assets under management and an average investment horizon of three months would generate $400 million to $800 million in transactions per year, comparable to a $1.2 billion equity fund with 33% annual portfolio turnover.)

---

[1] The Federal Reserve Board's Regulation T required investors to post 50% margin for "long" positions and 50% margin for "short" positions. This meant that for each $100 of invested capital, an investor could be both long $100 and short $100 worth of shares. When an acquirer was offering cash for a target, however, a short position would not be taken and, thus, an investor could own $200 of shares for each $100 invested.

Farallon's arbitrage analysts also would have conversations with the investor relations departments of companies affected by a merger announcement, and would participate in company conference calls that related to the merger. To assess the potential regulatory barriers, lawyers would be contacted early on to investigate potential antitrust or industry-specific issues. In addition, Farallon would avail itself of industry experts, competitors of the company, major institutional shareholders, investment bankers, political consultants, trade journals, newspaper reporters and other arbitrage funds. As David Cohen commented, "When a question is posed to the arbitrage community, it will normally find an answer."

The British Telecommunications/MCI Communications Acquisition

On Friday afternoon, November 1, 1996, information circulated about a possible merger between British Telecommunications plc ("BT") and MCI Communications ("MCI"). While the details of the potential merger were not released, a combination of these two telecommunication giants would represent the largest international merger ever. David Cohen and Bill Duhamel immediately started collecting information to prepare themselves for a potential position that Monday morning. Given the international complexity of a deal between BT and MCI, they could use the weekend to study the situation and the potential for initiating an arbitrage position. By the end of the day on Friday, Cohen and Duhamel had already had preliminary discussions with several Wall Street analysts; and they had contacted two domestic lawyers specializing in antitrust and communications, and a U.K. political consultant, to begin the massive task of unraveling the regulatory complications.

British Telecommunications was the primary provider of telephony services in the United Kingdom, with £14.4 billion in revenue and £2.0 billion in net income for its 1996 fiscal year.[2] As a former government-owned monopoly, BT had been privatized in 1984 and, since the government's deregulation of the market in 1992, was facing increased competition. Nevertheless, as of September 1996, BT still had 91% of the exchange lines in the United Kingdom and garnered 79% of the market for national calls. Beyond standard telephony services, BT had expanded domestically into Internet services and internationally into major European markets as well as Asia and Latin America.[3] As part of its international strategy, BT entered into a joint-venture in August 1993 with MCI Communications to provide global enhanced and value-added telecommunications services throughout the world. BT also purchased 20% of MCI for $4.3 billion. The recent announcement by BT reflected its intention to purchase the remaining 80% of MCI that it did not currently own. For additional information on BT, see the Value Line sheet in **Exhibit 4**.

At the time of the announcement, MCI Communications was the second largest provider of long-distance services in the United States with almost $18.5 billion in revenues and $1.2 billion in net income for its 1996 fiscal year. While involved in additional communications services domestically, MCI's major strategic thrust in 1996 was to enter the local telephony market, which had historically been dominated by the seven Regional Bell Operating Companies ("RBOCs") and GTE. This opportunity in the local telephony market had become available as a result of the February 8, 1996 passage of the Telecommunications Act of 1996 which helped to deregulate the domestic telecommunications industries. In addition, partly through its joint-venture with BT, MCI had a strong presence internationally, ranking as the third largest carrier of telecommunications services.[4] For additional information on MCI, see the Value Line sheet in **Exhibit 5**.

---

[2] $23.6 billion revenue and $3.3 billion net income given an exchange rate of $1.64.
[3] Background information on British Telecommunications comes from 1997 Annual Report.
[4] Background information on MCI Communications comes from 1996 Annual Report.

Farallon's Initial Trading Position

On Sunday, November 3, 1996, BT announced that it had come to an agreement to acquire the remaining 80% of MCI for $25 billion. (See **Exhibit 6** for excerpts from the press release.) In exchange for each MCI share, BT would offer 0.54 shares of BT's American Depositary Receipts, or ADRs (1 ADR = 10 BT ordinary shares), and $6 in cash. The combined company would be named Concert plc. In addition, BT shareholders would receive a special dividend of 35 pence (equivalent to $5.74 per ADR at an exchange rate of $1.64/£) prior to the closing of the merger. BT also announced that, following the merger, it would cut its dividend approximately 10% and that it might repurchase up to 10% of its common shares. Preliminary estimates were that the merger would be completed within nine to twelve months.

By Monday morning, David Cohen and Bill Duhamel had reached some conclusions about the prospects for the merger. In their opinion, this deal represented a transformation in the world of telecommunications to a more integrated international market. Given that BT already owned 20% of MCI, the two appeared well-suited to be the pioneers in this new market. BT knew MCI extremely well, and it was in a good position to assess the ease or difficulty of integrating the two firms. With deregulation being a trend in both countries, Farallon believed that antitrust concerns in the U.S. and the U.K. would not be a major barrier to the deal. Furthermore, in 1993, BT had received regulatory approval for its 20% investment which included non-compete clauses that precluded MCI from the European markets and BT from the U.S. market. Hence, there now existed little, if any, overlap that might raise antitrust concerns.

Cohen and Duhamel thought that the only additional regulatory complication involved the Federal Communications Commission's ("FCC") limits on foreign ownership of U.S. telecommunications carriers to 25%. Despite this limit, there appeared to be some flexibility in that the FCC had granted a waiver of up to 35% foreign ownership in MCI when BT had made its initial investment in 1993. In addition, the FCC had recently issued an order – the Equal Competitive Opportunity (ECO) test – which outlined circumstances where the FCC would waive foreign ownership restrictions relating to U.S. telecommunications. These ECO tests focused on the degree of opportunities for competition and foreign ownership in the acquirer's home market. As Britain was arguably more open and competitive than the U.S., Cohen and Duhamel felt comfortable that BT would be granted the waivers necessary for it to acquire MCI. Moreover, the U.S. and Britain were allied in World Trade Organization (WTO) negotiations aimed at eliminating foreign investment restrictions in telecommunications globally. Cohen and Duhamel reasoned that this setting would make it difficult politically for the United States to deny BT's investment in MCI.

In assessing the trading mechanics of the BT and MCI shares, Farallon expected a large natural spread to exist between the BT and MCI shares. Cohen and Duhamel based this opinion on the fact that the deal was a cross-border transaction which would make the hedging aspects of the transaction more difficult. In addition, a $25 billion deal appeared too large for the arbitrage market to provide sufficient demand to eliminate the spread. Lastly, they anticipated "forced selling" by the MCI shareholders. Current low-dividend, growth-oriented U.S. investors in MCI shares may not want, or be allowed, to own the higher-dividend, lower-growth, international BT shares. Also, given the recent historically poor performance of MCI shares, most investors would probably prefer to take an immediate profit over waiting around for the resolution of the merger.

Cohen and Duhamel thought that the appropriate gross spread for the deal should be about 12%. Yet, when the markets opened with MCI and BT at $31.88 and $61.50, respectively, the initial spread was considerably less. Farallon's assessment was that the market had not properly assessed the complications of the U.K.'s Advance Corporation Tax ("ACT"). The ACT was a 25% tax credit on BT dividends which had been instituted in the U.K. to help lessen the effect of double taxation on distributions to shareholders. In the case of selling short BT shares, the borrower of the shares would need to pass along 125% of any net dividends to the lender of the shares. Any risk arbitrageurs who were ignoring ACT in calculating the economics of purchasing MCI shares and selling short BT shares were underestimating the cash outflows to the lenders of the BT shares. For capital markets information from November 4, 1996, see **Exhibit 12**.

As a result of the narrow initial spread, Farallon decided to take the opposite of the usual merger arbitrage position by going long BT shares and selling short MCI shares. Eventually the spread widened, and Farallon more than reversed its initial position by going long MCI shares and short BT shares to establish an initial position representing approximately 0.5% of its assets under management. Over the next few months, the regulatory hurdles became less of a concern and Farallon continued to add to its position. By the end of December 1996, Farallon's position had grown to 3% of its assets under management. By July 1997, with a number of regulatory clearances already received, the merger expected to close in just a couple of months, and with the gross spread having narrowed to approximately 7%, the BT/MCI investment had grown to Farallon's largest position, representing almost 9% of assets under management. Throughout, Farallon hedged its purchase of MCI shares through the short sale of either BT ordinary shares or BT American Depositary Receipts (ADRs). In addition, Farallon also hedged the currency exposure in BT's dividends.

The MCI Announcement

On Wednesday, July 9, 1997, MCI called an unscheduled teleconference in which it went to the unusual step of announcing that it would meet the market's second quarter earnings expectation, but that the costs associated with entering local telephone markets would be substantially higher than expectations. (See **Exhibit 8** for the press release, and **Exhibit 9** for a related press report.) In particular, MCI guided future earnings expectations down almost 50% due primarily to losses in excess of $800 million associated with local entry, more than twice as large as it had earlier projected. As a side note, MCI also said that heightened competitive pressures would lead to lower than expected earnings in its core long distance business.

After the call, Bill Duhamel spoke with MCI's finance staff, who assured him that BT was fully aware of the situation and would soon issue a press release that reaffirmed BT's commitment to the merger. Anxious about Farallon's largest position, Duhamel stayed in the office that night expecting to receive the press release at 4 a.m. (9 a.m. London time). Later in the morning, BT informed Duhamel that no such press release would be issued.

Immediately, debate raged on Wall Street regarding the prospects of the MCI merger. At the heart of the debate lay the "material adverse change" clause in the merger agreement (see **Exhibit 7**). The clause referred to specific exemptions that were outlined in an undisclosed exhibit. From disclosures in the merger proxy, it was apparent that MCI and BT had been unable to agree upon projections for MCI's new local business. Thus, Duhamel and Cohen surmised that adverse changes in the local business were probably excluded from the "material adverse change" clause. This conclusion was confirmed by subsequent press reports. However, it was unlikely that changes in the core long distance business were excluded. Therefore, the issue was whether or not losses at MCI were really in the local telephony expansion, or whether they were being used to mask actual deterioration in its core long-distance business. Cohen and Duhamel spent an inordinate amount of time trying to understand developments in the business to answer this issue. If the changes were only in the local business, BT did not have a legal out from the merger contract. However, if the core business had declined materially, then it might have a basis for terminating the contract.

From among the leading Wall Street equity research analysts, Bill Duhamel often sought the insights of Jack Grubman at Salomon Brothers and Dan Reingold at Merrill Lynch. Unfortunately, the two were diametrically opposed on their outlooks for the deal. Grubman came out in support of the deal, stating, "there really is no chance of this deal being renegotiated."[5] He insisted that MCI was a unique and valuable asset, and, even if the deal were terminated, there likely would be other (undisclosed) buyers ready to acquire MCI.

Reingold, on the other hand, claimed that the losses at MCI stemmed from problems in its core long-distance business. He remarked, "it's one thing to have trouble getting into the local phone business, where you're not expecting any revenue; it's another thing to have trouble in long distance, which is your bread and butter."[6] He believed that MCI's shares were worth only $20, not the current price of $35, and, therefore, BT would be smart to use the opportunity of this announcement to walk away from the deal or, at least, to adjust the price it was to pay for MCI.

In the U.K., where most of BT's shareholders were located, the media was coming out against the deal calling on BT to revise its bid, arguing that the original deal had always been too favorable for MCI. In the U.S., where most of the MCI shareholders were located, research analysts and the media were divided on the situation. In addition, a number of prominent investors had large positions in MCI. On June 30, 1997, positions by active investment managers included 35.8 million shares ($1.43 billion at a price of $40) by Fidelity Investments and 15.9 million shares ($636 million) by The Capital Group. Despite these large investments, The Capital Group had reduced its position from 26.5 million shares just three months earlier while, over the same time period, George Soros had more than doubled his hedge fund's position from 6.0 million to 13.3 million shares ($532 million). In addition, Wall Street suspected that Salomon Brothers and Long Term Capital Management had sizeable positions as well. For a list of large publicly-disclosed positions in MCI, see **Exhibit 13**.

On July 31, 1997, while Salomon's Grubman was still steadfast in his support for the deal, Merrill Lynch's Reingold released a report on MCI in which he predicted a revision in the terms of the merger:

> We continue to believe the pressures are building for a renegotiation of the merger terms, with BT shareholders compensated for the reduction in MCI's near-term earnings power…. We have estimated a compromise of 15%-25% reduction in the exchange value. A renegotiation would avoid a reversion back to BT owning only 20% of MCI, with MCI trading standalone, likely in the $20 range. Another BT option, albeit low probability, would be for BT to use its capital to expand its partnerships with others…rather than to buy the other 80% of MCI. The counter-argument is that MCI might receive buyout offers from others (e.g., GTE, as speculated last fall). Today, however, we believe MCI would attract fewer buyers and a significantly lower valuation given…changes since last November's merger announcement.[7]

The next day, on August 1, 1997, BT announced it was conducting an in-depth review of the MCI acquisition. BT claimed it was surprised by developments at MCI and needed time to study the situation. MCI claimed that there was nothing new or unexpected in the announcements and that it was at BT's encouragement that MCI had disclosed these developments to the market.

To Cohen and Duhamel, one of the great mysteries of the situation was how BT could be surprised by recent developments at MCI. BT had three representatives on MCI's Board of Directors, had owned 20% of MCI since 1993, and had participated in joint planning committees regarding

---

[5] Bloomberg, July 14, 1997.
[6] Bloomberg, July 15, 1997.
[7] Daniel Reingold, MCI Communications Company Research Report, Merrill Lynch & Co., July 31, 1997.

MCI's strategy for local telephony expansion. What had gone wrong? How had BT been surprised? Had MCI's core business changed? Was there a clash of personalities between the brash, entrepreneurial MCI management and those of the staid, government-owned BT? Had MCI been caught trying to hide business developments from their partners, or was BT using the market to negotiate down the terms of the acquisition? Cohen and Duhamel were spending days reading the press and talking to people trying to fathom exactly what had happened and what might transpire.

With all of the negative press over the previous month, MCI shares had dropped from as high as $43 on July 8 to a current price of $34; BT ADRs had dropped from as high as $82 to their recent level of $70. Up to this point, Farallon had lost money on the position. Tom Steyer looked away from the lights of the Bay Bridge and asked David Cohen and Bill Duhamel what they thought Farallon should do with the position and with the hedge.

Exhibit 1 Risk/Return Analysis of Selected Hedge Funds, January 1, 1990 to December 31, 1997

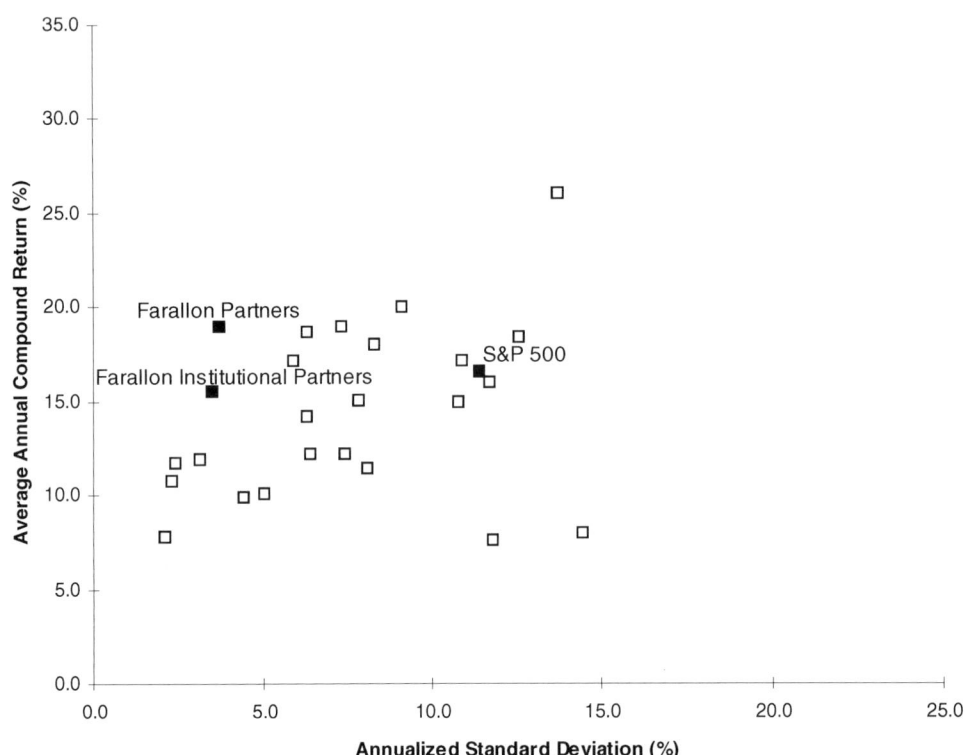

	Average Annual Compound Return (a)	Annualized Standard Deviation	Sharpe Ratio (b)
Farallon Capital Institutional Partners	15.5%	3.5%	1.38
Farallon Capital Partners	19.0%	3.7%	1.75
Average of 25 Hedge Funds (c)	14.5%	7.4%	0.73
Merger Fund	10.9%	4.6%	0.77
S&P 500	16.6%	11.4%	0.50

(a) After performance-related and other fees.

(b) Sharpe Ratio = (manager's quarterly average return - T-bill return)/(manager's quarterly standard deviation)

(c) Funds specializing in corporate events such as merger arbitrage.

Source: Cambridge Capital Advisors, Inc.

Exhibit 2 The Merger Fund

The following excerpts were selected from The Merger Fund prospectus dated December 30, 1997.

THE MERGER FUND
CONDENSED FINANCIAL INFORMATION

	Ten Months ended Sept. 30, 1997	Year ended November 30,								
		1996	1995	1994	1993	1992	1991	1990	1989	1988
Net assets, end of period (mm)	$446.0	$489.1	$243.1	$170.3	$25.2	$11.6	$10.3	$9.6	$11.0	$8.4
Ratio of operating expenses to average net assets	1.4%	1.4%	1.4%	1.6%	2.2%	2.8%	3.1%	3.3%	2.8%	2.6%
Portfolio turnover rate	271%	277%	290%	390%	186%	231%	312%	357%	430%	187%
Total return, Merger Fund	9.7% (a)	10.3%	14.3%	8.4%	17.2%	4.5%	16.8%	4.6%	5.7%	18.2%
Total return, S&P 500	27.2% (a)	27.5%	38.4%	1.0%	10.2%	16.5%	19.6%	(4.7)%	31.4%	23.2%
Total return, 3-month t-bills	4.3% (a)	5.2%	5.6%	3.7%	3.0%	3.6%	5.8%	7.8%	8.4%	6.1%

(a) Not annualized

Source: The Merger Fund 1997 Prospectus; Bloomberg

INVESTMENT OBJECTIVES AND POLICIES

The Fund seeks to achieve capital growth by engaging in merger arbitrage. The Fund's investment adviser is Westchester Capital Management, Inc. (the "Adviser").

Under normal market conditions, the Fund will invest at least 65% of its assets in the equity securities of companies which are involved in publicly announced mergers, takeovers and other corporate reorganizations ("merger arbitrage investments"). Depending upon the level of merger activity and other economic and market conditions, the Fund may temporarily invest a substantial portion of its assets in cash or cash equivalents....

Merger arbitrage is a highly specialized investment approach generally designed to profit from the successful completion of proposed mergers, takeovers, tender offers, leveraged buyouts, spin-offs, liquidations and other types of corporate reorganizations. Although a variety of strategies may be employed depending upon the nature of the reorganizations selected for investment, the most common merger arbitrage activity involves purchasing the shares of an announced acquisition target at a discount to their expected value upon completion of the acquisition. As compared to conventional investing, merger arbitrage results are considered by the Adviser to be less sensitive to the overall trend of stock prices. Over the last three-year period, the Fund's "beta" (a statistical measure of market-related risk, whereby a fund's sensitivity to movements in the Standard & Poor's 500 Stock Index is expressed relative to the Index's beta of 1.0) has averaged less than 0.2. The Adviser believes that this number is significantly lower than comparable figures for other equity mutual funds seeking capital growth. While some periods will be more conducive to a merger arbitrage strategy than others, a systematic, disciplined arbitrage program may produce attractive rates of return, even in flat or down markets. The principal risk associated with the Fund's merger arbitrage investments is that certain of the proposed reorganizations may be renegotiated or terminated, in which case losses may be realized.

Exhibit 3 The Merger Fund – Portfolio positions as of September 30, 1997

#	Position (Long/Short)	Company	Value
1)	Long	Equitable of Iowa Companies	$30.3 million
	Short	ING Groep NV ADR	$(11.6) million
2)	Long	Barnett Banks, Inc.	$23.7 million
	Short	NationsBank Corporation	$(24.6) million
3)	Long	APL Ltd.	$19.8 million
	--	Cash bid by Neptune Orient Lines Ltd.	N/A
4)	Long	MCI Communications Corporation	$18.7 million
	Short	British Telecommunications plc ADR	$(15.9) million
5)	Long	Medic Computer Systems, Inc.	$18.2 million
	--	Cash bid by Misys plc	N/A
6)	Long	American States Financial Corporation	$18.0 million
	--	Cash bid by SAFECO Corporation	N/A
7)	Long	Signet Banking Corporation	$17.0 million
	Short	First Union Corporation	$(17.2) million
8)	Long	CommNet Cellular, Inc.	$15.3 million
	--	Cash bid LBO	N/A
9)	Long	Energy Group plc	$14.6 million
	--	Cash bid by PacifiCorp	N/A
10)	Long	Bergen Brunswig Corporation, Class A	$14.5 million
	Short	Cardinal Health, Inc.	$(19.3) million
11)	Long	Enron Global Power & Pipelines L.L.C.	$14.3 million
	--	Stock bid by Enron Corporation	N/A
12)	Long	Washington National Corporation	$14.2 million
	--	Cash bid by Conseco, Inc.	N/A
13)	Long	Wheelabrator Technologies, Inc.	$14.0 million
	--	Cash bid by Waste Management, Inc.	N/A
14)	Long	Chauvco Resources Ltd.	$12.2 million
	Short	Pioneer Natural Resources Company	$(10.5) million
	Short	Chauvco International	$(1.8) million
15)	Long	Western National Corporation	$11.5 million
	Short	American General Corporation	$(2.7) million
16)	Long	Northrop-Grumman Corporation	$10.3 million
	Short	Lockheed Martin Corporation	$(10.8) million
17)	Long	ITT Corporation	$10.0 million
	Short	ITT Corporation – Call Options[8]	$(0.6) million
	--	Cash and stock bids by Hilton Hotels Corp. and Starwood Hotels & Resorts Worldwide, Inc.	N/A

---

[8] The Merger Fund had written October 1997 call options on 78,300 ITT common shares with an exercise price of $65.00 and November 1997 call options on 90,000 ITT common shares with an exercise price of $65.00. As of September 30, 1997, ITT's common shares closed trading at $67.75.

Farallon Capital Management: Risk Arbitrage (A)

#	Position (Long/Short)	Company	Value
18)	Long	Readings & Bates Corporation	$9.8 million
	Short	Falcon Drilling Company, Inc.	$(9.8) million
19)	Long	Beacon Properties Corporation	$9.3 million
	Short	Equity Office Properties Trust	$(9.9) million
20)	Long	Pennzoil Company	$9.2 million
	Short	Pennzoil Company – Call Options[9]	$(1.0) million
	--	Hostile cash bid by Union Pacific Resources Group Inc.	N/A
21)	Long	Kansas City Power & Light Company	$8.3 million
	Short	Western Resources, Inc.	$(4.3) million
	Long	Western Resources, Inc. – Put Options[10]	$0.0 million
	Short	Western Resources, Inc. – Put Options	$0.0 million
22)	Long	Pacific Forest Products Ltd.	$8.1 million
	--	Cash bid by TimberWest Forest Ltd.	N/A
23)	Long	Figgie International, Inc., Class A	$7.6 million
	--	Cash bid by HEICO Corporation	N/A
24)	Long	Boston Technology, Inc.	$7.3 million
	Short	Comverse Technology, Inc.	$(7.4) million
25)	Long	Louisiana Land and Exploration Company	$7.1 million
	Short	Burlington Resources, Inc.	$(7.1) million
26)	Long	Monterey Resources, Inc.	$6.9 million
	Short	Texaco, Inc.	$(7.0) million
	Long	Texaco, Inc. – Put Options[11]	$0.0 million
	Short	Texaco, Inc. – Put Options	$0.0 million
27)	Long	Tejas Gas Corporation	$6.8 million
	--	Cash bid by Shell Oil Company	N/A
28)	Long	Freeport McMoRan, Inc.	$5.7 million
	Short	IMC Global, Inc.	$(6.0) million
29)	Long	Standard Financial, Inc.	$5.7 million
	Short	TCF Financial Corporation	$(3.0) million
30)	Long	Cairn Energy USA, Inc.	$4.8 million
	Short	Meridian Resource Corporation	$(4.9) million
31)	Long	Fisher Scientific International, Inc.	$4.7 million
	--	Cash bid LBO	N/A

---

[9] The Merger Fund had written October 1997 call options on 80,000 Pennzoil common shares with an exercise price of $70.00 and October 1997 call options on 36,000 Pennzoil common shares with an exercise price of $75.00. As of September 30, 1997, Pennzoil's common shares closed trading at $79.69.

[10] The Merger Fund had purchased May 1998 put options on 73,700 Western Resources common shares with an exercise price of $29.09 and written May 1998 put options on 73,700 Western Resources common shares with an exercise price of $34.90. As of September 30, 1997, Western Resources' common shares closed trading at $34.38.

[11] The Merger Fund had purchased November 1997 put options on 652,400 Texaco common shares with an exercise price of $49.50 and written November 1997 put options on 652,400 Texaco common shares with an exercise price of $60.50. As of September 30, 1997, Texaco's common shares closed trading at $61.44.

#	Position (Long/Short)	Company	Value
32)	Long	USLD Communications Corporation	$4.9 million
	Short	LCI International, Inc.	$(4.9) million
	Long	LCI International, Inc. – Put Options[12]	$0.1 million
	Short	LCI International, Inc. – Put Options	$(0.3) million
33)	Long	Palmer Wireless, Inc.	$4.6 million
	--	Cash bid by Price Cellular	N/A
34)	Long	The Limited, Inc.	$3.3 million
	Short	Abercrombie & Fitch Company	$(0.6) million
	Short	Intimate Brands, Inc.	$(2.4) million
35)	Long	SFX Broadcasting, Inc.	$3.2 million
	--	Cash bid LBO	N/A
36)	Long	Syratech Corporation	$2.4 million
	--	Cash bid LBO	N/A
37)	Long	Mosinee Paper Corporation	$2.2 million
	Short	Wausau Paper Mills Company	$(2.2) million
38)	Long	Data Documents, Inc.	$2.1 million
	Short	Corporate Express, Inc.	$(2.1) million
	Long	Corporate Express, Inc. – Put Options[13]	$0.0 million
	Short	Corporate Express, Inc. – Put Options	$0.0 million
39)	Long	Integon Corporation	$1.7 million
	Long	Integon Corporation – Convertible Preferred	$1.7 million
	Short	Cash bid by General Motors Corporation	N/A
40)	Long	Salomon, Inc	$1.1 million
	Short	Travelers Group, Inc.	$(1.2) million
41)	Long	Quick & Reilly Group, Inc.	$1.1 million
	Short	Fleet Financial Group, Inc.	$(1.1) million
42)	Long	Circon Corporation	$0.9 million
	--	Hostile cash bid by U.S. Surgical	N/A
43)	Long	Advanta Corporation, Class B	$0.8 million
	Short	Advanta Corporation, Class A	$(0.9) million
44)	Long	Great Financial Corporation	$0.6 million
	Short	Star Banc Corporation	$(0.4) million

Source: The Merger Fund 1997 Prospectus

---

[12] The Merger Fund had written January 1998 put options on 243,900 LCI common shares with an exercise price of $26.40, written January 1998 put options on 243,900 LCI common shares with an exercise price of $20.40, and purchased January 1998 put options on 243,900 LCI common shares with an exercise price of $21.60. As of September 30, 1997, LCI's common shares closed trading at $26.63.

[13] The Merger Fund had purchased December 1997 put options on 101,000 Corporate Express common shares with an exercise price of $18.20 and written December 1997 put options on 101,000 Corporate Express common shares with an exercise price of $20.00. As of September 30, 1997, Corporate Express' common shares closed trading at $21.13.

Exhibit 4 Value Line sheet for British Telecom from July 11, 1997

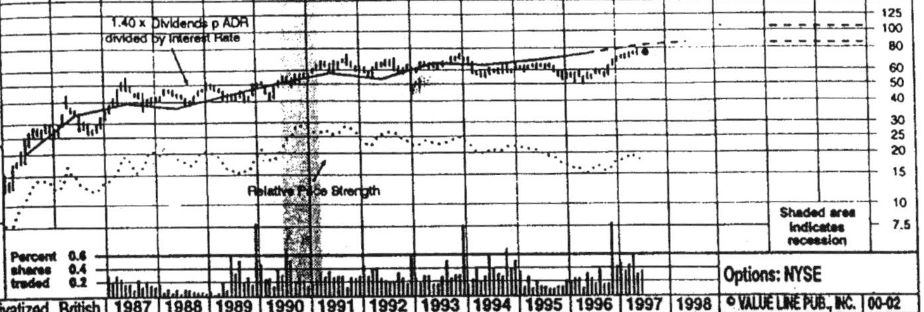

Exhibit 5 Value Line sheet for MCI Communications from July 11, 1997

MCI COMMUNICATIONS NDQ-MCIC

RECENT PRICE	P/E RATIO		RELATIVE P/E RATIO	DIV'D YLD	VALUE LINE
39	22.9	(Trailing: 22.5 / Median: 16.0)	1.35	0.1%	758

TIMELINESS — E (Relative Price Performance Next 12 Mos.)

SAFETY 3 Average (Scale: 1 Highest to 5 Lowest)

BETA .95 (1.00 = Market)

High:	6.6	6.1	12.3	24.3	22.4	15.9	20.4	29.9	29.0	27.5	33.9	41.9
Low:	3.0	2.5	4.7	10.8	9.3	8.9	14.8	18.8	17.3	17.4	22.4	32.4

Target Price Range 2000 | 2001 | 2002

2000-02 PROJECTIONS

	Price	Gain	Ann'l Total Return
High	65	(+65%)	14%
Low	45	(+15%)	4%

Insider Decisions

	A	S	O	N	D	J	F	M	A
to Buy	0	0	0	0	0	0	0	0	0
Options	0	0	0	1	2	0	0	0	0
to Sell	2	0	1	0	2	0	0	0	1

Institutional Decisions

	3Q'96	4Q'96	1Q'97
to Buy	185	189	149
to Sell	180	209	242
Hld's(000)	388075	374247	357861

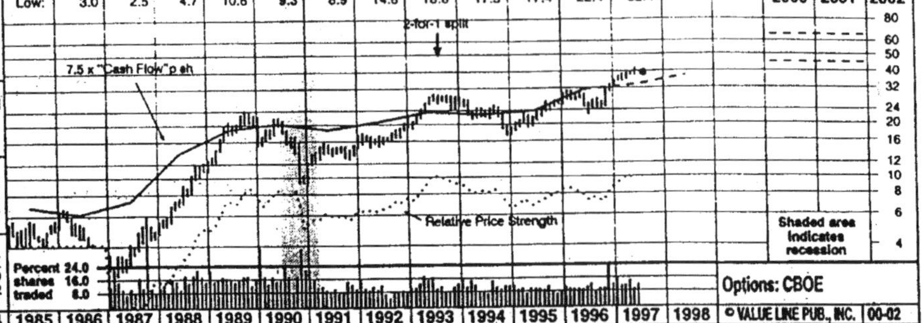

1981	1982	1983	1984	1985	1986	1987	1988	1989	1990	1991	1992	1993	1994	1995	1996	1997	1998	© VALUE LINE PUB., INC.	00-02
1.30	2.32	3.57	4.17	5.39	6.30	6.86	10.57	12.94	15.08	16.25	20.08	22.04	19.61	22.25	27.00	29.20	31.65	Revenues per sh[A]	43.80
.37	.60	.81	.82	.90	.82	.97	1.84	2.50	2.71	2.50	2.78	3.14	3.04	3.17	4.18	4.45	4.95	"Cash Flow" per sh	7.25
.23	.42	.39	.19	.17	.03	.15	.64	1.18	1.26	1.01	1.11	1.30	1.47	1.26	1.73	1.70	1.95	Earnings per sh[B]	3.45
--	--	--	--	--	--	--	--	--	.05	.05	.05	.05	.05	.05	.05	.05	.05	Div'ds Decl'd per sh[C]	.10
.70	1.35	1.91	2.47	2.12	1.88	1.01	1.64	2.08	2.50	2.65	2.42	3.20	4.26	4.18	4.89	3.90	3.55	Cap'l Spending per sh	2.75
.62	1.65	2.44	2.55	2.80	2.21	2.36	1.97	3.19	3.81	4.93	5.99	8.71	13.24	14.00	15.56	16.65	17.15	Book Value per sh	21.30
389.93	462.83	466.05	469.37	471.26	570.00	574.00	486.00	500.00	509.26	519.09	526.00	541.00	680.00	686.00	685.00	690.00	700.00	Common Shs Outst'g[D]	730.00
14.5	17.3	22.2	46.9	29.7	NMF	25.9	12.5	15.3	13.6	13.6	15.4	19.4	16.0	17.9	16.1	Bold figures are	Value Line estimates	Avg Ann'l P/E Ratio	16.0
1.76	1.91	1.88	4.37	2.41	NMF	1.73	1.04	1.16	1.01	.87	.93	1.15	1.05	1.20	1.01			Relative P/E Ratio	1.15
--	--	--	--	--	--	--	--	--	.3%	.4%	.3%	.2%	.2%	.2%	.2%			Avg Ann'l Div'd Yield	.2%
						3939.0	5137.0	6471.0	7680.0	8433.0	10562	11921	13338	15265	18494	20155	22170	Revenues ($mill)[A]	31975
						17.9%	22.1%	25.8%	24.9%	22.1%	19.7%	18.8%	19.7%	19.3%	21.5%	21.5%	21.5%	Operating Margin	23.0%
						471.0	549.0	655.0	743.0	776.0	873.0	970.0	1176.0	1308.0	1664.0	1905	2115	Depreciation ($mill)	2700
						85.0	356.0	626.0	666.0	551.0	609.0	727.0	891.0	866.0	1237.0	1230	1420	Net Profit ($mill)	2580
						19.8%	15.6%	25.4%	32.7%	35.0%	36.8%	30.4%	30.4%	38.9%	37.8%	40.0%	40.0%	Income Tax Rate	40.0%
						2.2%	6.9%	9.7%	8.7%	6.5%	5.8%	6.1%	6.7%	5.7%	6.7%	6.1%	6.4%	Net Profit Margin	8.1%
						150.0	d201.0	d296.0	d611.0	d542.0	d283.0	d600.0	1751.0	d323.0	d330.0	d350	d325	Working Cap'l ($mill)	d150
						2663.0	2677.0	2241.0	3147.0	3104.0	3432.0	2366.0	2997.0	3444.0	4796.0	5300	5755	Long-Term Debt ($mill)	8200
						1353.0	1359.0	1995.0	2340.0	2959.0	3150.0	4713.0	9004.0	9602.0	11411	12235	12755	Net Worth ($mill)	16300
						5.0%	11.8%	18.0%	14.4%	11.1%	10.8%	11.5%	8.1%	7.1%	8.2%	7.5%	8.5%	% Earned Total Cap'l	11.5%
						6.3%	26.2%	31.4%	28.5%	18.6%	19.3%	15.4%	9.9%	9.0%	10.8%	10.0%	11.0%	% Earned Net Worth	16.0%
						6.3%	35.9%	37.4%	31.5%	19.4%	17.6%	14.8%	9.5%	8.7%	11.0%	10.0%	11.0%	% Retained to Com Eq	15.5%
						--	3%	5%	8%	10%	9%	4%	4%	4%	6%	8%	7%	% All Div'ds to Net Prof	5%

CAPITAL STRUCTURE as of 3/31/97
Total Debt $5180 mill. Due in 5 Yrs $2835 mill.
LT Debt $4984 mill. LT Interest $230.0 mill.
Incl. $504 mill. capitalized leases.
(LT interest earned: 9.7x;
total interest coverage: 9.4x) (30% of Cap'l)
Leases, Uncapitalized Annual rentals $247 mill.
Pension Liability None
Pfd Stock $750.0 mill. Pfd Div'd $60.0 mill.
Incl. $750.0 mill. 8.0% Cumulative Quarterly Income Preferred Securities, Series A due 6/30/26. (4% of Cap'l)
Common Stock 687,067,321 shares
(Incl. 135,998,932 shs. of Class A common.) (66% of Cap'l)

CURRENT POSITION ($MILL.)	1995	1996	3/31/97
Cash Assets	844.0	348.0	215.0
Receivables	2954.0	3480.0	3617.0
Other	749.0	888.0	1013.0
Current Assets	4547.0	4716.0	4845.0
Accts Payable	706.0	992.0	895.0
Debt Due	500.0	203.0	196.0
Other	3664.0	3851.0	3874.0
Current Liab.	4870.0	5046.0	4965.0

ANNUAL RATES of change (per sh)	Past 10 Yrs.	Past 5 Yrs.	Est'd '94-'96 to '00-'02
Revenues	16.0%	9.0%	11.5%
"Cash Flow"	15.0%	6.0%	13.0%
Earnings	28.0%	5.5%	15.0%
Dividends	--	8.5%	12.5%
Book Value	19.0%	20.0%	7.0%

Calendar	QUARTERLY REVENUES ($ mill.)[A] Mar.31	Jun.30	Sep.30	Dec.31	Full Year
1994	3221	3309	3407	3401	13338
1995	3561	3706	3862	4136	15265
1996	4491	4565	4685	4753	18494
1997	4883	4975	5110	5187	20155
1998	5370	5470	5620	5710	22170

Calendar	EARNINGS PER SHARE[A B] Mar.31	Jun.30	Sep.30	Dec.31	Full Year
1994	.36	.37	.38	.36	1.47
1995	.36	.38	.11	.41	1.26
1996	.42	.43	.44	.44	1.73
1997	.42	.42	.42	.44	1.70
1998	.47	.49	.49	.50	1.95

Calendar	QUARTERLY DIVIDENDS PAID[C] Mar.31	Jun.30	Sep.30	Dec.31	Full Year
1993	--	.025	--	.025	.05
1994	--	.025	--	.025	.05
1995	--	.025	--	.025	.05
1996	--	.025	--	.025	.05
1997	--	.025			

BUSINESS: MCI Communications Corporation, the second largest long-distance carrier, offers long-distance services domestically and internationally. Primary business is U.S. voice, using MCI's 3,556 million circuit-mile microwave and fiber network. Offers 800, 888, & 900 services, operator assistance, worldwide direct dialing, and fax service. Connected 23,365 billable calls in 1995 vs. 19,411 in 1994. 1996 deprec. rate: 8.9%. Est. plant age: 4 years. Has 55,285 employees, 50,050 stockholders. British Telcom. holds 100% of Class A common stock representing a 20% voting interest. Officers and Directors own less than 1% common shares, Mellon Bank, 5.3% (3/96 proxy). Chrmn.: Bert C. Roberts, Jr. Inc.: DE. Addr.: 1801 Pennsylvania Ave., Washington, D.C. 20006. Tel.: 202-887-2028.

British Telecom's acquisition of MCI appears on schedule to be completed this fall. Last April, both MCI and BT shareholders approved the deal, whereby MCI investors will receive .54 American Depositary Receipt in the combined company, Concert, and $6.00 a share in cash. Concert will pay an annual dividend equal to 90% of BT's 1997 gross payout (see page 794). The European Commission gave its consent, calling for divestiture of certain assets to reduce market influence. Other rulings are pending from the Federal Communications Commission and the Department of Justice in the United States. BT will give MCI the financial wherewithal to aggressively pursue the local sector of the U.S. telecommunications market. MCI will contribute its marketing savvy and substantial customer base to Concert. The two companies have already worked together in a successful partnership in Europe, through which BT gained a 20% stake in MCI. At this juncture, we see no major hurdles to completion of the deal.

Two important international alliances were recently formed. Shortly after our last report on MCI, management announced a lucrative 50/50 joint venture with Telefonica de Espana to provide communications services to the $36 billion Latin American market. MCI will have a fiber-optic link stretching from Alaska to South America, and an oceanic connection to Spain. The companies expect to gain much from the current privatization trend in Latin America. Also in April, MCI and BT made public their plan to form a second alliance with Portugal Telecom. Aside from providing access to the sizable U.S.-Portugal route, the venture will boost MCI's access to the Brazilian market, which accounts for 40% of Latin America's communications revenues. Moreover, as per the alliance, BT and MCI will hold 1% and .5% equity interests, respectively, in Portugal Telecom.

MCI shares are now trading close to an all-time high, but growth-oriented MCI investors might want to wait to cash in their shares until the completion of the acquisition. Concert, which will have considerable clout in the global market, will likely find favor among investors seeking steady dividend income.

David M. Reimer *July 11, 1997*

(A) Fiscal year ended March 31st of following year prior to '85. Excludes Telecom USA prior to '90. (B) Based on fully diluted shares. Excludes extraordinary losses: '88, 2¢; '89, 8¢; '95, 46¢. Excludes special items: '83, d6¢; '84, 5¢; '85, 17¢; '86, d79¢; '89, d5¢; '90, d72¢; '93, 26¢. Next egs. report due late July. (C) Semi-annual div'd. Next div'd meeting about Nov. 3. Goes ex about Nov. 20. Approximate div'd payment dates: June 21 and Dec. 6. (D) In millions, adjusted for stock split. (E) Timeliness rank suspended due to pending acquisition.

Company's Financial Strength	B+
Stock's Price Stability	55
Price Growth Persistence	70
Earnings Predictability	75

Exhibit 6 Excerpts from press release announcing BT/MCI merger dated November 3, 1996

MCI AND BT ANNOUNCE LARGEST INTERNATIONAL MERGER IN HISTORY

Move Creates First Global Communications Company For the 21st Century

WASHINGTON, DC, November 3, 1996 - British Telecommunications plc (BT), the U.K.-based telecom giant, and MCI, the second largest U.S. telecommunications company and the world's third largest international carrier, today announced that they have signed a definitive merger agreement.

The merger combines the substantial financial resources and global position of BT with the growth momentum and competitive market expertise of MCI. The combined company will be headquartered in London and Washington, D.C., and will be called Concert...

The Board of Directors of Concert will comprise fifteen members, eight from BT and seven from MCI. The Board will be jointly chaired by Sir Iain Vallance, the current chairman of BT, and Bert C. Roberts, the current chairman and chief executive officer of MCI. Sir Peter Bonfield will be Concert's chief executive officer. Gerald H. Taylor will be president and chief operating officer of Concert. Messrs. Bonfield and Taylor will comprise the Office of the Chief Executive Officer...

This merger creates the world's first global communications company, with trans-global customers, a multinational management team, dual transatlantic headquarters and shares traded on three stock exchanges globally.

This communications powerhouse will have revenues of over $42 billion, cash flow of $12 billion and 183,000 employees who support 43 million business and residential customers in 72 countries. Based on the most recent fiscal net income of both companies, the combined company would be the sixth most profitable in the world.

The decision to merge MCI and BT follows the investment by BT in 20 percent of MCI in 1993 and the creation of the Concert Communications Services joint venture between the two companies. The joint venture has been touted by industry analysts as having a one-year lead over its competitors in providing global services and solutions to the world's multinational companies. Concert Communications Services has sold more than $1.5 billion in contract revenue, and recently announced that it would break even one full year ahead of original forecasts.

The new merged company will provide an integrated set of local, long distance, and international services including voice, data, wireless, Internet and intranet, information technologies and outsourcing. Under the terms of the agreement, MCI and BT will continue to sell and service customers under their own names in their respective home countries. MCI will continue to aggressively support the opening of the U.S. local telecommunications market.

Sir Iain Vallance, Chairman of BT said: "Concert will be exceptionally well placed to play a leading role in the major growth areas of the changing global communications marketplace. The complementary strengths and skills of BT and MCI will enable Concert to take full advantage of the tremendous opportunities provided by the forthcoming liberalization of telecommunications markets in the U.S. and Europe. We believe this merger will provide major benefits for the shareholders, customers and employees of both BT and MCI."

Bert Roberts, Chairman and CEO of MCI, said: "This merger creates the first telecommunications company of the new century. Financial muscle, global customers and brands, and customer-driven innovation will trump the competition as we open up communications markets both domestically and around the world. Concert's scale will allow it to pursue major opportunities in new markets while maintaining the financial stability that comes from strong core businesses in the developed markets of the U.S. and U.K."...

Significant Benefits to Merger

The merger creates a first-of-its-kind global telecommunications company and is expected to bring major benefits to its customers by providing greater reach, integrated end-to-end services and the combined strength of the two global companies. The merged companies already address the biggest and fastest growth markets in the world, including the local market in both the U.S. and Europe, European and U.S. wireless, global systems integration, Internet/intranet and international services.

For MCI, financial strength and stability are essential as it pursues the U.S. local telecommunications market, opened to competition by the Telecommunications Act of 1996. This market is the largest and most profitable segment of the U.S. market and represents the company's largest opportunity, with annual revenues of nearly $100 billion and EBITDA...of $43 billion. In this market, MCI will benefit from BT's 90-year experience in providing local telecommunications services.

BT's broad range of international relationships around the world will enable Concert to capture an increasing share of the rapidly growing global telecommunications market.

Concert will capitalize on MCI's tremendous growth record. In the last five years, MCI has captured over 40 percent of the growth in the U.S. long distance market. BT will gain access to the North American telecommunications market, which represents 40 percent of the world's international telecommunications traffic. In addition, Concert will take advantage of MCI's expertise and proven success in opening up new markets to competition.

Both companies have significant investments in intelligent networks and information technology. This technology will be shared by the companies and used to develop new services for multinational customers. With this merger, the companies will combine their international networks and expect significant synergies from common technology platforms...

Additional Revenues and Reduced Costs

Immediate opportunities will be created for significant revenue enhancements and savings in operating costs and capital expenditure. The two companies are targeting cumulative synergy benefits arising from a full integration of the two businesses at approximately $2.5 billion within five years following the closing of the merger. Annual pre-tax synergy benefits are estimated at nearly $850 million by the fifth year following the merger. The transaction is expected to use purchase accounting.

Dividends

Dividends will continue to be an important component of shareholder value. BT's dividend policy will not be affected by the merger. BT's directors believe that its earnings and cash flow will continue to be strong enough to support a growing dividend, as adjusted for the effect of the special dividend (valued at $3.6 billion), although the policy will be to grow earnings at a higher level, which would lead to an increase in dividend cover over time. Provided that the merger closes before March 31, 1998, MCI shareholders will receive in full the BT dividend for that year...

Exhibit 7 Excerpts from BT/MCI merger agreement dated November 3, 1996 relating to the material adverse change clause

ARTICLE III

REPRESENTATIONS AND WARRANTIES

3.1. Representations and Warranties of MCI. Except as set forth in the MCI Disclosure Schedule delivered by MCI to BT at or prior to the execution of this Agreement..., MCI represents and warrants to BT as follows:...

(i) Except as disclosed in the MCI SEC Reports filed prior to the date of this Agreement: (A) since December 31, 1995, MCI and its Subsidiaries have conducted their respective businesses in the ordinary course consistent with their past practices and have not incurred any material liability, except in the ordinary course of their respective businesses consistent with their past practices; (B) since December 31, 1995 to the date of this Agreement, there has not been any change in or effect on, or any event or circumstance involving a prospective change in or effect on, the business, financial condition or results of operations of MCI or any of its Subsidiaries, that has had, or would have, a Material Adverse Effect on MCI; and (C) since December 31, 1995, there has not been any change in or effect on, or any event or circumstance involving a prospective change in or effect on, the business, financial condition or results of operations of MCI or any of its Subsidiaries that has had, or is reasonably likely to have, a material adverse effect on the business, operations, assets, liabilities (including, without limitation, contingent liabilities), financial condition or results of operations of MCI and its Subsidiaries, taken as a whole, other than as a result of (1) changes after the date of this Agreement in general economic conditions or the securities markets, and (2) legal or regulatory changes effective after the date of this Agreement affecting the telecommunications industry generally.

(ii) As of the date of this Agreement, no plans or proposals are under consideration by MCI to announce or implement any restructuring or other similar actions by MCI or any of its Subsidiaries which would be reasonably likely to result in material charges or write-offs to the consolidated financial statements of MCI or material reductions in the anticipated consolidated revenues or operating income of MCI...

ARTICLE VI

CONDITIONS PRECEDENT

6.2. Additional Conditions to Obligations of BT and Merger Sub. The obligations of BT and Merger Sub to effect the Merger are subject to the satisfaction of, or waiver by BT, on or prior to the Closing Date of the following additional conditions:

(a) Representations and Warranties. Each of the representations and warranties of MCI set forth in this Agreement that is qualified as to materiality shall have been true and correct when made and shall be true and correct on and as of the Closing Date as if made on and as of such date (other than representations and warranties which address matters only as of a certain date which shall be true and correct as of such certain date), and each of the representations and warranties of MCI that is not so qualified shall have been true and correct in all material respects when made and shall be true and correct in all material respects on and as of the Closing Date as if made on and as of such date (other than representations and warranties which address matters only as of a certain date which shall be true and correct in all material respects as of such certain date), and BT shall have received a certificate of the chief executive officer and the chief financial officer of MCI to such effect.

(b) Performance of Obligations of MCI. MCI shall have performed or complied with all agreements and covenants required to be performed by it under this Agreement at or prior to the Closing Date that are qualified as to materiality and shall have performed or complied in all material respects with all other agreements and covenants required to be performed by it under this Agreement at or prior to the Closing Date that are not so qualified as to materiality, and BT shall have received a certificate of the chief executive officer and the chief financial officer of MCI to such effect…

ARTICLE VII

TERMINATION AND AMENDMENT

7.1. Termination. This Agreement may be terminated at any time prior to the Effective Time, by action taken or authorized by the Board of Directors of the terminating party or parties, whether before or after approval of the matters presented in connection with the Merger by the stockholders of MCI and by the shareholders of BT:…

(g) By BT, upon a breach of any representation, warranty, covenant or agreement on the part of MCI set forth in this Agreement, or if any representation or warranty of MCI shall have become untrue, in either case such that the conditions set forth in Section 6.2(a) or Section 6.2(b) would not be satisfied (a "Terminating MCI Breach"); provided, however, that, if such Terminating MCI Breach is capable of being cured by MCI prior to October 31, 1997 through the exercise of its best efforts and for so long as MCI continues to exercise such best efforts, BT may not terminate this Agreement under this Section 7.1(g);…

ARTICLE VIII

GENERAL PROVISIONS

8.12. Definitions. As used in this Agreement:

(d) "Material Adverse Effect" means, with respect to any entity, any adverse change, circumstance or effect that, individually or in the aggregate with all other adverse changes, circumstances and effects, is or is reasonably likely to be materially adverse to the business, operations, assets, liabilities (including, without limitation, contingent liabilities), financial condition or results of operations of such entity and its Subsidiaries taken as a whole.

Exhibit 8 MCI Press Release on July 9, 1997

MCI Calls for Regulatory Action to Bring the Benefits of Competition To Local Phone Customers; MCI Reports Financial Impact of Local Monopoly Stall Tactics

MCI today called on federal and state regulators to end anti-competitive tactics practiced by the local phone monopolies. These tactics are preventing MCI from fully executing its local strategy and, most importantly, delaying consumer benefits intended by the Telecommunications Act of 1996. As a result, MCI faces higher than expected costs to enter the local market and today outlined the impact of these costs on short-term financial performance.

Consumers Denied Benefits of Competition

"In their efforts to delay local competition, the local monopolies are obstructing the Telecom Act, sabotaging the FCC's objectives and undermining the power of Congress," said Timothy F. Price, MCI's president and chief operating officer. "Regulators must move swiftly to remove the anti-competitive obstacles that are preventing local phone customers from enjoying lower prices, innovative products and better customer service."

MCI cited a wide range of anti-competitive practices by the local monopolies, including delay tactics, disruption of service and disparate treatment of new entrants. Examples include:

> Failing to enter into interconnection agreements, preventing MCI from realizing the revenue potential of its more than $1 billion investment in local facilities. In the 17 months since the enactment of the Telecom Act, the local monopolies have signed interconnection agreements in less than a third of the arbitration proceedings with MCI.

> SBC challenging the constitutionality of the provisions in the Telecom Act requiring the local monopolies to open local markets before they are permitted into in-region long distance.

> Demanding exorbitant non-recurring installation charges for local services and facilities. For example, in New York, NYNEX imposes a $75 installation fee on MCI for a single network element necessary to connect an MCI customer. This cost is $20 higher than NYNEX charges a customer for the entire installation of its local service.

> Failing to have operationally ready electronic support systems on January 1, 1997, as mandated by the FCC. To date, not one of the local monopolies has met this requirement. "We urge regulators to enforce the Telecom Act with specific remedies against continued anti-competitive tactics that violate the law," said Price.

MCI proposed a variety of specific actions to the FCC:

> Urging prompt final action by state regulators on local interconnection agreements.

> Bringing all non-recurring charges to forward-looking costs and ensuring permanent, pro-competitive pricing is in place before local monopoly entry into in-region long distance.

> Setting national performance standards and deadlines for electronic ordering systems and imposing automatic penalties for failure to meet these standards and deadlines.

> Closing the $200 million gap between the access charge reductions filed by the local monopolies and the FCC's $1.7 billion reduction announced in May.

Exhibit 8 (cont)

Impact on MCI Financials

Due to anti-competitive tactics, MCI said local market losses for the year could reach $800 million, more than twice what was originally planned. The bulk of the losses will occur in the second half of the year as MCI's local investments are underutilized. MCI said 1998 losses in its local business could exceed the levels incurred in 1997.

Ongoing competition in MCI's core business continues to intensify with pricing trends continuing to decline. Furthermore, MCI is experiencing negative impacts on its core business due to re-deployment of marketing, operations, and product development resources from the core business to local. To the extent that state and federal regulators fail to act aggressively to open local markets to competition, MCI could experience negative impact on core revenue growth and declining profits in 1998. However, MCI remains optimistic that effective regulatory leadership can de-monopolize the local markets and fulfill the promise of the 1996 Telecom Act.

Nonetheless, MCI expects Q2 1997 earnings to be in line with analyst expectations. As a result of the developments described above, MCI expects earnings for the remainder of 1997 and 1998 to be lower than current market expectations.

The company is also exploring a series of steps to improve financial performance. While these decisions have not been finalized, if taken, they could result in material charges to MCI's 1997 results of operations.

"For 1998, swift regulatory action at the state and federal level could make a major difference in MCI's results," said Price. "The local market remains MCI's number one strategic objective. This is not only because the economics are compelling, but because customers are demanding freedom of choice."

"MCI leads the market in meeting fast-growing customer demand for integrated communications solutions, but won't achieve the full potential of this position until we can offer local service to our customers on a national basis," said Price.

MCI, headquartered in Washington, D.C., provides a full range of integrated communication services to more than 20 million customers. On November 3, 1996, MCI announced a definitive agreement to merge with BT to form Concert, the world's first global communications company.

Source: MCI Communications Corporation

Farallon Capital Management: Risk Arbitrage (A)   299-020

Exhibit 9   Excerpts from July 11, 1997 news article relating to MCI's disclosure of local losses

BT, MCI SHARES FALL AFTER FORECAST OF LOCAL LOSSES

Shares of British Telecommunications Plc and MCI Communications Corp. plunged after MCI surprised investors by saying that it expects local phone losses of $ 800 million, or double its forecasts, threatening the companies' $ 25 billion combination.

BT's American depositary receipts fell 5 1/4, or 6.4 percent, to 76 5/16, the largest one-day drop since Oct. 26, 1989. MCI shares fell 7 3/8 to 35, a 17 percent drop and the biggest since November 1990. The declines lopped about $ 8 billion off the companies' combined market value.

MCI's warning prompted concern that BT may renegotiate its purchase of the No. 2 U.S. long-distance provider. While the acquisition was designed to give the combined company a boost in the local phone market, investors were startled by how much the price to do that had gone up.

"This came as a bolt out of the blue," said John Hatherly, head of research at U.K.-based M&G Ltd., which owns 1 percent of BT stock.

BT said it learned yesterday of MCI's loss in its local operations and the prospect for lower earnings next year. "We were disappointed," said Ted Graham, a BT spokesman.

MCI declined to say if the forecast will mean a change in terms of the sale.
……………..

"I would appreciate a renegotiation because what I'm buying appears to be worth less—but I don't expect it," said Alex Crooke, fund manager at Henderson Investors, who owns 3.5 million pounds ($ 5.9 million) of BT stock. He said he isn't planning to sell the shares at such a low price.

While MCI's second-quarter earnings are likely to meet analysts' expectations, results for the second half of 1997 and 1998 will be lower than estimates, MCI said. Profit could also decline in 1998.
…………….

The new forecast underscores the high cost of tackling the Bells to enter local markets, even 18 months after sweeping telecommunications deregulation designed to promote competition in the local phone business.

Renegotiation?

If the terms of the acquisition were changed, some believe the companies would have to seek shareholder approval again. The acquisition has already gotten approval from both companies' shareholders and certain regulators. It still needs approval from the U.S. Federal Communications Commission.

"There's no way on Earth they'll renegotiate these terms," said Jeff Heil, a director at Society Asset Management Inc., which owns 1.34 million MCI shares, according to recent filings. "There'd be such an uproar from MCI shareholders that the deal would fall through."

There's a $ 150 million termination fee if the companies don't complete the sale.

Investors aren't as sure the acquisition will be completed. The difference between the value the offer and MCI's actual share price jumped to more than 24 percent today from about 15 percent yesterday.

"It's not as safe as it was," said arbitrager Ben Hoyer of Palestra Capital.

Exhibit 9 (Cont.)

Investors and analysts said they were surprised that BT was caught off balance by MCI's announcement. They cited BT's three seats on MCI's board as well as BT's 20 percent ownership in MCI.

In addition, they said the two management teams have been working closely. At a recent MCI analyst conference in New York, top-level BT executives spoke about how BT was using successful MCI marketing campaigns in the U.K.

"BT has people on MCI's board. They're actively involved in the running of the company," Heil said. "I'd be very surprised if this was a real big unknown to them."

The news for MCI comes at a particularly tough time, analysts said, as its long-distance growth is slowing and its spending billions of dollars to get into new markets.

Instead of concentrating on completing its sale to BT and fighting new competitors in its core long-distance business, MCI management is engulfed in legal and regulatory battles to enter the U.S. local market, analysts said.

Source: Bloomberg News

Exhibit 10 Daily stock price history of British Telecom ADR and MCI Telecommunications Common from January 2, 1996 to August 1, 1997

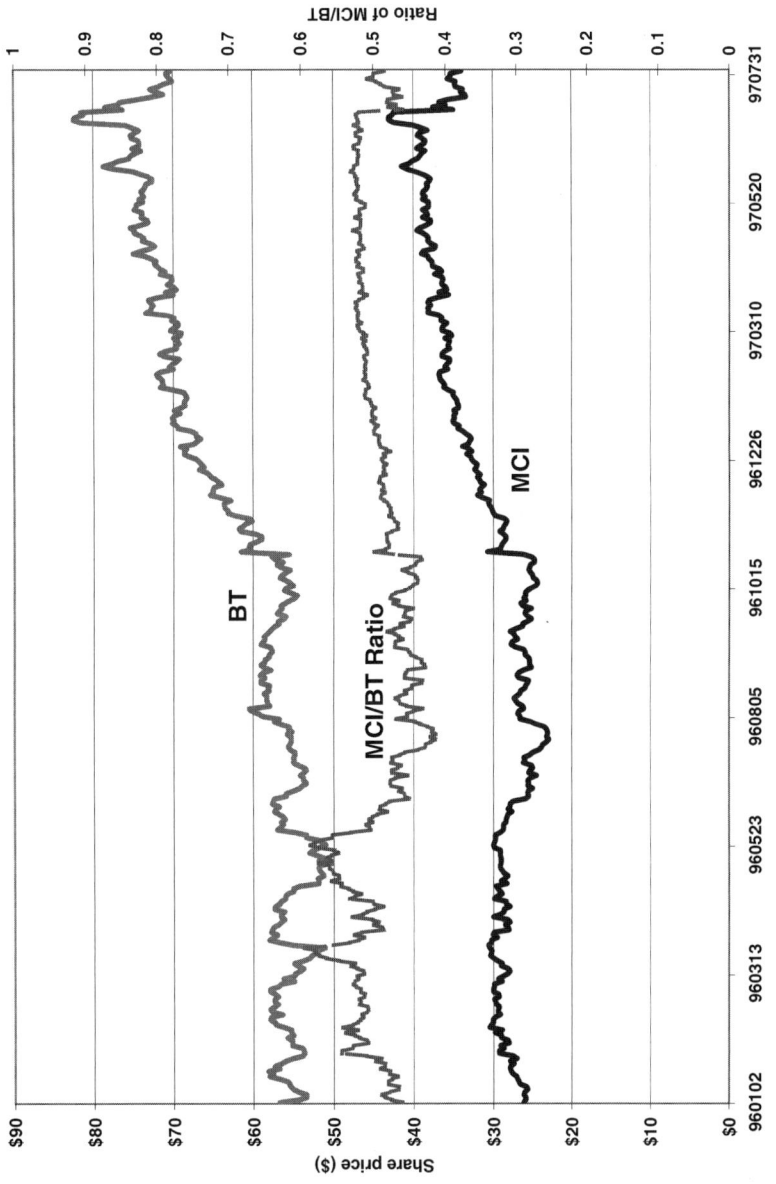

Source: Bloomberg

Exhibit 11 Summary terms of the British Telecom acquisition of MCI Communications

Date:	November 3, 1996
Acquirer:	British Telecommunications plc
Target:	MCI Communications
Consideration:	0.54 BT ADRs (1 ADR = 10 ordinary shares) and $6 in cash for each MCI share
Special Terms:	BT shareholders will receive a special dividend of 35 pence per ordinary share prior to the closing of the merger. Following the merger, BT will cut its dividend (estimated at around 10%) and may repurchase up to 10% of its common shares.

Exhibit 12 Capital markets information on November 4, 1996 and August 1, 1997

	November 4, 1996	August 1, 1997
U.S. Treasury securities:		
3 month	5.131%	5.267%
1 year	5.423%	5.494%
5 year	6.080%	6.070%
Approximate rebate on BT shares (£ 3-month LIBOR – 200 bps)	4.313%	5.133%
BT stock price at close of market	$61.625	$70.3125
MCI stock price at close of market	$30.75	$34.00
$/£ Exchange Rate	$1.6442/£	$1.6314/£

Source: Bloomberg; Farallon Capital

Farallon Capital Management: Risk Arbitrage (A) 299-020

Exhibit 13 Large holders of MCI stock over six quarters ending June 30, 1997 (number of shares)

	3/31/96	6/30/96	9/30/96	12/31/96	3/31/97	6/30/97
Hedge Funds						
Soros Fund Management				62,500	6,007,800	13,273,100
Baker Nye				372,597	1,238,706	1,979,206
Jeffrey N. Greenblatt				771,403	1,823,194	1,948,194
Halcyon/Slifka Mgmt. Co.					324,100	1,046,200
Angelo Gordon & Co.				451,500	646,500	670,000
AAL Capital Mgmt. Corp.	200,000	319,000	319,000	394,000	396,900	516,500
Harvest Management Inc.				80,000	78,530	344,030
J. Ezra Merkin					301,561	256,200
Leon G. Cooperman		899,700		510,000	693,500	
Active Managers						
Fidelity Investments	6,532,275	5,583,275	10,487,475	36,370,495	44,058,995	35,836,804
The Capital Group	24,768,800	24,586,700	25,485,500	27,145,500	26,532,800	15,853,500
Putnam Investments	9,974,051	8,013,348	22,019,173	12,774,434	12,665,992	12,660,336
Sanford Bernstein	13,863,359	14,093,827	14,185,373	14,032,473	10,216,587	8,524,605
Lord Abbett & Company	9,203,656	9,666,150	8,130,725	6,416,375	6,143,217	4,779,665
Harvard College	330,710	348,000	354,700	811,410	2,160,600	2,873,400
SIT Investment Assocs.	1,441,900	1,097,000		1,071,600	1,388,000	1,263,500
John A. Levin & Co. Inc.		500,000	500,000	1,110,100	1,059,800	1,204,200
Westchester Capital Mgmt.				657,100	799,574	907,074
Legg Mason	878,765	900,095	1,019,766	1,040,541	1,108,008	822,650
Thompson, Siegel & Walmsley			18,250	1,369,490	714,040	687,540
T. Rowe Price Associates	2,122,306	385,106	397,706	529,106	573,710	627,413
Sound Shore Mgmt. Inc.			742,000	1,749,000	1,861,500	563,600
Wellington Management	5,076,065	6,029,265	6,744,925	1,887,295	1,120,400	376,115
Fund Asset Mgmt. Inc.	910,608	819,541	1,177,479	943,267	337,188	353,455
Invista Capital Mgmt. Inc.	4,053,714	4,836,122	5,237,040	5,089,011	2,513,098	297,270
Investment Counselors/MD	2,011,029	1,990,229	2,082,529	1,740,929	1,370,749	213,029
RCM Capital Management	2,491,850	2,462,000	3,582,550	3,225,250	66,750	68,400
PIMCO Advisors L.P.	8,911,936	7,742,500	7,567,705	280,805	97,705	26,677
Jennison Assoc Capital	9,927,350	9,116,350	2,774,050	1,311,250	1,462,650	
Passive Managers						
Barclays Bank	17,268,110	16,896,408	16,848,540	17,214,547	16,716,302	16,946,726
J P Morgan & Co. Inc.	14,707,525	15,591,685	17,288,031	17,524,348	16,792,687	14,695,236
Bankers Trust NY Corp	11,163,411	10,934,109	10,819,111	11,461,456	10,716,973	11,030,671
State Street Corp.	6,247,611	6,041,347	7,309,384	6,600,701	6,699,843	6,617,876
Vanguard Group					6,246,723	6,566,874
Mellon Bank Corporation	10,513,714	11,435,766	12,282,365	10,518,764	6,519,870	6,435,967
National Westminster Bank	948,604	821,093		1,081,996	1,367,680	3,602,653

Note: Excludes Farallon Capital. Excludes investment banks since they are not required to file 13(f)s. Excludes investors that use synthetic strategies, such as equity swaps. Cells are left blank if investment fund did not report a position at end of indicated quarter.

Source: CDA/SPECTRUM, Institutional 13(f) Common Stock Holdings & Transactions

 **Harvard Business School**

9-295-094
Rev. May 27, 1997

Syscom Computers

In January 1994, Jane Watson settled into her chair in her new office overlooking San Francisco Bay. With the new year came her first chance to catch her breath since Syscom Computers had hired her to be their new CFO. At the top of her to-do list was addressing the Board's concerns about Syscom's foreign exchange (FX) risk management. After her first Board meeting ended, a senior Board member pulled her aside to say: "Our business is to make world class information solutions for our customers. We should not be doing fancy financial deals. Let's keep it simple and stay out of the headlines."

Given her experience with the complexities of FX management, Watson shared some of the Board's concerns about risk management practices at Syscom. One of the sales subsidiaries, Far Eastern Sales, was trading currency derivatives in large volume, and potentially mixing speculation with hedging. Other divisional and corporate exposures were managed centrally at the corporate office.

To date, Syscom had not had any major problems with its use of derivatives. However, several prominent companies had announced large losses from derivatives, generating widespread concern about devising mechanisms for corporate control. Furthermore, an influential study[1] by an international financial institution (the Group of Thirty), made explicit recommendations for risk managers on topics such as the management of credit exposure, the independence and authority of risk management operations, and the use of appropriate personnel and information systems for risk management activities. In light of these changes, Watson believed the Board was wise to be concerned about the company's risk management processes.

Watson was also aware that the board's concerns were sparked by internal developments. Watson's predecessor, Joe Thursgood, had asked a major investment bank, Swiss Bank Corp., to evaluate Syscom's risk management practices. Its report had argued for extensive changes. Watson knew that a comprehensive response from her office was expected, and that she would need to pay particular attention to several issues: the persons who had control and decision making authority over hedging policies and their execution; the means by which speculation would be defined and detected; and the systems used in collecting and aggregating information about business and financial exposures. As her gaze shifted from her window to the reports on her desk, she wondered

---

[1] *Derivatives: Practices and Principles,* Group of Thirty, Global Derivatives Study Group, July 1993.

Research Associate Christopher L. Marshall prepared this case under the guidance of Professor Kenneth A. Froot and Professor Peter Tufano with the help of several individuals affiliated with Swiss Bank Corp. including Katie Updike, Marty Reiner, Jim McNulty, and Dave Weinberger. The case is to be used as the basis for class discussion rather than to illustrate either effective or ineffective handling of an administrative situation.

Copyright © 1995 by the President and Fellows of Harvard College. To order copies or request permission to reproduce materials, call 1-800-545-7685, write Harvard Business School Publishing, Boston, MA 02163, or go to http://www.hbsp.harvard.edu. No part of this publication may be reproduced, stored in a retrieval system, used in a spreadsheet, or transmitted in any form or by any means—electronic, mechanical, photocopying, recording, or otherwise—without the permission of Harvard Business School.

whether Syscom had taken the right approach to risk management, and whether the firm's dedicated systems and operations were doing what they were supposed to do.

History of Syscom Computers, Inc.

In early 1980, two engineers from Hewlett-Packard, Dave Baxter and Bob Ransome, met for lunch at an Oakland coffee shop. They sketched out what would be their new firm's first product—an early workstation for engineering design and development. Shipped just a year later, the Syscom PRISM was a huge success, and quickly set the benchmark for competition in the industry. Ransome left in 1987 to teach engineering in his native England, and Baxter became the firm's acknowledged leader and CEO. In just five years, Syscom became a Fortune 500 company, reaching a sales figure of over $2.5 billion in 1990 (see **Exhibits 1** and **2**). By 1994, Syscom employed nearly 8,000 people and marketed systems in over 30 countries. International sales had enjoyed remarkable growth since 1985, when Syscom began marketing its products in the United Kingdom, France, and Germany, increasing fivefold from 1987 to 1990. The company entered the Asian market in 1988, acquiring a major stake in a successful Japanese company that specialized in selling U.S. computer systems. This acquisition, which became Syscom's Far Eastern Sales division, had spearheaded much of the firm's recent growth.

Syscom's strategy was based on its technological leadership. The challenge was to develop systems of very high quality that would become industry standards. This approach had produced consistently successful products, allowing Syscom to charge a premium price for its products. In 1993, Syscom had received 13 industry product awards, including several for its new file servers. Syscom believed that the new servers would consolidate the firm's leadership in high performance systems. But because the technology was developing rapidly, the pace of change gave no respite even to industry leaders, Syscom, Compaq, Sun, IBM, DEC, and Hewlett-Packard. A number of other U.S. and Japanese firms were also hard on their heels.

Syscom's products were sold mainly to large and medium-sized engineering and design businesses. However, earnings in the industry were increasingly volatile, as the intensively competitive market for workstations forced shorter product cycles. Syscom was also sensitive to macroeconomic conditions, since networks of workstations were significant capital investments and could easily be postponed.

Organization and Control at Syscom

Syscom had five major divisions (see **Exhibit 3**): **Manufacturing**, based in California; **North American Sales,** located with the corporate offices near San Francisco's Candlestick Park; **European Sales** and the **R&D** division, both based in the United Kingdom; and **Far Eastern Sales,** based in Japan.

Syscom had a tradition of allowing the regional divisions to make their own decisions. As Dave Baxter explained, Syscom's rapid growth had been generated in part by its emphasis on hiring very smart people who were also willing to make and act on their own decisions:

> In a dynamic business like this no one has all the answers: what you need are managers who are very bright and very flexible, able to react intelligently to the problems that come their way. The product cycle for our products is very short; six months is a long time in this industry. We have to delegate a lot of control to the

local divisions to allow them the flexibility to adapt to the changing realities of their marketplaces.

Distributing control to the operating divisions meant that Syscom's corporate staff worked hard to monitor divisional activities, making extensive use of their own computer technology to do so. Baxter went on:

> The ability to monitor heartbeat, blood pressure, and fifty other measures of the business is absolutely critical. 95% is normal rhythm and we ignore it, but every now and then you'll see a crisis. Constant watching prevents major expensive events. Yet computers can make your life very complicated very quickly. I call this "the illusion of management by spreadsheet." A manager comes in with this immensely complicated spreadsheet and twenty full-color graphs. It all looks under control. But if you ask five tough questions about what's going on, then you find out whether the manager is on top of what's going on or is basically confused. Very few people will be between the two extremes.

Manufacturing at Syscom

Workstations were assembled at Syscom's sprawling 750,000 square foot state-of-the-art facility near Oakland, California. Thousands of different components and subassemblies were built in-house or purchased from suppliers, most of them American. In 1993, these suppliers accounted for 78% of all purchases. Increasingly, however, a number of components were being purchased from suppliers outside the United States: memory chips from Japan; and most circuit boards from Singapore. In line with Syscom's stress on total quality management in product development, Syscom's Oakland factory used an advanced system to keep its inventories at almost half the level of many of its competitors. Purchase orders for critical supplies covered two to three months of the firm's requirements.

Although the Oakland factory was less than a year old, it was already at full capacity in the face of unexpectedly high demand for the file servers. As a consequence, Syscom was considering the acquisition of an assembly and packaging facility in the Philippines from a Japanese corporation. Locating a facility in the Philippines was attractive because Syscom's 1993 labor costs were nearly $1 billion, higher than many of its competitors (at about 32% of total costs of goods sold), and Filipino labor costs were low. Syscom expected to pay as much as ¥20 billion for the facility.

Manufacturing was treated as a cost center. Although its labor and most raw material costs were predominantly dollar denominated, the divisional Controller was concerned about the impact of exchange-rate fluctuations on foreign sourcing costs, especially as these were becoming a larger part of the firm's cost of goods sold. Such concerns would only intensify if, as seemed likely, the proposed acquisition of a Filipino plant were to proceed. Like the European and North American Sales divisions, all of the Manufacturing's divisions FX exposures were handled by the corporate office.

Research and Development

Syscom's success relied heavily on a stream of new products from the firm's R&D facility outside Cambridge, England. Drawing on a pool of highly trained, but relatively inexpensive, computer scientists and engineers, the firm had created a research center that analysts believed was Syscom's crown jewel. Baxter justified the strategic plans that called for large and consistent R&D spending over the next five years:

> Clearly, with 35% gross margins, some big profits are possible if you win the technology war. Our estimate is that over 8% of 1994 revenues will be spent on R&D.

This seems high, but it's an essential expenditure. Scrimping on R&D in this business destroys long-run profitability. Winners and losers are determined by very small differences in relative position.

North American and International Sales

The company sold extensively abroad, and as a consequence, was sensitive to fluctuations in FX rates. Typically, three to four months passed between initial price commitment, invoicing, and ultimate receipt of funds. Syscom was also subject to competitive economic FX risks. Several small companies had begun producing low cost clones of Syscom's systems in Asia and South America, and they had targeted specific high growth international markets. In addition, Syscom's U.S. and Japanese competitors were increasingly producing and assembling their products in low-cost countries.

Syscom's sales divisions purchased from the Manufacturing division in dollars. Sales divisions' SG&A expenses were paid in the subsidiary's local currency. Each of the divisions faced its own distinct exposures.

European Sales shared office space in the United Kingdom with the R&D labs. While the European division had been the dominant source of sales growth in the past, its growth had been eclipsed by that of the Far Eastern division. Hedging was generally perceived by divisional executives as unnecessary. In the words of the division Controller:

> We are not interested in hedging our downside because that would also mean limiting our upside. We might make a little money this year on a strengthening D-Mark but lose it next year on the French Franc. We can't predict these things and should not kid ourselves that we can. If corporate wants to do this stuff they can have our numbers. But then it's their responsibility, and not ours.

European Sales had outlays in British pounds and U.S. dollars, and received most of the major European currencies. National sales managers wrote reports describing expected sales, then passed them to the U.K. office, frequently adjusted the estimates in light of its experiences with individual managers. Final estimates were passed to the corporate planning group to adjust divisional sales targets. Booked sales and expenses were entered into the European component of Syscom's general ledger (called the Integrated Financial System, or IFS) and downloaded monthly to the corporate office.

North American Sales shared offices with Syscom's corporate headquarters in San Francisco. Like European Sales, the division's competitors were predominantly U.S. distributors who outsourced much of their manufacturing overseas. This division had outlays in U.S. dollars and received U.S. and Canadian dollars. Booked sales and expenses were entered into IFS on a weekly basis. The division produced fairly accurate estimates of future North American sales, which it would pass on to the corporate office for consolidated revenue forecasts.

Far Eastern Sales was headquartered in Osaka, Japan. Far Eastern Sales had outlays in Japanese yen and U.S. dollars and received mainly yen as well as several other Asian currencies. Unlike the other sales subsidiaries, the Far Eastern subsidiary was only partly owned by Syscom, which had made a majority acquisition in 1988 of the small, but highly successful, Nichibei Computer Company, specializing in foreign computer distribution and sales. A little over a third of the subsidiary's equity was still owned by the subsidiary's original owners, Nichibei Corp. Pressure exerted by Nichibei made Far Eastern sales the most autonomous of the sales divisions.

Syscom Computers 295-094

The Finance Group at Syscom

As Syscom's CFO, Watson was responsible for financial and cost accounting, planning, budgeting, and compensation. Each function was complex in its own right, made more so by its linkages to the others. The previous CFO, Joe Thursgood,[2] experienced these complexities first hand when he tried to introduce a pay-for-performance program for Syscom's divisions. While the North American Sales division had been supportive, the International divisions (especially the European Sales division) had objected strenuously to the plan.

Financial and cost accounting The company's internally developed accounting system was originally built because ledger and journal systems that could run on Syscom's own hardware were unavailable. Although beginning to show its age, IFS remained central to North American accounting activities, providing materials planning, procurement, sales, order entry and processing, as well as some basic corporate accounting applications. Field Sales personnel in North America and Europe entered booked dealer orders into IFS weekly, while divisional accounting managers keyed booked expenses into IFS at irregular intervals. The Far Eastern division had a completely separate accounting system (called JIFS) that allowed local managers to enter both booked and contingent transactions. JIFS was loosely based on a package in use before Syscom acquired the subsidiary in 1988.

Planning and forecasting Syscom's formal financial forecasts extended out one year. Subsidiary managers were evaluated according to financial measures of their unit's business performance. Divisions independently developed and presented their numbers to headquarters. Monthly demand forecasts were made by the national field sales managers, based on the current sales levels as well as the ongoing changes in the firm's product line.[3] These forecasts were then analyzed, and in some cases adjusted by the divisional Controller. The Manufacturing division produced unit cost estimates. Sales and cost forecasts were consolidated at the corporate office (see **Exhibit 4**) and used to inform Syscom's strategic plan. This plan was in turn used as the basis for the following year's capital and operating budgets. In addition to this formal divisional planning and forecasting exercise, Syscom's corporate management built annually a strategic plan extending out three years.

Resource allocation and budgeting A budget committee, comprised of the senior divisional financial officers and chaired by the Corporate Controller, prepared new budgets annually in the light of changes to the strategic plan. The committee developed operating budgets and allocated resources to the three sales divisions according to the expected impact on the company's long-term dollar net income. To this end, the committee produced what it believed to be tough but feasible dollar net income targets for each of the sales divisions. At the senior divisional level, these dollar budgets would be converted into the local currency using the current forward exchange rates (see **Exhibit 5** for forward and spot exchange rates; see **Exhibit 6** for correlations among exchange rates). The Manufacturing division was a cost center, judged according to its ability to keep costs below budgeted dollar targets. The U.K.-based R&D group had costs that were primarily fixed in British pounds.

The capital budgeting process required the Corporate Controller to prepare proposals for project spending and appropriations every six months. These proposals served to update and validate Syscom's strategic plan. The budget committee would make its decisions and dictate expenditure allotments. The Finance group would then take responsibility for securing the necessary funding. For Syscom, this generally meant drawing on internal cash funds and specific lines of credit. If funds ran low, capital budgets could get very tight.

---

[2] Thursgood left Syscom after a mild heart attack prompted early retirement.

[3] Some of the forecasts were better than others. The North American Sales division had the most mature markets and the most reliable numbers, while the European Sales division's forecasts were often off target.

Compensation Divisional managers were compensated by salary plus a loosely-determined performance bonus. Performance targets were typically denominated in U.S. dollars. Thursgood, had struggled to introduce more objective pay-for-performance targets, but these efforts had largely floundered because it was difficult to develop and stick by target measures for very different markets. The European division CFO had argued persuasively against rigid targets. As a result, the current system allowed for extensive discretion in setting the compensation levels for divisional management. By contrast, the Far Eastern division had argued for—and received—strictly determined performance pay: its managers were evaluated according to the division's net income relative to target.

Risk Management at Syscom

Syscom's 1993 annual report described its rationale for FX hedging: "The purpose of the corporate hedging program is to protect Syscom from the risk that the anticipated dollar net income will be adversely affected by changes in the foreign currency exchange rates."

Because divisions were held to dollar budget targets, most of the FX risks lay with the sales subsidiaries. Thursgood had originally handed over the hedging decision to the sales subsidiaries themselves. In keeping with Syscom's commitment to distributed decision making, he argued that "the subs were closest to the business exposures so they should manage the risks." In some cases, the subsidiaries were able to adjust their product prices, passing the price changes on to potential future customers. Sometimes competition limited the amount of transaction exposure that could be shifted in this way. This situation varied country by country.

As time went by, the problems of controlling this distributed approach to risk management became increasingly apparent to Thursgood. Two years earlier, he had begun efforts to centralize the risk management function. Although most divisions off-loaded their exposures to the corporate office for hedging, Far Eastern Sales continued to manage its own risks. Part of the problem, as Watson knew, was the fact that hedging was deeply embedded in many other financial processes within the firm (see **Exhibit 7**). Strategy, budgeting, and the day-to-day accounting process were all connected with risk management policies. Traders would hedge against budgeted net income targets derived from the corporate planning process. These targets comprised both booked transactions, which were downloaded from the IFS general ledger, and expected transactions, which emerged from the forecasting process. Both booked and expected transactions were hedged completely.

Risk Management at the Far Eastern Division

Unlike the other divisions, Far Eastern Sales was a heavy user of risk management techniques, thanks to the efforts of one man, Sam Cheng, an MIT-trained engineer. Cheng managed the division's significant FX exposures; he also worked closely with the sales organization to give them a strategic edge on the pricing of major product deals. During 1993, Cheng was involved in sales to the Australian Revenue Service totaling A$35 million, Syscom's largest single corporate sale. Not only did Cheng succeed in fixing the Australian dollar purchase price during the nine-month bidding process, he also finished with a A$2.3 million net gain on the position. Cheng was currently advising Corporate Risk Management about a longer term strategic hedge on the possible acquisition of the Filipino factory, with the blessings of his boss, Chen Fujita, the Far Eastern division's Treasurer. Fujita had pointed out that the appreciating yen would increase the chance that Syscom's most formidable Japanese competitor would enter the acquisition contest.

Most of the hedging was performed by Takuma Ohmae, who had taken over most of the operational trading once Sam began managing the division's larger strategic hedges. Ohmae and two other traders aimed to hedge all divisional FX cash flows, both booked and projected, using a variety of exchange-traded and over-the-counter FX instruments, in order to limit the volatility of the division's estimated dollar-denominated net income up to one year out. Describing the group's operating strategy, Ohmae noted:

> Our job is mainly to immunize divisional profits from adverse foreign exchange fluctuations, particularly a fall in the yen against the dollar. Many of the other currencies we receive, such as the Hong Kong dollar, are formally linked to the U.S. dollar. Our strategy on hedging the $/¥ exposures is to use either currency forwards or the options markets. If we feel confident about our opinions on the market then we will use forwards or FX swaps. If we are less certain, then we will use options.

The hedging group had also been trading currencies on a complex model of interest rate and FX fluctuations that Cheng had developed. The reported results were impressive, showing significant profits. The group was attempting to have its trading limits increased.

Gathering exposure information Far Eastern divisional exposures were stored in a commercial front-office database package running on a file server, and were updated weekly by Jiro Kamuki, the most junior of the trading group. There were several sources for these data (see **Exhibit 8**): booked sales and expenses were read every week from the on-line JIFS system and typed in by Kamuki, revenue and cost projections were obtained from monthly reports produced by the divisional accounting office, while changes to the division's capital budget were communicated to the trading group by hard copy quarterly.

Trading Cheng and Ohmae were the only traders authorized to commit the division to one of the division's five preapproved counterparties. They obtained quotes from counterparties on potential deals. If possible, the traders would try to mix the counterparties to prevent any undue concentration of credit risks. All trades were entered into the front-office package, which, at close of trading, would download details of the trades to the back office. The front-office system also generated a real time profit-and-loss statement (P&L) based on the current market value of positions.

Measuring market and credit risks Portfolios were valued at market levels on a daily basis. Values of the hedge ratio (delta) were also calculated for the entire portfolio. The group's trading strategy called for delta-neutral hedges, i.e., hedges which fully offset the underlying currency exposures.[4] Occasionally, however, market conditions led traders to deviate from this policy. Cheng's group often ran simulations for one another, in an effort to assess the portfolio impact of abnormally large swings and periods of prolonged inactivity. In order to manage the division's credit risks, the current market value of all the group's derivative positions was calculated monthly. Every year, the group's traders would hold a meeting with senior financial staff in the division to set credit limits for each of the pre-approved counterparties. The current exposure for each firm was compared against its credit limit on a weekly basis by the divisional accounting staff. To further mitigate credit exposures, the group had also begun to use a standard multiproduct master agreement[5] with close-out netting provisions for all its transactions with a specific counterparty.

Back office Clearance and settlement of the group's trades were managed within the divisional accounting group using a commercial back-office system. The system recorded confirmations, counterparty payments and receipts, and expiration dates, and it confirmed the daily portfolio P&L. Journal entries for the JIFS system and transaction reports for traders and division management were produced by the system, but had to be transferred manually. There was a weekly reconciliation

---

[4] The delta of an FX portfolio describes the extent to which the value of the portfolio changes with increases in specific exchange rates.

[5] A master agreement between financial counterparties provides comprehensive documentation of standard terms and conditions covering all transactions.

between the back- and front-office systems. The back office system ran on an accounting group workstation and, like all the data on the local network servers, was backed up three times a week.

Responsibility for verifying the hedging group's compliance with the market and credit limits rested with a member of the divisional accounting staff. The same person was also responsible for ensuring the subsidiary's compliance with external laws and regulations. Occasionally, the divisional accounting staff would review the strategies and models used by the trading group (the last review was in 1992).

Organizational control and compliance   Divisional reports were almost entirely the responsibility of the back-office staff. Weekly position reports went to Fujita and to corporate risk management. Fujita also received a reconciled weekly P&L.

Ostensibly organized as a cost center, the trading group had nonetheless also enjoyed a four-year run of positive earnings. Their success in the market earned the group superior compensation (a fact that caused some irritation within the corporate risk management group). Fujita justified these arrangements, arguing that "at least in his division, people are paid for what they contribute to Syscom's bottom line."

Corporate Risk Management

The corporate office received dollars from its subsidiaries and paid dollars for local corporate expenses. The corporate FX group tracked both booked and expected (not-yet-booked) transactions (see **Exhibits 9** and **10**). To do this they would use total estimated revenues, obtained monthly from the corporate planning group, together with booked exposures in the IFS and JIFS systems. Other exposures tracked by the group included some expected yen exposures from manufacturing costs, the net exposures from the Japanese division, and a few strategic hedges.

The group's traders, Doug Hammers, David Winters, and their supervisor Frank Krugman, were recruited two years earlier from the procurement group, and, from scratch, they developed the corporate hedging program. On being asked the differences between the hedging at corporate and what went on in Cheng's group, Krugman commented:

> Generally, you could say that we try to use derivatives to smooth the earnings of the organization. From what I hear, Cheng is given more freedom to manage the operating exposures. He is also given more resources than we are. Apart from myself, only Doug is authorized to trade, while David is slowly getting up to speed with the hedging process. It takes time to set a risk management group up, and without sufficient resources, you have to make some compromises. One compromise is that we don't do all the trades that we might. We try to keep it simple, largely because we have to.

Krugman, Winters, and Hammers formed a close-knit group, doing everything from data entry to trading, modeling, confirmations and even on occasion helping with the clearing and settlement of their transactions.

Gathering exposure information   Every month, the Manufacturing division would e-mail Winters an updated list of expected purchases from foreign suppliers. The Japanese hedging group sent net positions every week, which were entered manually into the exposures spreadsheet. The divisions passed their new estimates to the group via Corporate Planning every month. Booked transactions were downloaded from IFS every week. Exposures were stored in an exposures and posititions spreadsheet, updated weekly by Winters, the most junior of the three-man trading group. Winters was responsible for managing the exposure data. Winters confided that the task took about two days a week of his time:

> I am run ragged getting information from the divisions, checking up on their exposures to see if they make sense. That said, it has been a lot better since we hooked up the position table directly to IFS. Before, there could be errors in the data entry, usually at the division, and tracking down those errors was tricky. The divisions don't seem to realize that there is real money riding on these numbers. Sometimes the numbers are late. Sometimes they don't come at all, and we have to start calling people up. The U.K. guys are the worst at this.

Once the exposure data had been entered, another part of the same spreadsheet, the Positions table, was updated. Positions contained information about the divisional exposures as well as the forward and options positions held to mitigate those exposures.

Trading Doug Hammers did most of the corporate trading, using primarily FX forwards and futures contracts as hedges. Swiss Bank Corp. was a major counterparty, accounting for well over $2 billion of traded notional value. Hammers entered trades into the trades spreadsheet, which, after counterparties faxed their confirmations, was used to update the exposures and positions spreadsheet.

The traders estimated the current P&L based on prices read off the computer screens supplied by various data services. A more precise front-office P&L was also calculated from the exposures and positions spreadsheet at the daily close of market, using prices read from the market monitor screens in the trading room. An oversight group that was composed of Krugman, Hammers, the Corporate Treasurer, the CFO, and several other senior officers from the accounting and finance groups met every three months or so to determine position limits. The Corporate Treasurer had to formally authorize every transaction over $10 million.

Measuring market and credit risks Corporate exposures were defined as the dollar impact of an increase in the value of a given currency (against the dollar) on an account. The risk management group reported only the netted positions and portfolio values using the market prices. Credit risks were managed by using counterparties rated AA or higher.

Back office Two junior staff members in the accounting group managed clearance and settlement of the group's trades. Jim Monty, an accountant who was friendly with Krugman, was charged with checking compliance and reconciliation with the trading group. Once the hedge transactions had cleared, accounting staff manually keyed them into the IFS General Ledger.

Organizational control and compliance The group produced a variety of management reports describing their trading operations. A printout of the trade report was posted in the trading room at the close of trading each day. The report used data culled from the TRADES spreadsheet. A weekly position report (from the POSITIONS table—see **Exhibit 10**) went to Krugman's boss, Phil McIntyre (and eventually to his boss, the CFO). Copies also went to the Accounting group. Every week, the CFO and the Treasurer received a copy of the reconciled weekly P&L and positions reports generated from the back office. The increased demand for information about hedging and exposures was beginning to cause problems for the group and its systems, Krugman admitted:

> I spend nearly three days a month producing reports for everyone from the Board down. Perhaps a couple of days confirming exposures with the subs and getting authorizations. Add to that a couple of days sorting out clearing problems, and you see how little time I spend actually watching the market.

Mandates for Change

Some months before Joe Thursgood left, he set up an internal task force to review risk management at Syscom. The task force's report argued for building a bottom-up approach to risk management:

> Since the divisions are judged on dollar targets, it makes sense to put the hedging operation as close to the source of the exposures as is possible, namely at the divisional level. But adequate performance requires better front office systems with better analytics to allow us to concentrate on the job of hedging Syscom's huge operational (and largely division-based) FX exposures.

None of the report's conclusions had been implemented in part because Thursgood believed the internal report incomplete. Before leaving, he called in a group of consultants from Swiss Bank Corp.'s Capital Markets and Treasury group, which specialized in corporate risk management to suggest alternatives.

The Capital Markets and Treasury (CM&T) group was comprised mainly of professionals from Chicago-based O'Connor & Associates (OCA), and was organized when Swiss Bank Corp. acquired OCA in the late 1980s. OCA itself was established in 1977 as a proprietary equity options trading firm and quickly became known in the industry for its use of advanced trading technology, quantitative research, and risk management tools. By 1987, it was the leading market maker in U.S. equity and FX options.

The SBC proposal (see **Exhibit 11**) was critical of Syscom's existing risk management process and advocated increased control through a partnership between the Bank and Syscom. Krugman was defensive, arguing that additional control was unnecessary for Syscom's limited needs. Cheng added that there might be risks in outsourcing such an important financial function.

Watson knew that any recommendations she made could have major political ramifications, and, as a new hire, she was concerned about prematurely upsetting the divisions. However, she also knew that is was her job to set sound policies and procedures for managing financial risk, and that the Board—and ultimately shareholders—would have to approve of these policies and procedures.

Syscom Computers

Exhibit 1 Syscom's Consolidated Income Statement (millions of US$)

	1987	1988	1989	1990	1991	1992	1993	Est. 1994
Revenues								
N. American sales	$607	$843	$951	$1,167	$1,322	$1,737	$2,007	$2,569
European sales	$403	$562	$784	$762	$889	$1,002	$1,122	$1,338
Far Eastern sales	$80	$243	$452	$652	$782	$997	$1,328	$1,781
	$1,090	$1,648	$2,187	$2,581	$2,993	$3,736	$4,457	$5,688
Costs & Expenses								
Cost of goods sold	$543	$856	$1,221	$1,491	$1,850	$2,306	$2,882	$3,863
SG&A expense	$367	$533	$600	$698	$710	$827	$939	$1,005
R&D	$125	$201	$222	$238	$253	$316	$332	$489
	$1,035	$1,590	$2,043	$2,427	$2,813	$3,449	$4,153	$5,357
Earnings from Operations								
Other expenses	$5	$9	$13	$16	$20	$28	$32	$53
Income before taxes	$50	$49	$131	$138	$160	$259	$272	$278
Provision for taxes	$14	$14	$37	$39	$45	$73	$76	$78
Net Income	$36	$35	$94	$100	$115	$187	$196	$200

Notes:

Syscom uses the U.S. dollar as its functional currency for consolidated reporting. Foreign currency assets and liabilities are translated into U.S. dollars at end-of-period exchange rates except for inventories, prepaid expenses, and property, plant and equipment, which are translated at historical exchange rates. Revenues and expenses are translated at average exchange rates in effect during each period except for those expenses related to balance sheet amounts that are translated at historical exchange rates.

Translation gains and losses relating to the financial statements of Syscom's subsidiaries are included in other income and expense, and were a net loss of $1.3 million in 1993, a net gain of $3.6 million in 1992, and a net loss of $6.5 million in 1991.

The Far Eastern division is 65% owned by Syscom. Other expenses includes the 35% of the division's net profit paid to the Nichibei Corporation, from whom the division was part acquired in 1988.

Exhibit 2 Consolidated Balance Sheet for Syscom Computers and Subsidiaries (millions of US$)

	1-Jan. 1993	1-Jan. 1994	Est. 1-Jan. 1995
Assets			
Current Assets			
Cash	$89	$106	$155
Short term investments	$98	$101	$110
Accounts receivable	$448	$579	$739
Inventories	$448	$513	$683
Other current assets	$29	$5	$17
Total current assets	$1,113	$1,304	$1,704
PP&E	$152	$205	$279
Other assets	$5	$6	$8
	$1,270	$1,515	$1,991
Liabilities and shareholders' equity			
Current Liabilities			
Accounts payable	$509	$662	$888
Accrued liabilities	$1	$1	$1
Income taxes	$9	$7	$55
Total current liabilities	$519	$669	$944
Long-term debt	98	98	101
Other liabilities	3	3	4
Total liabilities	$620	$770	$1,049
Stockholders' equity:			
Common Stock:$0.01 par value, shares outstanding: 59,457,284, 57,675,235 and 54,879,895, respectively	$1	$1	$1
Additional paid-in capital	$515	$585	$581
Retained earnings	$135	$159	$360
Total stockholders' equity	$650	$745	$942
	$1,270	$1,515	$1,991

Notes:

Long-term debt is denominated in a variety of currencies including US dollars (49%), British pounds (27%) and Japanese yen (34%).

Syscom Computers

Exhibit 3 Syscom's Organization Chart (1993)

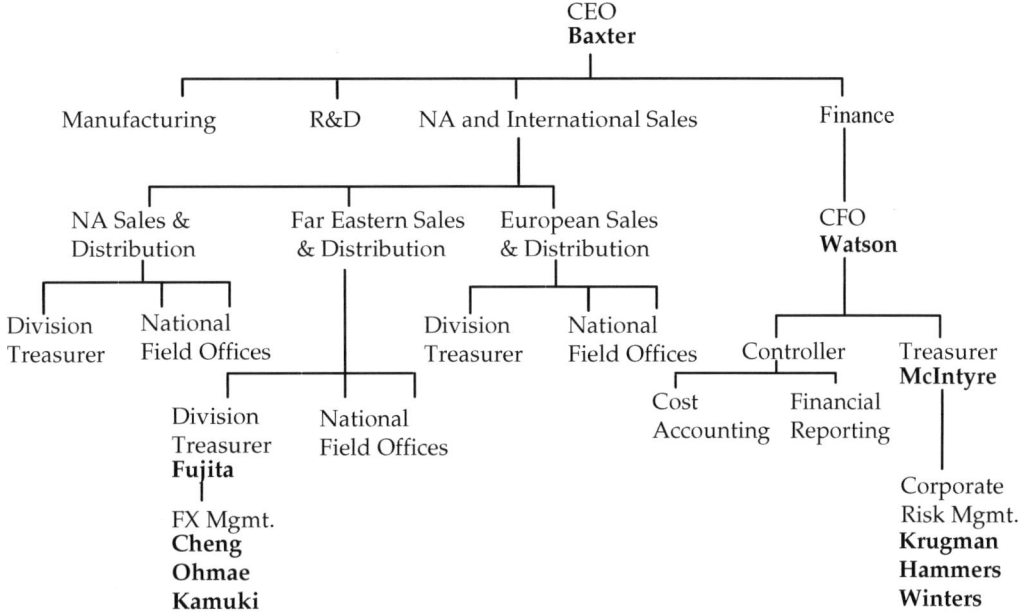

Exhibit 4 Booked and Estimated Income by Division and Country, 1993 (millions of US$)

	Q1 1994 Bkd.	Q1 1994 Est.	Q2 1994 Bkd.	Q2 1994 Est.	Q3 1994 Bkd.	Q3 1994 Est.	Q4 1994 Bkd.	Q4 1994 Est.	1994 Est. Total
North American Sales	$603	$110	$385	$294	$93	$451	$89	$544	**$2,569**
US (USD)	$517	$100	$323	$266	$76	$390	$73	$476	$2,221
Canada (CAD)	$86	$10	$62	$28	$17	$61	$16	$68	$348
Cost of goods sold (USD)	($381)	($70)	($298)	($228)	($84)	($408)	($65)	($397)	**($1,931)**
Marketing and sales	($52)	($13)	($52)	($16)	($53)	($16)	($52)	($17)	**($271)**
US (USD)	($45)	($11)	($46)	($13)	($46)	($13)	($45)	($14)	($233)
Canada (CAD)	($7)	($2)	($6)	($3)	($7)	($3)	($7)	($3)	($38)
Admin. & PP&E (USD)	($34)	($3)	($34)	($3)	($35)	($3)	($34)	($3)	**($149)**
Divisional income before taxes	$136	$24	$1	$47	($79)	$24	($62)	$127	**$218**
European Sales	$274	$101	$194	$105	$62	$233	$91	$278	**$1,338**
U.K. (GBP)	$64	$27	$41	$30	$16	$54	$25	$59	$316
Germany (DEM)	$94	$14	$61	$12	$4	$45	$14	$75	$319
France (FRF)	$45	$20	$35	$24	$10	$50	$15	$59	$258
Italy (ITL)	$51	$20	$37	$24	$12	$52	$19	$53	$268
Others (USD)	$20	$20	$20	$15	$20	$32	$18	$32	$177
Cost of goods sold (USD)	($173)	($64)	($150)	($81)	($56)	($211)	($66)	($203)	**($1,005)**
Marketing and sales	($33)	($14)	($34)	($16)	($33)	($18)	($31)	($22)	**($201)**
U.K. (GBP)	($12)	($4)	($11)	($5)	($11)	($5)	($11)	($6)	($65)
Germany (DEM)	($8)	($3)	($9)	($4)	($10)	($4)	($9)	($5)	($52)
France (FRF)	($6)	($2)	($7)	($2)	($6)	($3)	($5)	($4)	($35)
Italy (ITL)	($7)	($2)	($7)	($2)	($6)	($3)	($6)	($4)	($37)
Others (USD)	$0	($3)	$0	($3)	$0	($3)	$0	($3)	($12)
Admin. & PP&E (GBP)	($27)	($2)	($28)	($2)	($29)	($2)	($28)	($2)	**($120)**
Divisional income before taxes	$41	$21	($18)	$6	($56)	$2	($34)	$51	**$12**
Far Eastern Sales	$404	$168	$271	$117	$131	$214	$137	$339	**$1,781**
Japan (JPY)	$301	$105	$200	$64	$102	$142	$109	$237	$1,260
South Korea (SKW)	$35	$21	$25	$14	$9	$22	$10	$33	$169
Australia (AUD)	$30	$15	$25	$15	$4	$20	$5	$35	$149
Hong Kong (HKD)	$17	$12	$10	$10	$4	$18	$5	$14	$90
Others (USD)	$21	$15	$11	$14	$12	$12	$8	$20	$113
Cost of goods sold	($255)	($106)	($210)	($91)	($119)	($194)	($100)	($247)	**($1,322)**
Marketing and sales	($42)	($8)	($42)	($12)	($42)	($9)	($42)	($14)	**($211)**
Japan (JPY)	($31)	($7)	($31)	($7)	($31)	($7)	($31)	($7)	($152)
South Korea (SKW)	($4)	($1)	($4)	($2)	($4)	($2)	($5)	($2)	($24)
Australia (AUD)	($3)	($1)	($3)	($1)	($3)	($1)	($3)	($1)	($16)
Hong Kong (HKD)	($4)	($1)	($4)	($1)	($4)	($1)	($3)	($2)	($20)
Others (USD)	$0	$2	$0	($1)	$0	$2	$0	($2)	$1
Admin. & PP&E (JPY)	($26)	($2)	($26)	($2)	($26)	($2)	($29)	($2)	**($115)**
Divisional income before taxes	$81	$52	($7)	$12	($56)	$9	($34)	$76	**$133**
Corporate, R&D, & Mfg.									
Revenues (USD)	$810	$240	$658	$400	$259	$813	$231	$847	**$4,257**
Cost of goods sold	($830)	($122)	($790)	($170)	($700)	($273)	($700)	($278)	**($3,863)**
US Suppliers (USD)	($690)	($71)	($685)	($80)	($650)	($114)	($650)	($100)	($3,040)
Japanese Suppliers (JPY)	($140)	($51)	($105)	($90)	($50)	($159)	($50)	($178)	($823)
Corp. overhead (other than R&D)	($18)		($18)		($18)		($18)		($72)
R&D (GBP)	($90)		($90)		($90)		($90)		($360)
Interest expense (JPY,USD,GBP)	($2)		($2)		($2)		($2)		($6)
Est. cost of Filipino plant (JPY)	$0	($17)	$0	($17)	$0	($17)	$0	($17)	($66)
Divisional income before taxes	($130)	$101	($241)	$213	($551)	$524	($578)	$552	**($110)**

Notes: Booked revenues are those for which there is an existing contract. Estimated revenues are the difference between the booked revenues and forecasted revenues. R&D expenses (as well as small fixed-cost items) are allocated across divisional costs of goods sold. Figures above are income measures and do not reflect forecasted changes in working capital or other investment expenses.

Syscom Computers   295-094

Exhibit 5 Foreign Exchange Forward Rates

Prior exhibits were based on the following spot and forward exchange rates (in terms of US$) prevailing on 12/31/93.

	United States	Japan	Canada	Germany	United Kingdom	France	Italy	Australia	South Korea	Hong Kong
	USD	JPY	CAD	DEM	GBP	FRF	ITL	AUD	SKW	HKD
Spot		111.77000	1.3240	1.72630	0.67512	5.8995	1704.00	1.47688	808.1	7.71860
3 month		111.40499	1.3255	1.75100	0.68013	5.9464	1737.80	1.47680	NA	7.73400
6 month		110.86999	1.3274	1.75705	0.68257	5.9292	1756.05	1.48104	NA	7.73575
1 year		109.53500	1.3296	1.76360	0.68526	6.0025	1784.05	1.48970	NA	7.74450

Exhibit 6 Correlations Between Major Currencies

	JPY	CAD	DEM	GBP	FRF	ITL	AUD
JPY	1.00						
CAD	-.16	1.00					
DEM	.77	-.26	1.00				
GBP	.59	-.17	.83	1.00			
FRF	.75	-.23	.99	.85	1.00		
ITL	.66	-.25	.81	.70	.82	1.00	
AUD	-.28	.10	-.31	-.24	-.29	-.07	1.00

Note: This table shows the current correlations of the FX spot (in US$) using a 1 business day trading horizon.

Exhibit 7 Risk Management and Other Financial Processes at Syscom

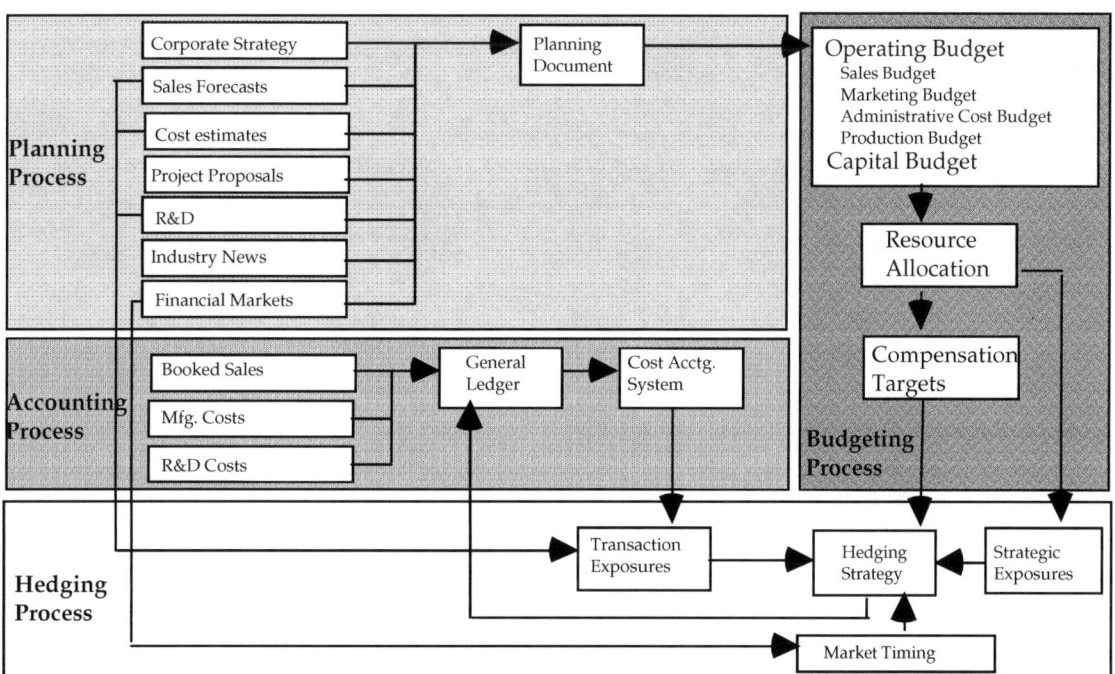

15

Exhibit 8 The Risk Management Process in the Far Eastern Division

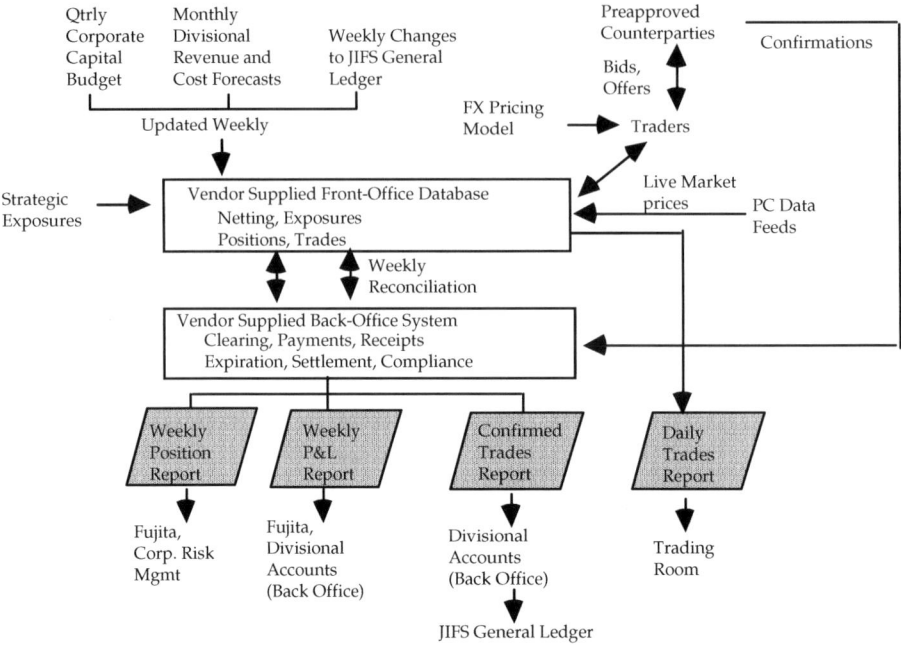

Exhibit 9 The Risk Management Process in the Corporate Office

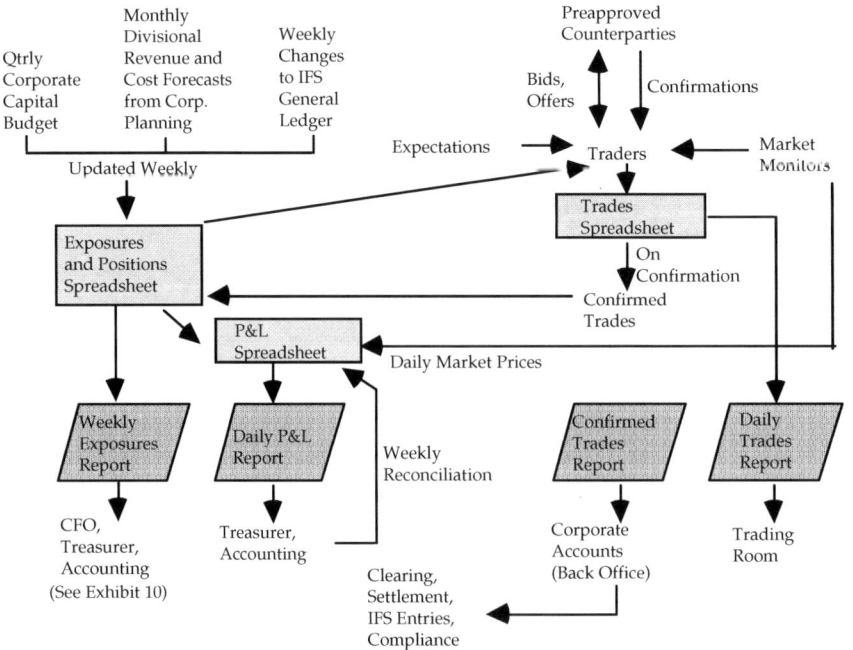

Syscom Computers   295-094

Exhibit 10 Corporate Risk Management Group Exposure Report for 1994 (as of 1/12/94)

Exposures to Net Income Before Taxes
(Millions of US $)

	First Quarter 10% FX Apprec.	Second Quarter 10% FX Apprec.	Third Quarter 10% FX Apprec.	Fourth Quarter 10% FX Apprec.
North American Sales				
CAD	$8.70	$8.10	$6.80	$7.40
European Sales				
GBP	$4.60	$2.50	$2.30	$3.70
DEM	$9.70	$6.00	$3.50	$7.50
FRF	$5.70	$5.00	$5.10	$6.50
ITL	$6.20	$5.20	$5.50	$6.20
Far Eastern Sales				
JPY	$34.00	$19.80	$17.80	$27.70
SKW	$5.10	$3.30	$2.50	$3.60
AUD	$4.10	$3.60	$2.00	$3.60
HKD	$2.40	$1.50	$1.70	$1.40
Corporate, R&D & Manufacturing				
JPY	($20.75)	($21.15)	($22.55)	($24.45)
GBP	($9.00)	($9.00)	($9.00)	($9.00)
Exposures of Far Eastern JPY Hedges				
JPY	($21.09)	($19.33)	($22.42)	($23.68)
SKW	($4.90)	($3.18)	($2.40)	($3.50)
AUD	($4.20)	($3.70)	($2.10)	($3.70)
HKD	($2.40)	($1.50)	($1.70)	($1.40)
Net Corporate Exposures Before Corporate Hedges				
JPY	($7.84)	($20.73)	($27.22)	($20.49)
CAD	$8.70	$8.10	$6.80	$7.40
GBP	($4.40)	($6.54)	($6.74)	($5.34)
DEM	$9.70	$6.00	$3.50	$7.50
ITL	$6.20	$5.20	$5.50	$6.20
FRF	$5.70	$5.00	$5.10	$6.50
SKW	$0.20	$0.12	$0.10	$0.10
AUD	($0.10)	($0.10)	($0.10)	($0.10)
Exposures of Corporate USD Hedges				
JPY	$7.84	$20.73	$27.22	$20.49
CAD	($8.70)	($8.10)	($6.80)	($7.40)
GBP	$4.40	$6.53	$6.74	$5.34
DEM	($9.70)	($6.00)	($3.50)	($7.50)
Net Corporate Exposures After Corporate Hedges				
JPY	$0.00	$0.00	$0.00	$0.00
CAD	$0.00	$0.00	$0.00	$0.00
GBP	$0.00	$0.00	$0.00	$0.00
DEM	$0.00	$0.00	$0.00	$0.00
ITL	$6.20	$5.20	$5.50	$6.20
FRF	$5.70	$5.00	$5.10	$6.50
SKW	$0.20	$0.12	$0.10	$0.10
AUD	($0.10)	($0.10)	($0.10)	($0.10)
HKD	$0.00	$0.00	$0.00	$0.00

Notes:

Each quarter's numbers describe the effect of the local currency increasing in value by 10% against the US dollar. Currencies are: JPY (Japanese yen); CAD (Canadian dollar); GBP (British pound); DEM (German mark); ITL (Italian lira); FRF (French franc); SKW (Swedish kroner); AUD (Australian dollar); and HKD (Hong Kong dollar).

Exhibit 11   Swiss Bank Corp. (SBC) Proposal (1)

Joseph Thursgood   October 21, 1993
Chief Financial Officer
Syscom Computers Inc.
San Francisco, CA

Dear Mr. Thursgood:

We are pleased to respond to Syscom Computer's request to evaluate and enhance the company's risk management system. Your internal task force report was helpful and highlighted some of the systems issues which we have discussed. As I mentioned to you, however the substance of this proposal will focus on the risk management "process" and not just the systems and spreadsheets that you are using.

Our approach is to **partner and co-develop** solutions with our clients. In order to get a truly integrated risk management approach, Syscom and SBC must work in partnership and co-develop the integration. We are prepared to tailor almost every element of our systems' interface to meet Syscom's needs. This is possible because all of the core underlying risk management tools are resident at SBC and are accessed by our corporate clients through client-specific interfaces. In this way, Syscom obtains a state-of-the-art risk management system which is continuously maintained by SBC, significantly reducing the largest expense associated with systems development - ongoing maintenance. More importantly, the systems elements are designed to integrate with your own in-house data and information processing flows, eventually culminating in a single entry system which significantly reduces errors and reconciliation problems, while enhancing controls and reporting.

One element which we emphasize is **training** as an integral part of any solution which we jointly develop with you. Several of your treasury management people have participated in our general seminars. Under the partnership development model we integrate the risk management training with the systems training in order to ensure that the process is understood and used properly. The training is co-developed with you so that Syscom's policies become part of the risk management training. It bears emphasis that this training is ongoing and should constantly be tailored to meet the needs of both newcomers and veterans within the organization. Our objective is to give the participants the language and skills to not only use the systems, but also to use the advice and counsel and market data which comes from third parties within the context of Syscom's policies and objectives.

The need for **global connectivity** is also recognized, particularly for foreign exchange capture, trading and risk management. As mentioned above, the system's architecture is designed to allow an external client to access the functionality of the SBC trading systems without the systems maintenance responsibilities. SBC also can retain the responsibility for managing third party software (*i.e.* Devon back office services for FX) and data sources (*i.e.* price feeds). As part of SBC's core business, the systems are constantly enhanced to meet the ever changing demands of the market place to handle new products and regulations.

While much of this discussion was reviewed with you at our recent meeting together with a demonstration of the key elements of the system, in order to give you a brief written document which can be shared easily with a few of your colleagues attached is the following:

! **Preliminary Observations for Discussion** - Comments on what policy and procedural issues need to be addressed as well as areas where we will need more information from Syscom.

! **Risk Management Implementation Path** - An initial suggestion regarding the specific steps we would take.

! **SBC Systems Functional Descriptions** - A description of the key elements which should be addressed in the initial review which we conduct.

! **Corporate Treasury Operational Flow Diagram** - An illustration of how information is gathered and processed between Syscom and SBC.

We appreciate that some of the recommendations that we may develop will entail changes for the operating subsidiaries in order to obtain the consistency and adherence to policy that you have established as an objective. Many of the recommendations we will develop jointly are quite similar to the Total Quality Management principles you have adopted in your own manufacturing environment. In fact, we hope that some of your colleagues involved with Syscom's TQM program will help us develop the standards to fit Syscom. As a starting point we would suggest standards that cover the following:

- Integration between systems (single entry)
- Continuous improvements (feedback of performance from operating units and the board)
- Training goals
- Ongoing maintenance responsibilities
- Global connectivity and communication

The initial review is estimated to take 2 to 4 weeks for 2 SBC personnel working jointly with 1-2 Syscom staff from the Corporate Finance and Accounting group. For the purposes of overall project sizing, based on our experience with other firms, we would expect to dedicate 3-4 full-time equivalent (FTE) SBC risk management and technology staff during the first year roll out phase. During this period we would need Syscom to dedicate 3 FTE staff for Joint Project Coordination, participation from Treasury and Accounting and limited time from Senior Management and Operating Managers. During the subsequent 2-4 years, enhancements and support requirements would probably require 2 FTE team members from Syscom and 2-2.5 FTE participants from SBC. By early conversion to SBC reporting (hard copy versus on-line) we would expect to free up time for your present staff to be available in the implementation phase and for ongoing support. Hardware and software budgeting should be accommodated within a budget of $250,000. Please keep in mind, that these estimates may change based on the results of the initial review. If existing processes are adequate or already integrated, the work plan may recommend incorporating these components without alteration. Additionally, given Syscom's extensive internal system's capabilities, we may design a larger share of the systems integration for Syscom personnel.

In summary, a risk management partnership is a way of doing business with Syscom rather than a "product" or "service." We look forward to the prospect of working with Syscom to create the most appropriate risk management process and system possible. Good treasury and risk management requires excellent systems, well trained individuals, and solid connections to the markets and market professionals. The failure to support any one of these elements results in a system that is constrained, expensive to support and at risk of obsolescence. Swiss Bank Corp. offers an integrated solution that provides the client with as much (but not more) functionality as is needed to attain these objectives.

Best regards,

James McNulty (Managing Director)

Robert Kunimura (Executive Director)

Preliminary Observations for Discussion

The approach to risk management is radically different between the Far Eastern and European divisions. There may be appropriate underlying fundamentals which can justify such differing risk management strategies, however, we would strongly advise Syscom to insure that the policies and the procedures are consistent.

The exposures monitored differ between entities. We suspect that the European division is not hedging in part because they are unaware of some of the exposures that underlie their operations, most notably the R&D expenditures. This would be true of any of the product areas that rely on the European R&D. Just providing the forum (maybe in-house training) for the various entities to discuss their approach to risk management could be illuminating.

Maintaining a focus on exposures, the task force report clearly identified and documented the exposure identification process, however we could not identify from the report the method of tracking the exposures over time. Specifically, we suspect that hedges may remain in place even if the underlying exposure has disappeared (*i.e.* a contract cancellation). As you know from the extensive accounting pronouncements on the subject, this has implications for reporting as well as for the economic impact on the company.

Although we need further clarification of the actual procedures, given our experience with other clients, we suspect that trades may be confirmed by the person who executed the trade. Although this rarely results in a loss, it does not conform to audit standards.

We would encourage Syscom to centralize information regarding exposure and hedging activity on a daily basis. The month end reports highlight activity, but the time delay prevents the central treasury function from advising the subsidiaries on available alternatives. Additionally, if a hedge is undertaken that is inconsistent with Syscom policy, the time delay could reduce options for reversing the transaction.

Consistent with the prior comment, a centralized view of exposure company-wide should permit Syscom to reduce hedging that is being attributed to inter company transactions. In fact if the headquarters operated like a "bank," Syscom could offset exposures directly between subsidiaries thereby minimizing the trades necessary and keeping the profit and loss statements focused on risks that are within their control.

The Far Eastern division has an excellent grasp of risk management concepts. These can be translated for broader use within the company. The active trading, however, raises significant policy and control issues which should be addressed within the context of a corporate risk management policy. If active trading is permitted, the activity should be segregated entirely from the hedging functions.

Although the task force did not comment on the back office support to the risk management process, we are aware that in the Far Eastern division the tremendous growth in the organization (and budget controls) has kept support staff to a minimum. Additional offshore outsourcing will increase FX exposure and the length of time that Syscom carries the exposure. Even now, we know that Sam Cheng is periodically frustrated by the processing backlog when he is actively trading with SBC and wants to monitor a given trade more closely. Improving the systems available to track exposures should prevent staff overloads, hopefully without staff increases.

Syscom Computers

Risk Management Implementation Path

Phase I	Process Review			
Phase II	Hardware/ Infrastructure Specification	Training Program Design	Market Data Services	
Phase III	Hedge Strategy Formulation	Exposure Modeling	Exposure Capture	Trade Entry
Phase IV	Risk Management Integration			
Phase V	Middle Office Integration	Back Office Integration	Netting/Payment Interfaces	

Exhibit 11 (continued)

SBC Systems Functional Descriptions

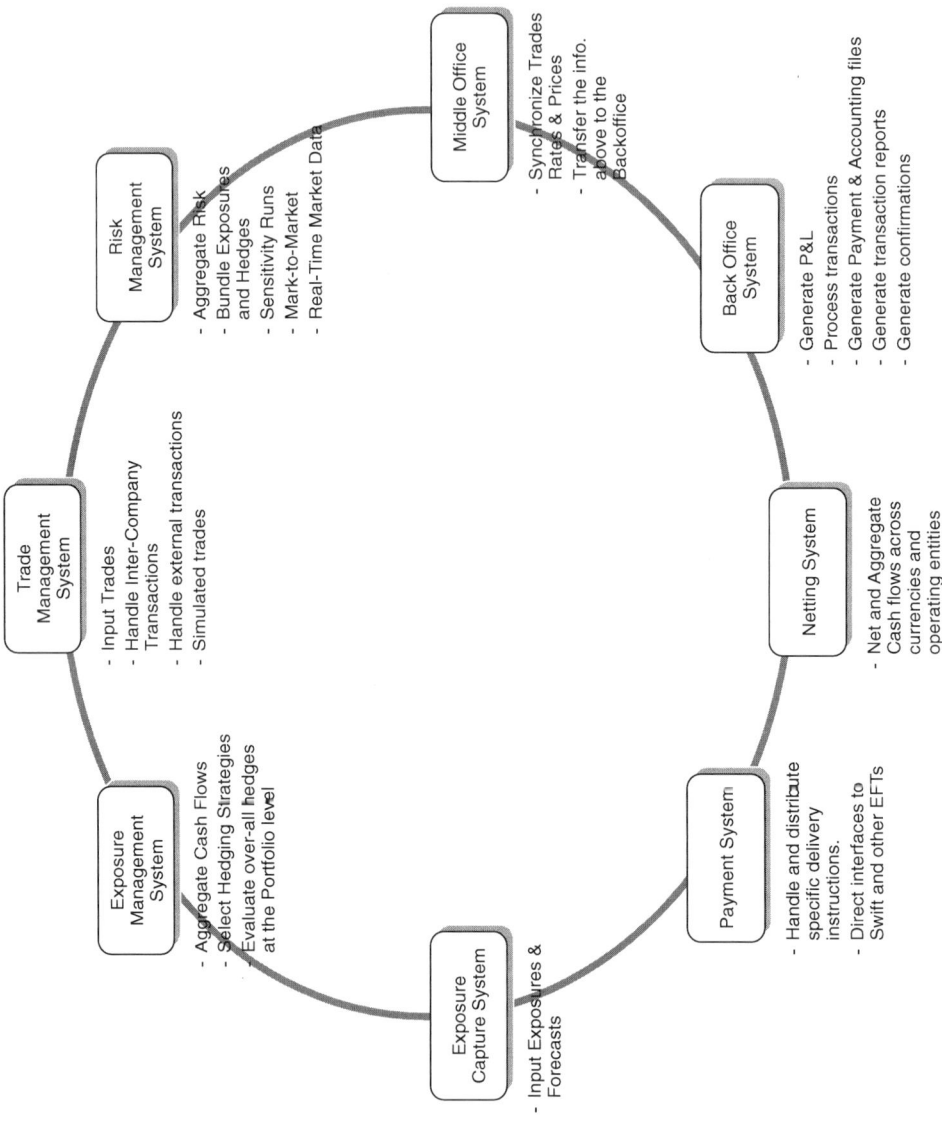

12/14/94

Exhibit 11 (continued)

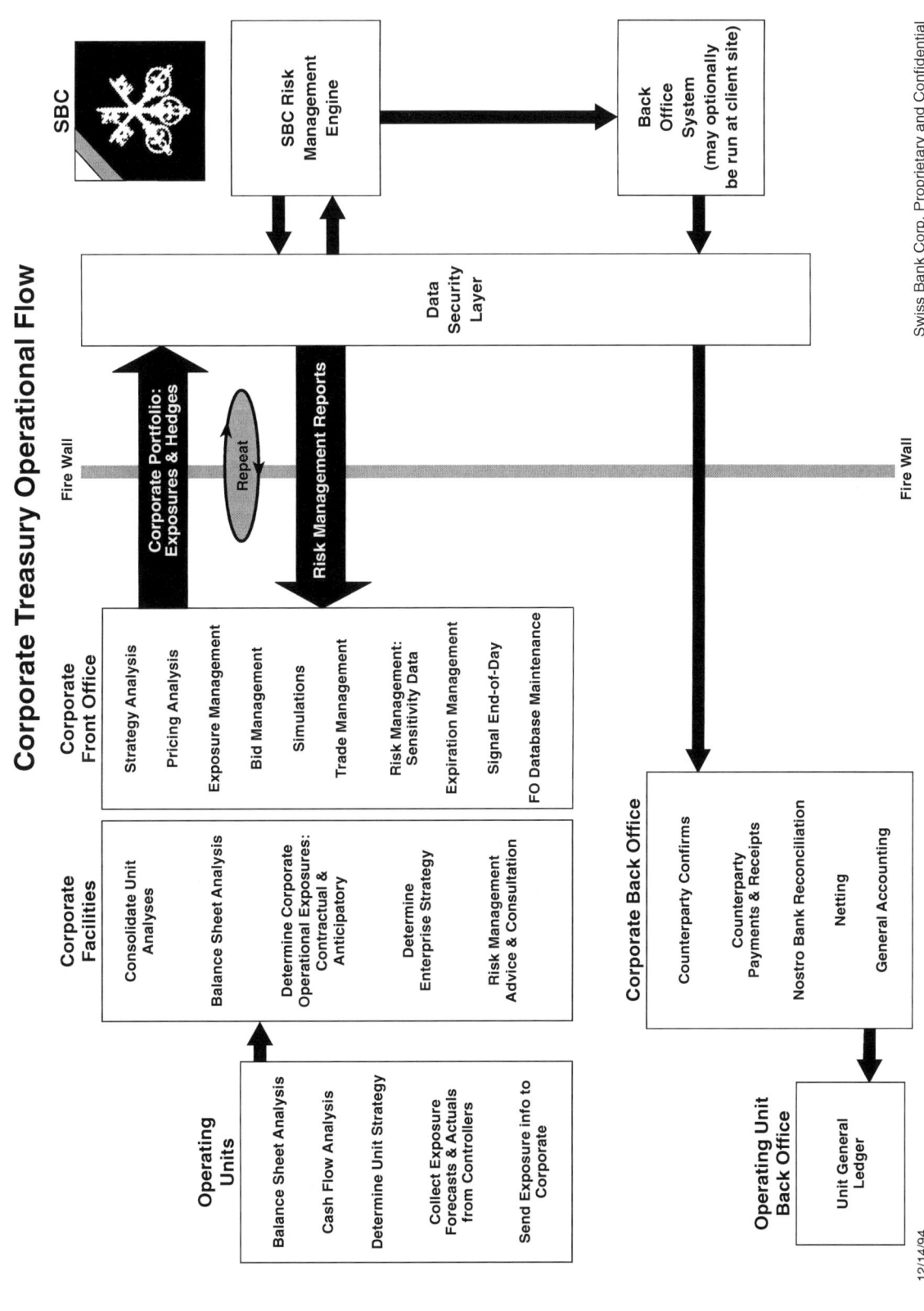